Mad Dogs and Englishmen
– A Bengal Adventure

The main building just before Opening Day. N.B. Little Abdul has lost control of his cow.

Mad Dogs and Englishmen
– A Bengal Adventure

Michael Pitt

The Pentland Press Limited
Edinburgh · Cambridge · Durham

First published in 1993 by
The Pentland Press Ltd.
1 Hutton Close
South Church
Bishop Auckland
Durham

ISBN 1 85821 046 1

Typeset by Elite Typesetting Techniques, Southampton.
Printed and bound by Antony Rowe Ltd., Chippenham.

To Helen and Baby Nickler, who shared it all

In Bengal,
To move at all
Is seldom if ever done
But mad dogs and Englishmen
Go out in the mid-day sun

Contents

List of Illustrations

Frontispiece: The main building before opening day.

1. 5.30 on a summer morning; the whole college limbers up for the day ahead.
2. Shopping in our village High Street. Arrival of the entourage always brought out the crowds.
3. Lamming into the curry – a business repeated twice a day, every day.
4. Prelude to a very eventful football match.
5. Our second Adjutant, the splendid Capt. Wasim Khan. In attendance: UNCLE.
6. Hanging the jute out to dry beside one of the great jheels near the college.
7. Baby Nickler leads the way. Bengalis of all ages love little children.
8. In the Geography Room.
9. A little quasi-military activity. The boys appeared to enjoy this aspect of the Soldier's Art.
10. Judging from the pomp and circumstance on the roof, this was Pakistan Day, '65.
11. Flowers of the Forest – in a jungle clearing near our garden fence.
12. Spotting the birds – twins and week-end visitors.
13. Principal's House – built in about fourteen weeks – wife, daughters and weekend visitors.
14. 'The silver, snarling trumpets' – a salvo from the College roof.
15. Founder and first pupil – the village school just outside the college boundary.
16. We lacked a gymnasium and swimming pool, but sports facilities were way ahead of other schools in Bengal.

Part One

Getting There

The seed is sown

What is the British Council

Birth of a nation

Bengal – a lot of people

A taxing climate

A sea voyage

Casing the joints

An astonishing achievement

The last lap

Getting There

It was a snide December day – the year 1963. The outlook from the little office window was as unpromising as the weather. I was in British Council headquarters, the murmur of Oxford Street an unheeded background to our talk.

'Pakistan is setting up new Cadet Colleges. We think this is the sort of job which'll suit you. They're asking for a Principal at – er – Momenshahi . . .'

Stephen Ward looked up; the ball was in my court.

'Where's Momenshahi?'

'It's in East Pakistan,' he replied, 'somewhere near the capital, Dacca. We're not sure exactly where, as it's not on any of our maps.'

'Sounds interesting. But what exactly is a Cadet College?'

'They're very much the creations of President Ayub Khan. He thinks that boarding schools run on British lines will give Pakistan the leaders she'll need in the future.'

We talked on far into the morning. I was taken round various departments of the Council, each one with its titbit of information. Gradually and painlessly the huge gap in my knowledge of Pakistan and of Cadet Colleges was plugged.

I left London that evening for my home in the West Riding. I would get a letter as soon as the Pakistan Government felt itself inclined – or disinclined, come to that – to approve my nomination by the British Council for this job.

My credentials were by no means spectacular. The son of a town parson, I was born within sound and smell of St. Pancras Station; the vicarage stood at the corner of a typical London Square which has since undergone its fair share of social ups and downs. When we lived in it,

5

dingy respectability about summed it up. We moved to Southampton soon after the General Strike, the sudden collapse of which prevented my father from realising a lifetime ambition to be a guard of a passenger train. This was our home until a Luftwaffe landmine landed slap on top of St. Barnabas Church, removing in an instant, so to speak, my father's *raison d'être*.

It was a good place to be young in – the tree-lined centre of a seaport then enjoying probably its most resplendent decade, with the great ships of the Cunard and White Star Lines vying with each other for commercial mastery of the Atlantic. We boys believed passionately that Southampton Docks were Number One, infinitely superior to Liverpool. To come out from Below Bar on to the quayside, and there to behold, a few furlongs away, the *Majestic* or the *Berengaria* in the Floating Dock – biggest in the world, we hastened to explain to visitors – is a memory which I reckon myself lucky to possess.

We lived within ten minutes' walk of the Dell, five minutes' of the County Cricket Ground, with Speedway even closer – a marvellous environment for two boys whose passion for watching games was stronger than their skill in playing them. In winter my brother and I were behind the goal every Saturday – 6d for first team matches, 3d for the reserves – with no thought of risk to limb or tender susceptibilities. In summer we would sit the long day through watching Phil Mead, George Brown, Alec Kennedy, Lord Tennyson – the last, I recall, constantly receiving telegrams on the field, the popular theory being that these were the latest racing results.

My father's stipend was £400 a year with a free house (not a very comfortable one, but the garden was big enough for two-man cricket and/ or football, with a bit left over for cultivation); this, together with my mother's small private income, was enough to keep us in fair style: no car, but two resident maids and a substantial table. Remarkably, my parents were able to send both of us to boarding schools – my brother to Sutton Valence, me to St. Edward's, Oxford.

For a basic fee of £90 a year I there received what I now believe was one of the best educations in the world. Life was fairly Spartan: cold showers, rather terrible food, Chapel twice a day, the cane if you put a foot even mildly wrong, very compulsory games, girls strictly taboo. Stiffest hardship of all, I see in retrospect, was lack of privacy. Yet we were marvellously well taught, in the classroom, on the river, in the field or in the common hurly-burly of adolescent life. Most of us emerged reasonably prepared for whatever the outside world had to throw at us. For my generation, that meant six years of war.

Although an infantryman and later on a parachutist, the time one spent fighting was very brief indeed. Boredom, rather than Fascist or Jap, was the real enemy. One's first thoughts on waking up most mornings were of the tedium and frustrations of the day ahead – no way to live a life.

Of course, there were compensations: I travelled widely – all over India, back and forth in North Africa, Syria, Palestine, the Lebanon, six months in delectable Crete, at the very end a hilarious eight weeks in Copenhagen – friendship, laughter, achievement – such things served to counteract the inescapable fact that one was doing something for which one was not intended either by nature or by inclination.

Pleased at the end of it all to find myself still in one piece, I headed, intent on teaching and complete now with wife and daughter, for Uppingham, a small market town in Rutland. The school was under the benign care of Martin and Kay Lloyd; it was a singularly happy place in which to learn the rudiments of one's job. Thence, after eight years, to the Yorkshire Pennines, to Rishworth School, where, for a like period, I contrived, in association with my Chairman of Governors, the late Fred Bentley – 'Bentley of the Halifax', a man of honour if ever I saw one – to turn a wilting plant into something rather more luxuriant.

In due time – only four weeks in fact – the letter from Pakistan arrived. My name was acceptable. Amid a welter of preparation, I had two contracts to sign, the first being with the British Council.

*   *   *

Nine out of ten Britons, if asked what the British Council is or does, would either confess ignorance or offer a hesitant opinion in which words like 'culture', 'the secret service' or 'something to do with the Foreign Office' would make their inadequate or downright inaccurate assessment. The very name, so reassuring, so ponderous, is the essence of vagueness. Not for nothing does it produce a trim, concise pamphlet called *What is the British Council?*

The head office – then in Davies Street, W.C.2 – reflected its curious personality. It was less plush than a business house, cosier than a government department. The architecture of the red brick building was safe and uninspired. In the canteen on the 5th floor (soup, macaroni cheese, treacle tart with custard, no lunch vouchers), place names like Bangkok, Teheran, Athens were muttered across the tablecloths with the indifference born of familiarity; over the lunchers there lurked a thin veneer of heartiness as at a parish breakfast. The names on the office doors carried their quotas of Smiths and Browns; out of any one of them might step a woman in a sari, a young Arab every inch the student, a gentle Siamese. Their business done, they vanished through the swing doors and were swallowed up in the chaos of nearby Oxford Street. They left behind them, in little square offices, men and women who were not quite civil servants, not quite schoolteachers, not quite old colonials. The atmosphere was neither frantic nor leisured. The murmur of discreet conversation was more insistent than the clack of typewriters, the files were bundled to and fro along the quiet corridors. Clearly something was going forward. But what?

Like so many things British, it was sired by private enterprise with Government creeping in as a latter day wet-nurse. From its birth in 1934 'The British Committee for relations with Other Countries' included among its objectives the teaching of the English language abroad and the care of overseas students in Britain. Its title was changed to something neater, if more obscure, and in the first year of the war the ultimate stamp of respectability was won with the granting of a Royal Charter. As the Council gets most of its money from the Government, it is naturally subject to scrutiny from the Treasury. But the Council jealously guards a considerable measure of independence from Government control. Broadly speaking, the Government decides where the Council shall work and on what scale; the Council decides what kind of work it will do.

The teaching of the English language is undertaken widely – the demand for a knowledge of English does not slacken; in many of the large cities of the world the Council has a headquarters and a library. It recruits teachers for universities, training colleges and schools overseas. Of these I was one, and found that the Council was in part my paymaster, hefting useful lumps of sterling into my bank at home (I was also paid in rupees by the Pakistan government, a seemingly happy arrangement, which in truth it was.) Tours outward and inward are arranged by the Council; the outward operation involves the sending of experts on short tours to make contact with their fellow boffins overseas; the inward operation is on a large scale and finds the Council helping and advising thousands of people who visit the U.K. each year for reasons various.

On occasions it looks after important foreign visitors, not always without embarrassment. The paramount Sheikh, inflated with oil, was on a week's visit with the Council as his guide and helpmeet. Not for him the staid programme arranged for his first evening; a night club it had to be, and off he went on his own to sample London night life. Calling at his hotel suite next morning, the Council man found his charge breakfasting with a blonde in a tattered evening dress. Her whole appearance betrayed not only her profession but also her status within it which was not of the highest. Accustomed to the pecadilloes of foreign potentates, the Council man was not perturbed until the Sheikh announced his intention of retaining Flossie's services throughout the week, insisting that she accompany him everywhere. His programme included an overnight stay in one of the stateliest homes, visits to universities and other commitments of a somewhat stuffy nature. All of which the Sheikh dutifully carried out, and Flossie came too. Moreover he had also insisted that she should wear all the time the tattered evening dress to which he had taken an unaccountable fancy. So together they trekked around, a colourful and enigmatic couple, with the Council man, presumably, driven at times to desperate and clandestine explanations. There was some speculation as to whether Flossie would be off to the sands of the desert. But no – a smacking kiss, a £1000 tip, and the Sheikh was winging back to the harem and the Cadillacs – alone.

Over the next three years I was to meet many Council officers, receiving from them much sound advice and encouragement. If at times we may have grumbled about the Council – who doesn't on occasions gripe at their masters? – we could not have received fairer or more generous treatment from first to last.

*   *   *

I also had to sign a two-year contract with the Government of Pakistan. Ian Stephens writes: 'The independent sovereign state of Pakistan was born into carnage and commotion. It was her first national experience.' It would have been surprising if things had been otherwise.

As soon as the British made clear their intention to quit a subcontinent they no longer had the resources to rule, the two main dissident factions in India, the Hindus and the Muslims, struggled to find an alternative form of government which would satisfy the aspirations of both. Out of this struggle, which became a civil war killing more people than the total casualties of all the Commonwealth forces in World War II, there emerged an India divided, with the Muslim communities concentrated into a new state, Pakistan.

Francis Bacon wrote: 'Prosperity is not without many fears and distastes, and adversity is not without hopes and comforts'. History has proved the truth of this a score of times; Pakistan, born to 'carnage and commotion', to adversity on a catastrophic scale, was to furnish another example. Those who reached her shelter after months of indescribable riot and terror were steeled to a fine courage, which not only proved of immense benefit to the new state in her earliest days, but also went some way to explain the extraordinary depths of patriotic emotion which this writer found in the country nearly twenty years later. Writing of the Muslim refugee-camps in the Old Fort at Delhi, Ian Stephens drives this point home in a striking passage:

> Many of these Muslims were Pakistanis-to-be: people who had opted for the smaller Dominion but had been unable to get there, because of the slaughter and derailments in the Punjab: the poor, mainly, but members of the Delhi aristocracy also, Government officials high and low, mercantile people of all sorts. They may have seemed demoralised in the camps, but the spirit of fortitude bred amidst these adversities, when eventually they were taken to Karachi by air, helped Pakistan to get through the daunting stresses and confusions of her first few months of life.
>
> There was, indeed, at the start, little but human will for her to live on. At Delhi the new Indian regime inherited all the splendid buildings and equipment of the Imperial Secretariat; but at Karachi, the Pakistan Government scarcely possessed typewriters, telephones, desks, ink or stationery, and its personnel struggled with urgent tasks of creative nation-building, not in palatial rooms of carved red sandstone, but temporarily in corners of shabby tin hutments and other structures left over from the war. They focused their glowing hopes, in this shared new venture, on the Quaid-i-Azam, their own Governor-General and fellow Muslim, Mr. Jinnah. It was inspiring to visit Pakistan, and to feel the enthusiasms that did away with difficulties, in those early days.

Pakistanis revere the memory of Mohammad Ali Jinnah with a deep and emotional fervour; in all sorts of places his picture hangs in the place of honour. He was without question a great man, dry, ascetic, resolute, and one who, Stephens observes, 'as a nation-builder future historians will have to reckon the Asian counterpart of Bismarck or Cavour'. It was his iron will and determination that won for the Muslims a state of their own, a state based exclusively on religious ideology. Jinnah had immense prestige, and among his own people, an unquestioned authority and control. He held at the same time the three offices of Governor-General,

President of the Constituent Assembly and President of the Muslim League. Just over a year after the creation of Pakistan he died at the age of seventy from pulmonary tuberculosis.

Jinnah's death was a blow heavy enough; it was followed three years later by the death, this time from an assassin's bullet, of Pakistan's remaining strong man, Prime Minister Liaquat Ali Khan. The new state simply could not afford the loss of these two eminent men. There is no doubt whatever that this double disaster led directly to the blackest period of Pakistan's short history, the years 1952 to 1958.

This is not a place for a description of the shoddy intrigues and squabbles that threatened during these years to bring the new state to collapse; Pakistanis refer to them as 'the bad days', days of muddle, frustration and confusion. The military coup of 1958 was not the first, but the third attempt to get the situation under some sort of control. Others had tried in 1953 and 1954, but these coups, mainly inspired by civil servants themselves tainted with corruption, failed to stop the rot. It was not until the Army, led by its Commander-in-Chief, stepped in decisively in the fall of '58 that an effective end was put to chaos and a new era opened up for the people of Pakistan.

'The most efficient and benign thing of its sort that the twentieth century has seen' is how Stephens describes the Ayub Khan military revolution. It was remarkable enough for its lack of blood-spilling and for the intelligent humanity with which antagonists were treated; it was altogether extraordinary for the manner in which the new President fulfilled the promises made in his first days of power. He said he would restore democratic forms as soon as possible, and did so four years later when martial law was abandoned and the new Constitution came into force; he said he would introduce badly needed land reforms, and did so exactly one year after the coup; he said he would clean up the Augean stable of corruption and jobbery, and, to a certain extent, did so without aid of firing squad or prison cell.

It is not surprising that under such intelligent and singleminded leadership, Pakistan should progress and prosper in a way which put to rout the views of the pessimists, who, in 1947, foretold that a country so weak and ungainly could never survive.

The ungainliness was shaped from a curious geographical circumstance that divided the country into two sections, the Provinces of West and East Pakistan. The latter was formed in order to bring within the Islamic fold the Muslim majorities of East Bengal. The two provinces were about a thousand miles apart with the great bulk of India between; in a number of important respects they were very different. The West Wing was of appreciable size – about 310,000 square miles; the East was small by comparison, little bigger than the British Isles less Northern Ireland. However, it was in the East Wing that the greater number of Pakistanis lived, making it one of the most densely populated areas in the world; the West Wing was on the whole dry, the East quite the reverse. In language they differed, mainly Urdu in the West, Bengali in the East (when the President of Pakistan made a speech to his people in the East Wing he had to have an interpreter in order to make himself understood). In dress, dietary habits, physique, culture, to some extent temperament, the two regions were dissimilar.

Above all, the citizen of West Pakistan considered himself a superior being to the East Pakistani, the Bengali. In no aspect was this more apparent than in the martial art; the higher ranks of the Pakistan Army were the exclusive preserve – with very few exceptions – of the West Pakistani. This was a situation which the British looked on with approval. The fighting troops of that splendid Indian Army in World War II were Punjabis, Pathans among others – seldom Bengalis, whose skills were exploited in echelons well away from the firing line.

To govern a country so varied and so geographically clumsy – the only way to bridge the gap between the two Wings was by air (three hours), or by sea (two weeks), India took good care that that inconvenience was never relaxed – called for leadership of exceptional quality. There were many critics of the Ayub Khan regime, especially among the politically-minded Bengalis quick to label his rule oppressive, but it is difficult to visualise how affairs could have been better managed or a nation brought more quickly to its feet than was achieved by this professional, Sandhurst-trained soldier who won for himself, along with Jinnah, the title of a Father of Pakistan.

President Ayub was not notably Anglophile, but he did have a lot of respect for the British education system, especially its private sector. He was keenly aware that Pakistan lacked men of managerial calibre. As suggested above, he thought that boarding schools run on British lines might help to solve the problem. It was carefully stipulated that these Colleges should be sited well away from cities where political agitators lurked, and that the pupils should not be under any obligation to join the Services. Entry qualifications were stiff; fees were paid only by those whose incomes suggested the means to do so. Of these two factors, much more anon . . .

The better to get such establishments launched, the President thought – rightly or wrongly – that the man to have on the bridge during the maiden voyage should be British; after two or three years, a Pakistani would take over. Which is, roughly speaking, where I came into the story.

Before leaving England we tried to find out as much as possible about these Ayub Khan creations – the Cadet Colleges. In West Pakistan, it appeared, there were then two, both well established. In East Pakistan there was one, at Chittagong, and about the Principal I heard much in my talks with British Council officers. 'Colonel Brown says this' and 'Colonel Brown does that' were phrases with which I became very familiar. I was shown photographs of V.I.P.s visiting the College with Colonel Brown prominent in the background. Clearly he was something of a legend, both in Bengal and in the corridors of Davies Street. In these earliest days, when I was groping my way to a clearer picture of what went on, he assumed in my mind a rather formidable aspect. He had reached, it seemed, a pinnacle of efficiency and know-how to which one could never hope to aspire. He was too good by half. I was later to get to know Maurice Brown extremely well; he was the kindest of men and a great help to a newcomer.

Momenshahi was to be the second of the province's colleges with a third close on its tail, Jenaidah. The East wing was in a hurry to overtake the West. As to general policy it was left to the Principal to decide to what extent the military ethos was brought into the life of the college. He had to assist him, apart from a large teaching and administrative staff, an Adjutant and five havildars (the Pakistani name for a sergeant) attached from the Army. But these were essentially schools designed to give a broad-based general education; the object was to produce young men capable of taking decisions and accepting responsibility. The number of pupils averaged about three hundred. In each college the Principal was responsible to a governing body for the entire running of the establishment. The Chairman of the College Governors was in all instances a serving officer, and a high ranking one at that. It seemed that this was a situation with which I was not entirely unfamiliar.

I had an interview with Sir Paul Sinker, the Director of the British Council. 'Don't be under any delusions', he said. 'You're taking on an extremely tough job.' He had just returned from an extensive tour of his parish; clearly he knew what he was talking about. Together we studied a huge wall map in search of Momenshahi. We did not find it.

*   *   *

Our pitch, our centre of operations, was to be in East Pakistan, or, as we preferred to call it, Bengal. At its population density I have already hinted; in fact, it was heavily overpopulated at 922 to the square mile. The effect of this on a stranger is at once apparent; he finds that he cannot move about the countryside by car or on foot without being in sight of, and acutely aware of, people (the Chittagong Hill Tracts, the Sundabans and the moribund river tracts of Jessore and Kushtia excepted). This is due to the fact that most Bengalis live in country villages, tied to the land by tradition and pursuing their rural business in a manner familiar to their great-great-grandfathers and many generations before that. There are, apart from Dacca, no big urban agglomerations, the jam is spread evenly, there is no relief from the pressure. It is almost true to say that every copse in Bengal – there are a million copses great and small – hides a village or a cluster of mud huts, each hut in turn giving shelter to more people than would commonly be thought possible. Thus one can move through the countryside unconscious of dwellings, but never unconscious of dwellers. This can, and does, become somewhat oppressive; the Bengali is a confirmed starer, a stranger-watcher *par excellence*; to stop one's car, to sit down under a pipal tree, is to attract a crowd. The spaces are wide open enough, but at times one wished that they were shared by rather fewer members of the human race.

Bengalis are called a riverine people because they live in a vast delta. The eminent geographer, Dr. Nafis Ahmad, called it 'the most remarkable network of rivers in the world . . . In the more easterly portions of the Himalayas all the water falling upon the Kumaon, Nepal, Bhutan and Assam sections finds its way ultimately into the Ganges, Brahmaputra and the Meghna, and through these mighty rivers it is washed down to the sea across the surface of East Pakistan.'

To fly over this area in the monsoon is to get the impression of looking down at a vast lake interspersed with clusters of trees, tracks artificially raised from the water and patches of green paddy not wholly submerged. For six months of the year the Bengali becomes a boatman, and a very picturesque job he makes of it. While the villager, accustomed to sedate and leisurely progress at all times, finds nothing incommodious about this, to the man in a hurry Bengal presents travel problems out of the ordinary. Distance as the crow flies means nothing; huge water barriers inhibit roadbuilding, compel vast detours. Happily for the hustler, air services went a long way to meeting his problem. Air buses and helicopters reduced journeys which at ground level would take days to a matter of minutes. Abetted by the singular terrain, the helicopter in Bengal was coming into its own.

People, water, trees, people, rich green plains, water, people, the spread of the sky, kutcha huts, trees, sun, water and again people – these were the impressions that the great alluvial plain of Bengal made on the foreign resident. There remains one other factor which dictated his dress, curbed his output, controlled his temper, threatened his blood-pressure and directed his thinking – the weather.

*   *   *

The climate of Bengal has an evil reputation. Before leaving England I was regaled, mainly by ex-14th. Army men, with horror stories about the famous South West monsoon. 'Ghastly, my dear chap, you'll be lucky to live through it,' roughly summarised their remarks.

In the event, we found it far less disagreeable than we had expected. Throughout the year, a great deal of rain falls over East Bengal, varying from a minimum of 60 inches to as high as 150-200 inches in the North-East. Most of this fall is concentrated into the monsoon period from June to September. The rain itself we found not unpleasant; it brought a profusion of green back to the parched landscape; it brought some relief from the heat. The poor drainage in the towns made walking a messy and unpleasant business, tolerable only if one was shod with gumboots. What does give the monsoon its peculiar sting is the humidity, a word which to so many people means nothing at all, but is everything to a resident of Bengal and some other areas East. It saps energy, reduces you to a perspiring hulk and raises your dhobi bills to formidable heights. Step out of the car after an hour's drive and the back of your cotton shirt is black with sweat; you sit on the verandah of an evening pouring beneath the electric fans; you are surprised that you have so much moisture to lose.

Chief weapons against the common enemy were air-conditioners and a massive consumption of liquor. Use of the former was confined, for the Britisher, to his bedroom, though quite a number enjoyed air-conditioned offices. These machines consumed a great deal of electricity which in Bengal was extremely expensive; the extent to which one used them was accordingly governed by whether you or your employer footed the bill. The Americans were less troubled in this respect, it was unusual not to find an American home fully air-conditioned. In this they were greatly assisted by the beneficence either of Uncle Sam or of the employer.

There is little doubt that air-conditioning made a very big difference to the life of the Westerner in Bengal; he could sleep at night in cool, dry air, needing, as like as not, at least one blanket on the bed. One awoke refreshed, the day ahead had already lost most of its terrors.

As for consumption of liquor, this was plain necessity, no hint of luxury here. One simply had to replace the moisture draining out of the system the livelong day. Some preferred the replacement to be substantially alcoholic, rather expensive and with possible deleterious effects. My own choice – though no teetotaller – was lime juice which I swallowed in vast quantities, and I put down my freedom from tummy ailments largely to this. Beer was scarce and mostly of a light, lagerish quality. Whisky and gin were not hard to come by, but wines, especially good vintages, were scarce and kept for royal occasions.

To return to matters climatic, quite the most exciting elemental displays were confined to the months of April and May, with the onset of the Nor'Westers, known locally as Kal Baisakj (calamities of the month of Baisakj, April-May). These are the tropical storms as portrayed by Hollywood; they are what one has been led to expect. On their approach the prudent bolt their windows, lock doors, clear the verandah of furniture, bring down baby; preparations are as for a siege.

I first experienced a Nor'Wester one April evening. I was playing tennis and watching with some concern the build-up of heavy black cloud to the North. I was for stopping, but my daughters, Drake-like, pooh-poohed the suggestion as senile fussing, and we played on. The wind struck with a suddenness and rage that defies description. One moment the air was balmy, quiescent; the next it was a fury that made standing upright difficult. The sudden chill was like stepping into a deep-freeze. We bolted for the house and beat the rain by a few seconds. The big climax came some fifteen minutes later; the house shook, the lightning dazzled, doors and windows, though secured, rattled and groaned; the noise was infernal. To add to the confusion, all lights went out; we groped for candles which when lit flickered protestingly in the icy draughts. Water was now pouring down the stairs, driven in beneath the verandah doors on the first floor. It was a case of all hands to the pumps; one was glad not to be at sea. All was over in a matter of minutes, though the storm lingered on fitfully with brilliant lightning and pulsating rain.

Dr Nafis Ahmad has this to say:

'They are called Nor'Westers because they often approach a station from the north-westerly direction; in fact they may come from all points of the compass, but the north-west is the most frequent direction. These thunderstorms are a striking phenomenon.

Occasionally a Nor'Wester rivals a tornado in its violence and destructive effects, but cyclonic circulation or wave motion in any form, such as is found in a tornado, is rare. For example, conditions approaching those of a tornado with similar destructive results, were witnessed in the storm which struck parts of Faridpur and Jessore districts on 12 May 1961.

All this having been said, the fact remains that for five months of the year – mid-October to mid-March, with slight seasonal variations – the climate of Bengal is quite delightful. The days are mild and sunny, the nights deliciously cool; the sky is clear and the atmosphere bracing. Of rain there is little or no evidence. Outdoor functions can be planned with the absolute certainty that the weather will be a formidable ally. In a Bengal winter it feels good to be alive.

*   *   *

'Fling a ten-month-old child straight into the Bengal monsoon? Ridiculous! You can't do it.' The voice of my mother-in-law, who knew her subcontinent, was authoritative and made sense. On 1 May 1964, I sailed alone; the family would follow in October.

In those days – a mere twenty eight years ago – there was no question of flying, sea-routes were still wide open to the intending traveller. One chose Anchor Line – or rather, the British Council Travel Department did the choosing; one merely followed their experienced instructions. Liverpool, Karachi, Bombay and back: Anchor Line had been churning over that route for generations, carting heaven knows how many missionaries, merchants, colonial servants, tea planters – many with their families – for service of one kind or another on behalf of the Jewel in the Crown. The ships were of moderate size – about 20,000 tons or thereabouts – no air conditioning, art deco, heavy menus, Indian stewards. If one enjoyed the sea, all well and good, and there was no denying the comfort of knowing that somewhere deep down in the hold rested one's brand new Ford Zephyr plus a formidable stack of crates heavily daubed 'Not Wanted on the Voyage'. Accompanied baggage gave one satisfaction which the traveller nowadays can rarely enjoy.

In the eyes of many who belong to what was once a sea-faring nation, there was about a long voyage an aura, a glamour, which in the event was seldom justified. The first few days wore the gloss of novelty – the smells, those long menus, the starting of huge books one had never had time to read, the massive onset of protracted leisure. But before long one was up against what Peter Fleming has described as 'the impact of too frequent recognition', the problem in short of too many people in a space too confined. Into the feasting there crept a taste of monotony; the deck games, the hearty evening entertainments became merely instruments for passing time (though of the former I would exclude deck golf, a magnificent game of the utmost skill and a devilish ingenuity); idleness, so recently at a premium, lost its attraction. Certainly, the voyage had its moments – that tiny delectable Mediterranean island (what was it called? One could retire there); the endless fascination of other ships, seventy per cent of them tankers; the cosy confines of the Canal, the control of which to a layman's eye seemed effortlessly efficient; the spindly Egyptian, one of the Canal pilot's crew, trying to flog filthy postcards in the darker corners of 'B' deck. And there was Jackie, carrying her fifteen years with a poise as graceless as a leaden collar, Jackie with her skinny little frame in a bikini of undaunted brevity, the pride of the Boat Deck – Jackie with her witless Mum ('She's such a delicate child, dear. I don't know what to do with her, I really don't!'), less successful than her daughter in concealing her North Country origins – Jackie whose affair with a young Persian ended with an abruptness which sent Mum to her cabin for a prolonged rest.

    Saddest moment came early at Gibraltar – the desperate humiliation of a wife and daughter, as, from their seats on the tender, they watched Papa, who had scarcely stirred from the bar since Liverpool, make his crazy drunken progress across the narrow gangplank. To shouts of laughter and encouragement from the ship's side, he reached the tender safely, but the pain of a mother and child was calamitous.

*   *   *

'Karachi has grown in ten years from two hundred thousand people to two million. Abject poverty side by side with huge modern office blocks and extreme wealth. There's a magnificent hotel opened last week by the President, a splendid chunk of architecture. But the place as a whole does not appeal, too hot, too noisy, too crowded, too dirty.'

This extract from a letter to my wife is certainly a superficial judgement. May in Karachi is not a welcoming month, nor was I long enough in the city to justify so forthright an opinion. Certainly my stay there was made most enjoyable in the beautiful and hospitable home of Jock Jardine, the

British Council Representative in Pakistan. I was to spend ten days in the West Wing awaiting a ship to Chittagong. The Council took good care that those ten days should be spent profitably, and duly packed me off to look at colleges further afield. I flew by Viscount to Rawalpindi where, twenty three years before, I had made my first parachute jumps.

To say that air travel has revolutionised the subcontinent would be an exaggeration; it would take more than a fleet of jets to do that. But it has certainly played a big part in opening up a slice of the earth, the main centres of which are vast distances apart. Pakistan was quick to realise the importance of the air, developing both a most efficient organisation, P.I.A., and a frequent service between the big cities. In the linking of East and West Pakistan, P.I.A. was indeed something of a lifeline. Tourist fares were heavily subsidised by the Government, which meant that Mr Ahmed, Mrs Ahmed and the children, once condemned to long and desperately uncomfortable journeys by rail, could afford to travel swiftly, luxuriously, 35,000 feet above the dusty plains. At Rawalpindi, we (I was lucky to have with me Derek Beard, the Council Education Officer) were met by Mrs Peter Harwood and driven into the Muree Hills up a mountain road leading us to the P.A.F. Cadet College, to a view of snow-topped mountains and to a climate which made us grateful that night for three blankets and a hot water bottle. Karachi – midday temperature over a hundred – seemed a good deal further away than it was.

To visit three Colleges in four days, questioning, listening and again questioning, was to invite an acute attack of mental indigestion. That no such inconvenience occurred was a tribute to the kindness of my hosts and to the lucidity of their many explanations; the Harwoods at the Pakistan Air Force College, its buildings cascading down a hillside so steep that one might suppose its pupils were being acclimatised for their later activities; the Michael Charlesworths at Lawrence College founded in 1860, originally as a school for the sons and orphans of British Army soldiers; Bill Winlaw at Hasan Abdul Cadet College, who had me out of bed at five thirty in the morning to take the salute at a march past – all these visits were invaluable in helping me to get a picture of school life in Pakistan.

*   *   *

Take a hundred acres of desert in one of the hottest spots on earth, assemble materials, build a school, select Colonel John Coombes to make the whole place tick, and you had Petaro Cadet College. In a scorching wilderness he fashioned not only an educational institution, but also a little world of its own, having a shopping area, farm, hospital with maternity wing, birth control clinic, primary school and staff welfare club. It was an astonishing achievement.

I arrived there after an early morning 120 mile drive from Karachi. With the shade temperature dribbling up to 118 degrees, I was taken round the College at a pace bordering on the suicidal. John Coombes seemed unperturbed as he galloped round shouting, 'My God, it's bloody hot!' and mopping himself incessantly with a towel which he carried with him as if it were a garment. Our progress was not without incident. Happening upon a minor engineering project which was clearly heading for disaster, he rent the air with language that would have won instant recognition in a barrack-room. It was a measure of his status that the man on the receiving end of this tirade – he was, I afterwards learnt, the Engineering Officer – showed neither surprise nor resentment.

I enjoyed sitting in on what amounted to a miniature court case with John acting as judge, jury and attorney. This, I felt, was how things were done in the days of the British District Commissioner. The case was, as so often, a complex one involving a girl, her husband and her brother. She was clearly something of a baggage and may well have deserved the beatings which her husband was wont from time to time to mete out, beatings which had caused the brother, in the improbable role of knight errant, to step in. There was much garbled talk of kidnap, and the husband was clearly aggrieved that he was no longer enjoying his wife's company in the marital bed. The whole case was spread with a thick layer of salacity, a fact to which John gave emphasis by dint of meaningful glances and prodigious winks in my direction. His judgement, I recall, was impeccable, and the parties shuffled off with as contented an air as strained relationships would allow.

With huge glee, John took me to the staff welfare club, there to feast our eyes on the work of a builder suddenly divorced from his wits. 'I told the bloody fool to build me a Ladies. Just look at it!' We were standing in front of a door bearing the legend 'Gents'. In order to reach her haven, the lady had first to open this and then walk down a narrow passage to a door marked 'Ladies', her way impeded by two urinals. One found it hard to imagine a more abrupt shock to the charming natural modesty of Muslim ladies.

John was full of anecdote. One day a housemaster came to him in a great stew. 'Sir, you must speak with the Dispenser. He is rude to me, he abuse me. He will not let me have his pisspot, but tell me to use a cigarette lighter instead'. From which astonishing statement, the following facts emerged. A boy was a suspect dysentery case, so the housemaster goes along to the dispensary to borrow a bedpan in which a sample can be sent to the local hospital. Lacking the word bedpan, he asks for a pisspot. But – here's the rub – the Dispenser has only one; it's made of china and is his pride and job. He's not going to have it broken by some damned coolie en route to the hospital. It is the usual custom for samples to be rendered in a cigarette packet, but in his agitation the Dispenser, also losing grip on his English, says 'lighter' instead of 'packet'. The Housemaster is outraged that he, a devout Muslim, should be asked to defile himself by contact with tobacco! Such incidents gave colour to the daily round.

Over lunch we replaced a good deal of the liquid lost earlier in the day, and then walked out to my car. Though it had been standing all morning in the shade, the metal-work was too hot to touch; the inside was an inferno. John's parting remark was characteristic: 'You ought to take a ride in the President's car, old boy. Air-conditioned. Only trouble is you can't fart in it!'

Streaking back across the Sindh Desert towards Karachi, I was horrified to see through the heat haze ahead the body of a man prone in the middle of the empty road. Of other humans there was no sign; the scene was deserted. Brigandage? A hit and run driver? Death from heat stroke? Here surely was an opportunity to test one's capacity as a Samaritan. My driver braked to sixty, flicked the wheel, and we were past the prostrate figure before you could say Levite. 'Driver, stop!' I cried. 'That man . . .' I glanced back through the rear window. Slowly the figure rose, stretched, rubbed its eyes and shambled off down the sun-baked road.

*   *   *

'To be sure of your baggage, stay with it.' Acting on this sensible advice, I took ship from Karachi to Chittagong. Writing diary-fashion to my wife:

S.S. Rustom, May 28th

We're well under way now for Colombo which we should reach on the evening of the first. This is a lovely ship, built by the Germans in 1953, and sold to a Parsee three years ago. She has two classes, *de luxe* and economy. Between the two there is a great gulf fixed. *De luxe* is as comfortable as its name suggests, economy rather less so. I have a palatial cabin with bathroom; the taps exude fresh water. The only snag is that the air-conditioning has broken down, but one can't have everything. There are only five

de luxe class passengers in accommodation for forty. We eat at a
long table with the master and the officers. Three of the latter are
British, the first mate, the chief engineer and the master himself.

May 29th

I am not likely to collapse from overindulgence on this ship;
it's a great pity there aren't more passengers. After dinner last
night the rest of the evening was spent in playing Scrabble with
the skipper and first mate. They are both pleasant men, and have
given me the run of the ship. I have plenty to read including a
thick pile of papers from the various schools visited. I can study
these and do some constructive (I hope) thinking. There is a
swimming pool on the ship, and the food is excellent.

May 30th

I've just been on ship's rounds with the master, first mate,
doctor and purser. Very interesting, especially the food stores,
and the accommodation for the economy class passengers, of
which there are about a hundred. Pretty grim, all herded together
in what is no better than a hold. But they pay only eighty rupees
for the voyage of nine days, including two big curry meals a day,
which is probably one more than they are used to. The mate told
me last night of the passenger who travelled *de luxe* class himself,
sending his wife and kids economy! I must try that one out on you
some time.
We are carrying the fattest purser afloat. Twenty four and a half
stone, and so wide that it requires nice judgement for him to get
down the corridors. He flies into vast rages with the stewards and
is something of a character. Weather very sticky, it's most trying
at night, and I find one sleeps with little depth. I generally doze
off about twelve for a couple of hours, then go on deck for an
hour to cool off. The best sleep is from about four till seven when
the tea arrives.

June 1st

There is much speculation as to what time we shall reach
Colombo; it rather looks as if the times will be awkward from the

point of view of getting ashore. A first class row flourishes between the skipper and the chief engineer, because the latter is not
giving the ship the power of which the boss thinks she's capable. I
spent a lot of time on the bridge last night watching a magnificent
electric storm. No thunder and very little rain, just sheet after
sheet of tremendous lightning with hardly a second's darkness
between each flash.

On a wet squally Sunday we entered the river Karnafuli and sailed up
towards the city of perpetual peace, Chittagong. Altogether a misnomer,
surely, for it has had a turbulent history in which the natural elements
have played their part. The spot was pointed out to me, half a mile inland,
on to which a 6,000 ton freighter had been lifted by a tidal wave in the
1963 typhoon. The sky was black and threatening; I had breasted the tape
with the monsoon.

Part Two

Getting the Show on the Road

Getting the Show on the Road

To arrive in a strange city late at night is to experience the sharpest of anticlimaxes, the more so if it is raining. No matter how diligently we peer through the sodden windscreen, the place refuses to take shape, defies our attempts to distinguish it from any other city in the warm wet darkness. Even the smells, inseparable from urban life in the East, are diffused by the damp and the closed windows. Noises too are muted, everyone is abed. It was so when we drove into Dacca after the long haul from Chittagong, Jim Chaffey at the wheel of a British Council car, my own following in the hands of a hired driver, for I was not yet licensed to drive in Bengal.

Jim had achieved what was generally recognised as a wonder; he had cleared my car from the docks only half a day after it had been landed. In Southampton or Cape Town, this would not have excited comment; in Chittagong it was a miracle of rare device, for Chittagong was one of the world's most effective bottle-necks. There were three methods of getting goods away into the interior, all of them inadequate – a slender road broken half-way by a three hour voyage in a car ferry (on this our journey over the water, a sudden violent storm whipped up, full of rain and wind; in the inky darkness, I hoped that our captain, whose appearance did not inspire confidence, knew what he was about – he did); secondly there was a railway but much of that was single-line; lastly an airline, decidedly expensive. As if these obstacles were not enough, Chittagong was cursed with a Customs authority whose motto was clearly 'What we have we hold'. The result was a dockside crammed to bursting with goods of every shape and size. I counted forty-eight tractors forlorn in a parking lot, captives, I was told, for over three months. Cars were too numerous for a hasty reckoning. The authority had become notorious for sloth among people not inclined to view sloth with much misgiving. Its ability to hang on to goods gave it power which on occasions seemed positively magnetic. A fortnight after the great May cyclone of '65, six sealed railway wagons full of rice were sent up country for relief of the disaster victims. They disappeared – lost, it seemed, without trace. Ten days later they turned up back at Chittagong as tightly sealed as when they had left. By dint of persistence, patience and not a little palm-greasing, Jim had got papers through, and my own vehicle was free to essay the open road. In his triumph, I was happy to stand aside and cheer.

My first impression of Dacca, when morning light gave substance to the city, was one of verdancy. The rains had come early that year, allowing the grass and trees to take on a lushness, cool and pleasing after the aridity of Karachi. But let an appraisal of Dacca begin with the travel brochure:

'Dacca, known the world over as the city of mosques and muslim, has a history going back to the earliest times. The exact date of its foundation is not known, but it is first mentioned in recorded history as the new provincial capital under the Moghul governor, Islam Khan, who shifted his headquarters here from Rajmahal in 1608. Much of Dacca's great past is preserved in rich monuments of impressive beauty whose exquisite structural pattern, intricate design and workmanship bear witness to the high standards of art and architecture achieved by the Moguls who ruled here from 1575 to 1707'.

So far, so good. The writer is on safe factual ground here. Dacca certainly has an exciting history, but the 'rich monuments' have been allowed to fall into the most depressing decay. Soon, however, the writer really warms to his task:

'Although Dacca is essentially Oriental in outlook and atmosphere, yet it is a truly cosmopolitan city. Side by side with the old Dacca of Mogul mosques and monuments, Buddhist pagodas and monasteries, Hindu temples and shrines, a new Dacca is fast developing – a thriving monument to the comforts and pace of modern living. The hotel Shahbagh, with its stately modern pillars, stands like a grand mansion, offering most modern amenities. Just across the road the new building of Radio Pakistan rises up from green grounds like a citadel, gleaming in white harmony with the Shahbagh. The sprawling lawns, the modern swimming pool, the lovely tennis courts, the rich library, the well stocked cellar and the friendly atmosphere of the Dacca club invite one to laze away an evening in perfect leisure and comfort. Modern cinemas screen latest movies from Hollywood as well as from British and Continental studios. The latest addition is a fully air-conditioned super-structure rising into the sky, with two auditoria, one on top of the other, showing two different films at the same time.

The writer was on dangerous ground here in his eulogies of the Dacca club; he overlooked the mangy dogs and chickens which pecked at the rubbish on the lawns, the slippery carpets of damp moss oozing on to the tennis courts; he was not there in the early morning to see the servants doing their washing in the modern swimming pool; he was unconscious of the general air of grubbiness and neglect which pervaded the 'friendly atmosphere'. In fairness it should be added that the Dacca members deplored their club, and periodically tried to get something done about it. But let the travel man take up the tale again:

'The University Museum is full of precious relics and exhibits. Its library contains latest books in all fields of literature and science as well as rare old editions. Its classrooms are filled with eager students. Even a tourist is welcome to attend a lecture and learn at first hand of the glorious traditions and proud aspirations of Pakistani youth.'

Eager they certainly were, though some of their traditions were less glorious than others, for Dacca University, situated slap in the middle of the city, is given over more than most to students' riot and tantrums. Shortly before my arrival, a degree-giving ceremony was enlivened by activities hardly appropriate to the occasion. The guest of honour was the Provincial Governor to whom the students had taken a violent and unaccountable dislike. The procession of V.I.P.s across the lawns to the big marquee resembled the departure from Odsal Stadium of an Australian Rugby League team after winning a particularly dirty international.

Silence of a sort was maintained while the Vice-Chancellor made his speech of welcome, but as soon as the Governor arose to bestow the degrees, all hell broke loose. Not content with vociferous protest the students at the back of the marquee picked up chairs and hurled them pell mell toward the platform. Police became active; the rioters were driven out to form an immovable phalanx around the centre of operations. The few British on the platform sat tight, staring into space, a stolid example of the stiff upper lip; taut expressions betrayed their thoughts – this sort of thing could never happen at Oxbridge.

Degree-giving was abandoned, but, in spite of the whispered pleadings of the Vice-Chancellor who by now was looking his age, the Governor was plainly determined to have his say. He again rose to his feet to address an audience reduced to a handful by the stress of circumstances. It was a brave but futile exercise; the students, hearing his voice on the loudspeakers, set up a cacophony which effectually drowned every word of the speech. Occasional loud bangs that did no good at all to the nerves of those sweating it out in the marquee proclaimed the discharge of tear gas to which the police had resorted in an attempt to disperse the mob. At least the proceedings were not tarnished by dullness; they ended as they began, in tumultuous confusion. All the more credit to the Governor who, when I paid a courtesy call a few weeks later, enthusiastically discussed plans for the formation of two new universities. In silent admiration one could only give him ten out of ten for trying.

Unquestionably the Bengali is a politically-minded person. Perhaps it would be more accurate to say that he is more susceptible than most to irresponsible political agitators. It was not without significance that one of the two new universities mentioned by the Governor was to be located in the depths of the country, outside, so the authorities hoped, the range of the political hooligans who flourished in Dacca. These hooligans were, of course, exceptionally active at the time of an election. Our short stay in Dacca coincided with the first big elections held in the country for five years; at close hand we saw basic democracy at work. The people, all over twenty-one, including women, were electing the forty thousand basic democrats who in turn would be formed into union councils for the administration of local affairs, and would act with the forty thousand elected from the West wing as an *ad hoc* electoral college for the formal choice of the nation's President.

These elections were exceptionally noisy; clearly quite a lot of people were having quite a lot of fun – the explosion of fire-crackers, the din of strange musical bands, the shouts of processing mobs, all contributed to the general pattern of enthusiasm unrestrained. One feature was disturbing; every evening gangs of children, many of them not yet in double figures, would parade up and down the streets shouting and yelling political slogans that to most of them were quite meaningless. In this pursuit they were led by one or more adults, beating drums, waving time, exhorting the children to bigger and better ululations. These men were shabbily dressed fanatics of a rather nasty kind. We found the spectacle depressing, and wondered why the authorities, always loud in lamentation of political activity among the young, allowed such shameless exploitation of children.

If Dacca was a university city with, as has been demonstrated, a lively student community in its midst, it was also a capital – in conformity with the Central Government's policy of maintaining equality between the two wings, it was known as the Second Capital of Pakistan – with a plethora of government offices and an expanding commercial life. To house these goings-on, reinforced concrete was much in evidence. Little sky-scrapers rose in bleak profusion; new roads were cut, without, alas, adequate drainage; a vast new hotel gave rather overdue competition to the 'stately modern pillars' of the Shahbagh; there was a boom in house building for the affluent (not a few of them lay half finished awaiting the time when the intending owner could muster the funds to continue the good work). Meantime the old city defied progress and remained what it always had been – a seething jumble of shops, houses, hovels, markets, alleyways, mosques, animals, traffic chaos, people and open drains doing duty as public lavatories.

Dacca, then, was a restless place, an uneasy compromise between ancient and modern, between East and West. Against the walls of a half completed office block, the citizen squats to urinate; in the old city, a stark naked half-wit shambles past the colour film advert – a life-size cut-out of a blonde in a swim suit; the main streets are choked with Fords, rickshaws and bullock-carts; profitable building surges on, but the huge bulk of the population ekes out a threadbare existence in disgusting hovels; the urban refuse, pestiferous amid a cloud of vultures, is dumped beside the main road a mile from the heart of the city; new shopping centres are proudly advertised, but it is in a hundred and one ageless bazaars that the real business is done. Sometime, no doubt, Dacca would come to terms with itself; the planners were active and not without vision. But let us return to the travel brochure for the last word:

'In the crowded bazaars and market places tourists and diplomats from all over the world rub shoulders with the local populace. Smoothly-shaven westerners mingle freely with strikingly handsome bearded Bengalis while the Buddhists monks, wrapped in their saffron robes, stroll nonchalantly along. The winding, meandering rivers have a life of their own. Dacca's waterfronts are crowded with all kinds of craft: yachts, sampans, canoes, motor launches, fishermen's boats, all bubbling with activity, all going their separate ways.'

During the whole of my time in Dacca and its environs, I saw one Buddhist monk.

*   *   *

Along the marine parades of Bournemouth, Frinton and Torquay stroll the sahibs and memsahibs left over from the days when the British raj in India was drawing to its inevitable close. About those days they are, as like as not, nostalgic. They miss the sense of power which even the most undistinguished official then enjoyed; they miss the hunting, the cheap liquor, the easeful tropical day; above all they miss, the more so as they bend their ageing backs over yet another stack of washing-up, the servants. They sigh for Abdul who was at their side with a restorative at the flick of a finger, and who would cheerfully take off sahib's shoes and sweaty socks when he returned exhausted from tennis; they sigh for Mukhtar in the kitchen, who might be none too clean but who produced food hot and tasty often at the appointed hour; they sigh for Ali the sweeper, who would consider it an indignity to himself if the memsahib so much as bent to remove a crumb; they sigh for the perambulations round the garden to appraise the efforts of the malis, all day in the sun on fifteen rupees a month; some, who knows, may sigh for the tin pot into which they had defecated for years in the comforting knowledge that a fellow human would be on hand to clear the remains seconds after their departure. For India was – and to some extent still is – a stronghold, almost *the* stronghold, of the servant class – bearers, cooks, sweepers, misalchis, syces, malis and the rest.

There was no dearth of servants in Bengal; to find a good one was an altogether different matter. The iniquities of one's bearer, the slovenliness of the cook were number one topics of conversation wherever two or three of the affluent were gathered together. I was temporarily housed in the flat of David Bradley, a Council officer on leave in England, inheriting for the time being his bearer, Menahjuddin, and Abdul the Cook. The latter had worked in a ship's galley and considered himself superior to the parochial folk about him. He was endowed with culinary talents and a rich sense of the absurd. Each morning, breakfast done, Menahjuddin would stand by for the day's orders. As I was a frequent eater-out, these would often be negative. 'No lunch, no dinnah!!!' I would roar in a voice half shout, half song. From the kitchen Abdul would echo the refrain – 'no lunch, no dinnaah!' – followed by a loud yell of laughter.

My luncheon requirements were always both simple and scanty, a situation which shocked him deeply but did not prevent him producing the meagre food deliciously cooked. Once, returning early from the office, I found him asleep across the front door-step. A gentle poke with the foot, and he was round the corner in a flash, his wail of dismay lingering on the humid air like the trump of Germinal. Poor Abdul was ageing, he had a cough, his days must have been numbered. Somehow he would, I am sure, have made them cheerful ones.

On David Bradley's return, I had to seek out a new establishment. Unfailingly in Bengal everyone has a brother, in which respect Menahjuddin did not fail, proudly producing one as fat as he was thin, as self-confident as he was diffident. I set off to my new flat with the portly Isnahjuddin and a cook whose name I have forgotten quicker than his ghastly cooking; he did not last long.

While I was a bachelor, Izzy did me well, but with the arrival of the family in October the chinks in his armour became apparent. In his references, he was said to be a dab hand at organising parties; in the event he proved himself inept, losing his head with disturbing frequency, and, as he cleared up the debris afterwards, smiting the night air with a world of sighs. Izzy did not take to my family, nor they to him. We decked his portly frame in a uniform befitting the Principal's bearer; we provided him with Deenat as an assistant, but it was to no avail. Things did not improve when we moved to the College. The sighs and the 'much trouble' became increasingly repetitive, and on Deenat's all too willing shoulders more work was thrust. One morning the word was spoken; not without dignity, Izzy folded up his uniforms and walked away down the drive, having secreted somewhere in the ample folds of his apparel two of our best thermos flasks and three of his late master's white shirts.

We raised Deenat's salary to a hundred rupees and made him the head of the household. He was a delightful boy, quiet, hard working, devoted to our Nicola (known locally as 'Baby Nickler'). He and the new cook, Cyprian, became the keystones of our domestic life. Cyprian – the name betrays his religion, Roman Catholic – was, when the mood took him, a quite excellent performer. I remember one dinner of outstanding quality with John Wailes of UNESCO and Jim Chaffey as our guests. Soup – at which Cyprian excelled – butter fish with a mustard sauce, roast leg of lamb with mint sauce and garden peas, green mango fool. (Of all fools this is the king, the flavour hovering between gooseberry and apple, tart and smooth to the tongue). But Cyprian could have his off-days, and my wife had hard tussles with the obtuseness by which he demonstrated his distemper. His cook book caused us a good deal of puzzled amusement. How, for instance, was one to interpret *floare, supbons, bared, rades, cickins, carespace, fese, tabulpapar, calore, pasly, traneps, bets* and *raice*? The sporting flavour prompted by the last two meant, in fact, beetroots and rice. Have a guess at the rest if you wish – the only clue afforded is that all are commodities used in Britain.

*   *   *

It was important to make one's number with the military. One of my first appointments was arranged for me by Harry Forster, British Council No. 1 in Dacca: a meeting with the boss – Chairman of Governors and G.O.C.-in-C. East Pakistan, Major Gen. Agha Mohammed Yahya Khan. Harry accompanied me to effect introductions, to produce, as it were, the rabbit out of the hat. We drove past the airport into the rather special world of the Dacca Military Cantonment.

Military cantonments are associated mainly with the subcontinent; although built under the Raj, they bear scant resemblance to anything to be found in the U.K. – certainly not to barrack buildings, those Victorian edifices which cast their ponderous shadows in county towns and around the drill squares of Aldershot, Tidworth and the like. Cantonments resembled more closely the military camps that were thrown up all over Britain in such desperate haste during World War II – hutments flung together with no regard for landscape nor the aesthetic sense. Some resemblance, perhaps, save that cantonments were built with much more style, with a sense of permanence and with an infinitely keener regard for the surroundings. They were spaciously laid out, with trees, shrubs and flower beds to give shade and to please the eye.

The cantonments tended to be oases of calm and cleanliness; this was certainly the case in Dacca, where the transition from the lively, chaotic squalor of the city environs to the orderliness of the soldiers' world was a sharp reminder of what can be achieved by good order and military discipline. Pakistan prided itself on its army (on its Air Force – no less so); in Bengal, it was here, within the cantonment, that the West Pakistani felt really at home, exercising the command which tradition taught him was his by right. Certainly, as we drove into the General's Headquarters on a bright June morning in 1965, nothing seemed so wildly improbable as the events which, in fact, erupted six years later – the expulsion of West

Pakistanis in a bloodbath, and the creation of a new country, Bangladesh. As might be expected, access to the great man was only gained through a succession of lesser fry. We were conducted to the GSO 1 (Education) who conducted us to the GSO 1 (Operations), who conducted us to the Deputy Military Secretary, from whose office we at last, via an A.D.C.'s anteroom, gained the air-conditioned sanctum of the General himself.

Our interview was brief though agreeable enough; the General did most of the talking. A short, brusque man, Yahya Khan was a ruthless authoritarian who understood the Soldier's Art in so far as it applied to the field and the clash of arms. That was his special strength and the basis of his reputation. In his own Headquarters Mess – I later attended a Guest Night, which had adopted many habits from the old Indian Army days – he cut a somewhat horrifying figure, taking aboard a hefty load of whisky (rumour persisted that he was a bottle-a-day man), which turned him into a noisy, garrulous bully. He knew nothing about education, and I found, on the very rare occasions I could meet him to talk business, that there was little common ground between us. I was not at all sorry when, two months after my arrival, he was posted back to West Pakistan, to pass ultimately, albeit briefly, into the pages of Pakistan's history.

The military man with whom one was to have most dealings was the GSO 1 (Education). Understandably, the General delegated a lot of authority to him, and right gleefully did Lt. Col. Rahman take on the charge. As a member of the seven man Governing Body (three of the seven never attended a single meeting – indeed I never clapped eyes on them), he was in a good position to make himself just as helpful, or obstructive, as he chose. He was a Bengali, and an able fellow; unhappily for me, and for smooth administration, he hated my guts.

About Lt. Col. Rahman I later learnt two things: firstly, he wanted my job – in his eyes a foreigner as Principal of a prestigious establishment like a Cadet College was anathema; secondly, he never ceased in his efforts to get me kicked out, recruiting on to his pay-roll a miscellany of College staff ranging from one of the housemasters to a kitchen hand, whose job it was to keep him informed of everything I did, morning, noon and night, month in, month out, the year long. From this little espionage network he hoped, no doubt, to harvest enough dirt to see me on the next plane to Heathrow. That this cataclysm never happened was no fault of the worthy Colonel, who endeavoured, not without success, to put as many spokes in the wheel as only he knew how.

*   *   *

From the start my uneasy footsteps were guided by British Council officers, not least by the Chief, Harry Forster. The day after my arrival, he
suggested a drive out to the College. I needed no urging, for me it was a
case of the sooner the better. A seven thousand mile journey stretched
over five weeks had brought me at last to the scene of operations, the spot
marked X. The drive was not without anxieties, I was fearful of anti-
climax; after all, this was to be our home for the best part of at least two
years. Those who had visited the site had been loud with praise, some
unashamedly enthusiastic, but at the back of one's mind was the fear that
the grass, always greener on the other side, might once again turn out to
be an illusion.

After an hour's motoring we turned off the main road and drove up a
wide approach; ahead of us, bestriding the horizon, was a long white
building, in its centre a dome not yet completed. It was at once remarkable
for the fact that it was built on a 'hill', a good twelve feet above the level
of the surrounding country-side (a boy was later to write that he was
enjoying his new life 'in the hills'). This was the College building, housing classrooms, four laboratories, four lecture theatres and staff room. It
was certainly impressive, cool and spacious; two storeyed, it stretched out
on both sides of the entrance hall and main staircase leading to the flat
roof and dome. (The main structure of this dome was walled with panels
of latticed concrete – very artistic; through the panels in winter the fresh
breezes blew, in summer the rain poured, water cascading down two
flights of stairs in prodigious volume. It was an odd piece of planning for
one of the wettest places in the world.) Wide verandahs flanked both sides
of the classrooms, sixteen in number. So far, so good.

The main part of the College lay behind this building, the two boarding
houses, dining hall, staff quarters. These were ranged round a big playing
field; not yet finished, but very recognisable for what they were, the
buildings gleamed white in the sunshine. Everywhere there were trees,
around the seventy-acre plateau lay the jungle out of which this site had so
recently been hacked. Even allowing for the builders' rubble and for the
thick glutinous mud, one was elated. This was, after all, something; the
enthusiasm of earlier visitors was not misplaced.

We sloshed about in the mess, appraising this, criticising that; the administrative block hard by the College building was far too small, my own office
a risible cell twelve by twelve – something would have to be done about that.
No start had yet been made on library or assembly hall for the good reason
that no-one could make up their minds just where to put them. My own
house, too, had already been the subject of fruitless controversy.

Colonel Maurice Brown in the role of adviser had visited the site two months before, bringing to the scene a wealth of experience and common sense. 'The Principal's house must be there,' he had said pointing to a delectable site a furlong away from the south-east corner of the site. Officials had been inclined to agree, though with reluctance; in the blue-print the Principal's house was elsewhere sited. 'Let us wait and see what the Principal thinks,' they said, and there the matter rested. I had no doubts at all – Maurice Brown was right. But there was a snag – the new site was fractionally outside the boundary limit. Land purchase must be arranged before a sod could be turned. Accordingly, a meeting was arranged to be held on the spot, the Education Secretary, the Architect, the District Commissioner and myself; everything would be settled there and then. To this assemblage I made my way, feeding on hope.

I had envisaged a cosy businesslike conference, all details despatched in a few minutes of brief parley between men of decision. The outcome was very different – firstly the Architect failed to turn up, secondly I was swiftly to find out that there is no such thing in Bengal, especially out of doors, as a cosy businesslike conference. We grew into a throng, almost a rabble; contractors, government officials, building engineers, assistant building engineers, electricians and heaven knows who else gathered in front of the building.

We set off across the campus a good forty strong, all chattering at the tops of voices, myself in the van understanding never a word but trying, in view of the photographers scurrying about, to look like God's gift to Bengal education. Arrived on the site, the bedlam persisted, I trying to get a word in here and there amid the prevailing hubbub. We returned to the College building where tea, bananas, sweet cakes and glasses of danger-ous-looking water were dispensed in one of the classrooms; we ate nois-ily, what time the doors and windows filled up with gaping coolie faces, three deep, avid for a glimpse of the great men at food. Not for the last time in Bengal I had the feeling of being an exhibit in a zoo. At last cars moved off, but not before the Education Secretary had murmured assur-ances in my ear that all would be well; the purchase would now go ahead unimpeded. 'Soon your house will be built,' he said with a smile and an optimism that I could not entirely share.

The responsibility for the building of the College lay in the hands of a government department somewhat euphemistically named 'Constructions and Buildings', dubbed C. & B. for short. They were pleasant people but not notably efficient: there was too much red tape, and they were ham-pered at every stage by a cumbrous chain of command which ensured that no man need ever make a decision – there was always somebody one rung up the ladder who could carry the can. The department was divided into two – building and electricity. For delays they could, and did, heap blame on each other; for mistakes, which were legion, the buck was passed between them with mutual hatred and scorn. It was not a set-up which leant itself to speedy and effective building.

A problem that always faced me in these construction days was the difficulty of finding anyone on the site who could speak with a vestige of authority. There was, of course, no telephonic communication so that it was impossible to announce one's arrival in advance. The 'engineer' in charge on the job was a youth of about twenty-three, so thin that he seemed to have the utmost difficulty in remaining upright. He bent in peculiar places, which, added to a set of gigantic teeth, gave him the air of a discarded safety-pin. I was fascinated too by his Adam's apple, protuberant and a good half inch out of centre. He was completely and utterly incompetent, yet here he was in charge of a building operation costing millions of rupees. Moreover, he was very seldom there, for he commanded a jeep and used it freely to rid himself of the cares of site management. With his penchant for absenteeism and with the lack of know-how among his subordinates, many of my sallies to the College were completely wasted. I recall arriving unheralded rather early one morning – about 9.30 a.m. The youth was there all right – in bed, not yet at grips with the long day's problems. He emerged half-an-hour later, followed closely by an acolyte holding an umbrella over the willowy frame to protect it from the cruel rays of the sun.

At last, he left. Sacked? not a bit of it – promoted! What he really needed, if he was ever to be of any real use to his department, was a three-year course with a big civil engineering firm, learning the job from the bottom, getting his hands dirty and doing for the first time in his young life a really hard stint of work.

Lack of even average competence at the manager-foreman level was one of Bengal's biggest headaches. It was difficult to see how the situation could improve until such time as the prevalent attitude towards manual labour changed. To work with the hands was considered degrading; to sit under an umbrella watching others work was considered uplifting – my head gardener had been with me only a few weeks before he was asking to be allowed to 'stop working with his hands'. Since this attitude was deeply ingrained, the change may be a long time coming.

The construction processes made few concessions to new fangled devices; they were based substantially on an abundant labour force. The coolie scuttling up and down the rickety bamboo scaffolding with basket on head, hefting loads of bricks and wet concrete, was still the vital cog in the building machine. A concrete mixer was the only modern contrivance on the scene; else it was much as it had been for centuries.

One operation gave much pleasure. The final covering to the flat roof was a paste made from water and brick dust – it was meant to act as a sealer to keep out water. This was spread over the flat surface like jam on bread, and then beaten down hard and flat into the concrete beneath. To this end a gang of little boys was assembled, each with a wooden implement like a large butter pat. Squatting down shoulder to shoulder they smacked away at the floor in unison, chanting the while to assist rhythm. A chorus master walked up and down, attended sometimes by a drummer, beating time, and flicking at the laggard with a small innocuous whip. If I happened upon the scene with visitors, we would be given a benefit performance, louder voices, a livelier rhythm, more fervent exhortations, small faces alight with smiles as they sensed our pleasure.

It turned out that my good friend the Education Secretary was a little premature in his optimism about my own house. The business of concluding the land purchase dragged on interminably. Meanwhile I was continually on the lookout for the Architect, a government official and a Geordie. We will call him Carruthers. He was a figure straight out of the pages of Somerset Maugham, a man with the tropics so deeply soaked into his blood that he gave off a pungent aroma of whisky and spices. The main problem was to run him to earth, office hours meant nothing at all. I discussed this with Major Rashid (about whom more anon).

'Carruthers was out here long before Partition,' said the Major, 'he just carries on as he pleases.'

'Any chance of getting him at the office?'

'Not much. We'll have to try his house, twelve o'clock's the best time. He's generally come to by then.'

We drove through an unspeakable bazaar into a clearing backed by a garden, neglected and massively overgrown. Somewhere in the thicket was a bungalow.

The bearer was by no means optimistic. He sat us down and made off on tiptoe to the nether regions. A loud roar augured ill for our mission, but the bearer, apprehension in his gait, beckoned us into a bedroom. From a tangle of sheets, which invited no close inspection, a tousled figure, near naked, groped for a packet of Scissors (four annas for twenty).

'Bearer, beer!' he roared. We sat on the bed; gingerly I proffered plans of the house which I wanted altered. With a stub of pencil Carruthers sketched a line here, a line there, punctuating his efforts with sepulchral coughs and groans. The hangover lay thick about him.

'God, I feel bloody awful!' he cried, as if we needed telling – he looked ready for the tomb. Ten minutes later, fortified with beer, we were breathing fresh air and heading for home. The surprise came next day when I met Carruthers again; he remembered every detail of our conversation, every minute alteration.

It was one thing to get an architect surfacing from an excess of alcohol to approve interior alterations; it was quite another to get government departments to speed up negotiations for land purchase. It was September, three months later, before the deed was finally done, the last signature secured. Not that our troubles were then over. As closely as we could, from our temporary quarters in Dacca forty miles away, we kept an eye on the progress, but our vigilance was not close enough to prevent a hilarious disaster. On arrival, months later, to take up residence, we found that the builders had forgotten to provide us with a front door. Back door, yes, window bars fitted, all entries secured save one – where the front door should have been was a vast gaping hole. A blind man could have pillaged the house with impunity. We slept the first night with a huge packing-case across the aperture, a servant sleeping beside it on the inside. Next day a temporary gimcrack affair was put into use, and with this we had to be content until the triumphant arrival, some three weeks later, of the Front Door.

It was ironical that the smouldering war between the two branches of C. & B. should flame into activity over the matter of our water heater. The electricity branch was responsible for wiring and supplying the immersion unit, 'Buildings' was responsible for tank and piping. Between the two, venomous box-and-cox was played for weeks, each lamenting the other's ineptitude. To bring them together for sensible discussion was impossible. At length it grew almost funny, though my wife, with nappie-washing to supervise, seldom saw the joke. Certain it was that we were the main casualties in this farcical strife. For two winter months we simply went without hot water.

These setbacks apart, the house, when at last it was ready, was one which gave us a good deal of pleasure. The alterations for which I pleaded concerned the ground floor. It had been planned in conventional style – small entrance hall, living room, dining room. These we flung wide open, giving us one very large living space, and, just as important, cross ventilation. A wide verandah surrounded the ground-floor on three sides. Halfway up the stairs a small landing gave access through french windows to a balcony for winter sun-bathing. On the first floor were four bedrooms, three of them with their own bathrooms. The Bengali cook prefers things to be simple; he likes best of all to cook on an oil-stove; the kitchen hardly conformed to the standards advocated in the glossy magazines, but it served its purpose. We had, too, a small guest bungalow adjacent to the house which was very useful. Not the least remarkable thing about this substantial dwelling was the speed of its erection – about fourteen weeks . . .

Meanwhile the building work in the college proceeded in a series of fits and starts. Certainly very rapid progress had been made in the early months before my arrival. President Ayub Khan had laid the foundation stone in November '63, serious building was begun in January. When I first saw it in early June, the College had a good solid look about it. But as the rainy season got under way and as the work became more detailed, so things tended to grind to a halt. Unless one raised a hullabaloo – chose the right person to cajole, the right bottom to kick – nothing whatever would be done. Dealing with persons to whom passing the buck was second nature, this selection was not always easy. Nor, as buildings drew near to completion, did it pay to look too closely into the finishing work. This was dreadfully shoddy, and it was apparent that all too soon we would be running up big bills for repairs to premises. It was hopeless to complain though we did so and vociferously. 'I am so sorry, but what can I do? We have no skilled workers.' That reply, heard so often, contained, we knew, more than a grain of truth. As for painting inside and out, having seen the effect of a season's monsoon rain on buildings in Dacca, I preferred not to think of what we might be looking like in a year's time. More by good luck than by good management the buildings were ready in most essentials for the eventual opening in January, '65. But before that happy event, much had to be done . . .

*   *   *

It was necessary first of all to get some sort of a base from which to conduct operations. In this I was helped by a distinguished government educationist who very kindly gave me desk room in the office of one of his henchmen, Major Rashid. More important, he deputed the worthy Major to give me 'every possible assistance'. The Major was splendid: a portly, middle-aged Bengali, he was sceptical about everything around him. Moreover, he had a rich sense of humour to colour his scepticism. He would let loose an endless flow of pessimistic utterances, accompanying each with a deep belly laugh, in which I had no difficulty in sharing. He had only to mention the words 'C. & B. Department' to subside into contemptuous guffaws. He helped me to preserve my sanity at a time when it was put to severe strain.

The Major's office was not so splendid. It was on the second floor of a brand new block – the builders' scaffolding had not yet been removed – but already the walls, corridors and stair-cases were stained with filth. On my way up each morning I had to pass a room the purpose of which would have been obvious to a blind man; one 'counted two and seventy stenches, all well defined'.

Besides looking after me, the Major did some work the nature of which I never succeeded in fathoming, but it entailed an endless coming and going of miscellaneous characters who effectively put my concentration to rout and made efficient work difficult. However, it was a base, it had a telephone, and I was thankful at this stage for these small mercies.

One morning I was putting in some tasteful doodling on the blotter, wondering how best to use the next two hours, when a message arrived from the distinguished government educationist asking me to join him for tea in ten minutes. I said I would be delighted and sat back in anticipation of a cosy, constructive chat over the tea-cups. My anticipation was very wide of the mark. At the appointed moment I found myself being escorted downstairs to, of all places, the office staff-canteen. This, it must be said, was a dingy little room in the basement. It was absolutely bulging with people, overcrowded even by local standards.

As I was being shoved inside, my mystification was turned to sheer terror when a voice purred in my ear 'You will, of course, speech make?' This is such stuff, I felt, as nightmares are made on. Sensing my alarm, an official hastily put me into the somewhat crowded picture. 'Our Chief has received a big decoration. We are here to rejoice with him.' Here indeed we were, along with the whole of his staff of about two hundred in a space which would have uncomfortably housed fifty. The great man came in; there was a polite burst of clapping, and we all sat down as best we could to cups of cool weak tea and sticky cakes. The temperature, overlaid by a rich human aroma, rose by the minute. A man got up and recited a poem to loud applause, in praise, I presumed, of our distinguished government educationist.

The hero of the hour then made a speech, at one point referring to my recent arrival, and adding, to my complete amazement, that 'he has already endeared himself to everyone present.' As I had only set eyes on about half a dozen of them, I felt he was stretching a point, but such kindness must be suitably acknowledged, and, when my turn came, I laid it on thick. I got a good reception, and squeezed down into my seat shaking and adrip with sweat. A few minutes later we were out again in the fresh air; it had been a taxing tea-party.

*   *   *

Apart from building problems – already described – there were three other major factors to be dealt with: finance, the collection of material human and the collection of material vegetable and mineral. The last alone was a very considerable operation indeed, involving the acquisition of every single item of equipment from india rubbers to motor transport – a big enough task in any country – in Bengal, a gargantuan one.

Shopping in Dacca even for the simplest things was apt to be a debilitating experience, for all too often the attitude of the shopkeeper was one of complete indifference. He was the sitting, or squatting, epitome of 'couldn't-care-less'; even in the concrete purlieus of new Dacca, his premises, newly acquired, were usually scruffy and in a sorry muddle. No better illustration of this could be cited than the experiences of our Librarian, Mr Ahmed, and his Principal, when, many months later, we were in a position to order books for the College Library. We were prepared to spend money, to have a bit of a splash. To smooth the path of business, Mr Ahmed had the previous week visited two or three booksellers with news of our intentions and with a precise request that the managers themselves would be available on the morning of our joint visit. In the event not one manager kept his promise; each shop was staffed by a semi-literate numskull whose knowledge of the book trade would not have covered a postage stamp. I groaned aloud to Mr Ahmed as we drove off to pursue the search in another part of the city. 'They have no responsibility, these managers,' he said.

All things were made more difficult by the acute shortage of goods; in some respects it was like being back in the England of 1946. Such things as could be bought locally were of poor quality, while to import from abroad entailed not only fathoms of red tape but also the delays at that renowned bottleneck, Chittagong. I was, moreover, expected, by the elaborate rigmarole which embraces financial affairs on the subcontinent, to get no fewer than three estimates for every purchase, be it a bottle of ink or a groundsman's tractor. Over this last point I frequently defaulted; bit by bit the stuff was gathered in – stationery, crockery, cutlery, textbooks, pots and pans, teaching equipment, clothing (every boy was to be kitted out fully from underpants outwards) and furniture.

In itself, the acquisition of furniture was a little saga. To begin with I was assured that there was in Dacca no single furnishing firm capable of producing anything but rubbish; their honest dealing also, it seemed, was open to question. I got the names of two firms generally reckoned to be less bad than the rest, and set off in search of the showrooms of Messrs. Decorum Limited. These I found underneath the Stadium in premises new, but, as was the way in Dacca, already wearing the appearance of a slum. There were a few pieces of nondescript furniture, and a willowy lout lounging at a desk. He eyed me with languor akin to dislike; the feeling was mutual.

'Burra sahib hai?' I asked without hope.

The youth spat and shrugged. It seemed unlikely that our business relationship would prosper.

'Perhaps one hour,' he said, turning away to scratch somewhere beneath his trousers. Two hours later the manager showed symptoms of interest.

'You come see my factory very fine?'

'Where is it?'

'Two three minutes. You got car?'

We plunged into the old city. We dived down alleyways so slender that one was judging distances on both sides to the nicety of an inch. At last we could go no further. I shut off the engine, lit a cigarette and sat back resigned to anything.

'We are here,' cried the manager. 'You come with me'. I abandoned the car, and followed Mr. Decorum Limited, who by now was agog with excitement, down a narrow path between high buildings. An open drain lent our walk an aromatic distinction.

'Here my factory!' shouted Mr. Decorum, waving his arm majestically as one displaying a treasure house.

I could hardly believe my eyes. Beneath a straw roof supported by rickety pillars and open on all four sides, squatted a gaggle of shrivelled humanity, lackadaisically banging and planing and sawing. Of mechanical aids there was no sign; that the fifteen or so creatures crammed into this pestilential hovel could produce anything at all was something of a miracle. My inspection was brief, I turned and made for the car, Mr. Decorum in my wake, full of exhortation. I could find no enthusiasm, the halting conversation dribbled into silence. I left him at his showroom, alive with anticipations I could never satisfy. Poor Mr. Decorum! No doubt he is still trying to puzzle out why the bustling foreigner was so singularly dead to the splendours of his factory very fine.

I clutched like the drowning man at a straw. It was five feet ten high, and full of teeth; it was Mr. Alam. Nature had been sparing of its graces when it fashioned this gawky anthropoid. Out of a massive mouth sprouted gums and dentures which would have kept a dentist in petty cash for a lifetime; below it a chin lapsed into cruel decline. One was not conscious of much else. The eyes were heavily lidded, yet bright with cunning or alarm as the situation warranted.

'I make good furniture, all seasoned wood.' This I knew to be the most barefaced fib, for in East Bengal seasoned timber was hard to come by. 'You speak, I do. All prices very cheap. Best working men.'

He produced estimates, terms were agreed and a contract drawn up. The first round, honours about even, had been fought in what was to prove a long, hard war of attrition.

Mr. Alam was required to establish a factory at the college that we might the closer keep an eye on his activities. To this end he was provided with a concrete building which his ragtag gang of scalliwags speedily reduced to a shambles. In an atmosphere thick with dust, heat and flies, they worked, cooked, smoked, ate, gambled, spat and slept. From it oozed a trickle of desks, chairs and miscellaneous pieces at a rate far too leisurely to keep pace with Mr. Alam's contractual obligations. Some of the stuff produced was of matchstick quality.

One day, out of temper, I stalked into the so-called factory, seized flimsy chairs and tore them apart. Under my kicking feet desks wilted and collapsed, tables disintegrated with the harsh splitting sound of unseasoned timber. Mouths fell open, eyes popped in dismay; nothing like this had ever been seen before. It was a horrid display of raw anger, but it served its purpose admirably – for a time the quality of goods improved.

There was on the site a notable lack of supervision. The foreman – if the title can be so misused – was a gangling clerk with a weak giggle and an air of helplessness. Mr. Alam himself was far too astute to appear often on the premises; he had, it seemed, a factory in Chittagong as well as showrooms in Dacca, which situation he exploited to make his presence as scarce as only he knew how. He mustered reinforcements to strengthen his position; one day I received this letter from his Dacca 'manager':

'We beg to inform your honour that our propritor was contact to see you on last 24th November 64, but due to his attending in 'Timber Auction' at ctg. for mymenshing work, he failed to see you in the schedual date. In this connection he informed us by

Trunk Call that he will see you on 28th instant after finishing
Auction work. To day again by a special massanger he is inform-
ing us that the date of the auction extended up to 2-12-64 and he
is very busy to collect timber from Auction for mymenshingh
work. He must see you on 3-12-64 positively.
    He also advices us to request your honour not to mind anything
for his unintentional late of present.'

So the battle raged.
    'Where's Mr. Alam?' I would cry in desperation at some new piece of
crass folly.
    The clerk would giggle and shrug, 'He in Dacca. He come from
Chittagong.'
    'When he come here?'
    'He come to-morrow.' With the clerk it was always to-morrow; like to-
morrow Mr. Alam never came.
    Which is not strictly true – Mr. Alam did come, but only when he wanted
money. This was between us a raw bone of contention almost from the start.
'I am poor man,' he would plead with a histrionic flourish that would not
have deceived a newt. He had, in fact, hopelessly overplayed his hand; he
lacked the capital resources to tackle an enterprise calling for much raw
material and labour. The crisis came just before the Idh break, a fortnight
before the College was due to open. Unpaid for weeks, his workers made an
angry buzz as they bore down on my house with Mr. Alam in their midst, a
reluctant figure, tatty brief-case at the short trail. They stopped at a respect-
ful distance and shoved the boss towards my front-door.
    'My men, very poor men,' he wept, changing momentarily the angle of
approach. 'They have no happy time. Only Idh time happy time. No
money to pay wages.'
    'That's your affair, Mr. Alam,' I replied. 'It's no concern of mine if you
can't pay your men.'
    At this stage he resorted to yet another line of attack.
    'I have affection for you,' he sobbed. No remark could possibly have
put me so abruptly on guard; had he produced a gun, I could not have been
more alarmed. After what had passed between us over the months, this
was, even by his standards, an outsize fib.
    'I'm sorry, Mr. Alam. No furniture – no money.' He shambled off to
make what peace he could with his irate employees.
    I refused point blank to pay for goods not delivered; by now Mr. Alam
had fallen so far behind on his deliveries that his arguments sprang only

from weakness. But he was never at a loss for an excuse, never deficient in promises to do better next time. In the latter he resembled Charles II, on whose word no man could rely. I certainly didn't.

Soon the uneasy alliance had to be broken, something had to give. I wrote a stern letter declaring our association at an end. Unwilling to accept the inevitable, he bombarded me with letters deviously worded, with visits increasingly lachrymose – all to no avail. He had provided us with a good deal of furniture – 'all seasoned wood' he affirmed to the end – much of it of poor quality; he was weeks behind with his deliveries. We parted without affection.

*   *   *

Shortly after my arrival, I contrived by luck rather than by good management to lay hands on a brand new Chevrolet mini-bus. It was olive green and of hideous appearance but its acceleration was superb, and so good was the suspension that the numerous bumps and potholes held few terrors. I had the name of the college painted in white along its sides and felt that we were beginning to get somewhere.

Now having two vehicles, it was necessary to look at our manpower situation and to make a rapid one hundred per cent increase. The engagement of a driver in Bengal is no simple matter; there is no such thing as a driving test with the result that any creature who can press a self-starter, grind his gears and keep his foot on an accelerator considers that he merits the title of 'experienced driver'. A wrinkle newly sprung across my forehead was put down to acute anxiety neurosis brought on by road testing three aspiring drivers, before good fortune led to my office one day No. 357642 L/Naik Nazir, late of the R.I.A.S.C.

'I serve Breetish Army, sah. I go many lands.' From his pocket he produced a bundle of grubby testimonials signed by Colonel Browns and Major Smiths, all testifying to his excellent qualities. I liked the cut of him; he was engaged there and then.

Nazir was in many ways a most unusual person. To begin with he drove with quite excessive care; also he was utterly reliable and very conscientious. These three attributes put him in a class of his own. He became very attached to my family, a feeling that was mutual, and by virtue of being the oldest member of the staff he appointed himself their protector, guide and mentor. 'I take sisters to Dacca?' was his most urgent plea – my wife, incidentally, was counted among the sisters – and he would watch over their shopping with elaborate care and with volleys of army rebuke for the beggars and nuisances who were apt to molest them. On taking leave of my daughter and me at the airport, bound for Christmas shopping in Calcutta, he went into a swift wriggle of embarrassment, shot a letter into Angela's hand and fled. We opened it on the plane:

> My dear Sister,
> Thank you very much on the eve of your departure to India. I wish you satisfactory journey. However I shall be highly glad at the same time will feel oblige if you kindly arrange bring back a woollen chadur from India which is available there, at a comfortable price than Pakistan. Please don't mind. I must pay the price just when you will return back at Dacca. With best wishes . . .

We returned in triumph next day with the chadur, no purchase could have given greater pleasure. We also contrived to buy a second-hand transistor set, on which he had set his heart, at a price well below his maximum. Like a child with a new mechanical toy, he speedily reduced it to silence, and an extensive overhaul was needed to bring it back to life.

His knowledge of what went on under the bonnet of a car was rudimentary which did not prevent him tinkering in the works whenever opportunity afforded. Every month he would do a day's maintenance on my car, an operation from which it took several days to recover. His service training had taught him that a vehicle must have its regular dose of maintenance, and who was I to say him nay?

Nazir reacted strongly to any visits we had from V.I.P.s. He would polish his vehicle by the hour, and himself stand stiffly at attention beside it at the moment of arrival, four medals resplendent on his narrow chest. His command of English was sketchy, but this did not stop him using it prolifically. Out of his mouth would pour volleys of utterly incomprehensible nonsense, never more so than when he was elaborating on the claims of his brother to the appointment of College shopkeeper. 'My brudder blaa blaa blaa keep shop blaa blaa staishnery blaa blaa staishnery blaa blaa.' We never quite made out what his brother did or sold; one stalled with all the tact that courtesy demanded. Nazir was a great writer of letters, as this one, written to my wife while we were on U.K. leave, shows:

> From: Nazir Miah, Driver,
> Mymenshahi Cadet College,
> Mymensingh.
> June 27, 1966

My dear Madam,
   I became very glad having received your affectionate letter of
23rd ultimo which unfortunately received by me only 25th of this
month (June, 66) for which I could not reply you in time. However, I have been feeling much pleasure, knowing that you with
your family members are enjoying the holidays in your mother-
land with great pleasure. Kindly convey my best wishes to my
shahib and sisters. Madam, sincerely speaking that I have been
feeling uneasy since you flew for London, though now counting
the days with pleasure that within a very short time, I shall be able
to see you.
   All here going O.K. But the paddy crops in most of the districts
have badly been affected due to heavy flood. Madam, long since I
have been dreaming of going to London the most beautiful city of
the day. I don't know whether this long cherished desire of mine
will be fulfilled.
   Deanat and Cyprian are well and informed them regarding your
letter.
   No more to-day. I and my family are well. Hoping you are
keeping a good health.
   With supreme thanks,

                                        yours affectionately,

                                        Nazir Miah
                                        Driver.

Every evening he would visit us, slipping quietly into the living room
with the greeting 'Good night, sah. Good night, sisters.' He would stand
there looking a little sheepish while we racked our brains for a topic of
conversation. I had put the College transport – such as it was, two vehicles
and two drivers – under the charge of the Adjutant. This was a fact which
the loyal Nazir refused quite to accept; he was the Principal's driver, and
the Principal's family was his special responsibility. He was far too gentle
to cause any trouble over this; he simply wanted to make his position
clear, and these evening visits were proof of his allegiance. A halting
conversation, profuse 'good nights' and he would move quietly off into
the night. We could have done with more men the like of Driver Nazir.

Now that we had achieved a driver, it was time to cast about for the man
who could play a key part in the extensive shopping that lay ahead of us –

a Bursar. There was no shortage of applicants, but at least seventy five per cent of them were not worth a moment's consideration. It was astonishing how many men of twenty-one or so considered that they had all the qualifications for this difficult job; in fact they clearly had not the remotest idea what the word 'bursar' meant. 'Get a man who's been the head or deputy head of a big school. Someone who knows the dodges and the tricks of the trade.' That was Maurice Brown's advice, and I followed it.

Having found the man I wanted – apart from his experience and general suitability, the last words of his letter of application had endeared him to me: 'Hoping you are O.K. by the Almighty.' – I then ran into difficulties. Mr. Chowdhury was working in a State school, and was therefore classified as a government employee. He could either resign from government service, thereby forfeiting pension rights and other marginal privileges, or he could elect to be seconded. On the face of it, this seems a fair system, but in reality the dice is heavily loaded against the individual. Firstly, obstacles are put against him if he tries to resign; secondly, if he plumps for secondment, everything is done to delay his transfer and, far worse, he cannot earn more than ten per cent over and above what he was getting in his previous post.

Our Bursar decided on secondment, and the first of the snags was brought into force in full measure; it was weeks before we could avail ourselves of his badly needed services. In the matter of salary, the situation quickly became ludicrous. Unaware of this government rule, I offered a salary which was in keeping with his age, forty-three, with his experience, and with the nature of the office he was about to undertake. The exact figure I cannot recall, it was about Rs. 850 a month, to my mind by no means an over-payment. This apparently caused something of a furore, for the unlucky man had, in his last post, been in receipt of the princely salary of Rs. 420 a month (about £360 a year) as the deputy head of an 800-boy school. My offer about doubled this figure – a state of affairs which officials at the Ministry of Education regarded as heinous. I was not prepared at any price to have my Bursar on a salary of Rs. 460 – he would have been receiving little more than the most junior member of the staff – and a solution had to be found. We got round it in the end by giving him a chunky bursar's allowance, which raised the salary, if not to the giddy heights of my first proposal, at least to a figure which bore some relation to his value and status.

A less complex appointment was that of Adjutant for the simple reason that I had nothing whatever to do with it; he was seconded to the College from the Army, to add, one assumed, military tone to the establishment. I was lucky with Captain Ansar, a young Gunner and a Bengali from the Calcutta area. He was a smart and on the whole efficient officer who believed in getting things done. I put him in charge of all physical activities, of clothing issues, of transport, of security, and of interior economy. He also appeared at odd intervals in the classrooms to spread the doctrine of military history. He had scant respect for his fellow Bengalis, and, having spent a good deal of his time in the West wing, he voiced a contempt for most things peculiar to the East. This, I could see, might lead to trouble, and I felt it more than likely that he would ere long fall out with the Bursar. Which in fact happened. Shortly after I had returned from a two-day conference in Lahore, I found this on my desk:

Subject:- Duties and responsibilities – Army officer – Attached to this College.
Sir,
I beg to state the following to clarify my position and status in the college:
a. I am posted here by the Army as Officer Commanding Army detachment and NOT as an Adjutant.
b. As a commissioned officer in the armed forces of Pakistan I hold the status of a first class Gazetted Officer. Under any circumstances I cannot be put under or on equal footing with the persons who are junior to me in rank, status, seniority *and drawing much less pay than I am.* (Author's italics).

And much more in similar vein. To this pretty piece of claptrap, I did not reply, nor did either of us ever refer to it. Having worked off his spleen, he once again buckled down to his job, and I contrived to keep the peace between him and the Bursar, on the whole successfully.

Small though the staff was at this stage, I could not, with Mr. Ahmed about, complain that it lacked character. He came to me from a firm of solicitors as a stenographer; this in Bengal implies a knowledge of shorthand which in fact he had. He was familiar too with the workings of a typewriter. But it was in personality not in workmanship that he added colour and interest to our lives. In appearance he was a touch grotesque. His head looked as if it had at some time fouled a wine-press; from this elongation there popped two hooded eyes like the breasts of a classical nude. He had prominent teeth, a graveyard cough and an unassailable opinion of his own worth. As Principal's stenographer he plainly considered himself a man of affairs, the hub rather than a spoke in our little wheel. Many a time I had to shoo him out as he lingered coyly beside my desk to listen in on, or better still to make a contribution to, some confidential *tête-à-tête*. These rebuffs did nothing whatever to curb his curiosity. 'My work very good, sir?' was an overture to yet another request for some favour, usually financial. While prepared to admit the former, I was seldom inclined to grant the latter.

I failed Mr. Ahmed dismally when I was unable to stretch a point in favour of his nephew. The child put up a poor performance in the College Entrance written tests. 'He is very bright boy, sir. You see him, sir, you like him' was his last ditch effort to get me to grant the boy an interview. As to how much face he lost within the family circle for this failure to influence his employer only one better acquainted with the Bengali mind could properly tell. Without doubt from that day forward there was a marked decline in the warmth of our relationship. His excitability, always a weakness which led him into countless situations embarassing to others if not to himself, became more pronounced. Worse grew the sarcophagus cough which worried me more than him. 'You really must see a doctor about your chest, Mr. Ahmed,' I would exclaim after another harsh paroxysm. 'Is alright, sir. I take medicine,' he would gasp, bulbous eyes streaming. But in the end it was his grandiose self-esteem that broke the partnership.

'I would like B type quarter, sir. C type no good quarter.'

'Mr. Ahmed, I've explained to you before that A and B quarters are for lecturers only. I can't alter that for you or anyone else.'

'But, sir, you are Principal!' he would counter in a tone suggesting that I lacked the spunk to exercise the powers of office.

My obduracy deterred him not a whit. Every few days, as the time drew near for the move to the College, the request was made, and with increasing impatience turned down. One day, just when his services were most needed, he simply failed to turn up. I never saw him again.

*   *   *

One of the most intractable difficulties that faced us was the problem of money. In theory a Cadet College was autonomous, that is to say run solely by a Governing body with the Principal as its chief executive. In practice the Governing body did nothing of the kind, for control over money – or perhaps one should say control over the supply of money – rested entirely in the hands of Government. One's funds came from the

Treasury, and it is a pretty common axiom that treasuries the world over are jealous of their funds and reluctant to part with them. The Treasury of East Pakistan, known as the Accountant-General's Department, was positively no exception to this rule, safeguarding its resources by an elaborate, devious and incomprehensible system designed to obstruct with the utmost tenacity.

In the days before I had a Bursar to do it for me, I had to pay frequent visits to the Accountant-General's office in Dacca in search of funds, armed always with a letter which read like this:

Government of East Pakistan,
Education Department.

From: Section Officer,
　　　Govt. of East Pakistan.
To:　The Chairman, Governing Body,
　　　Momenshahi Cadet College.

Sir,

I am directed to place at the disposal of the Chairman, Governing Body of the Momenshahi Cadet College, a further sum of Rs. 50,000 (Rupees fifty thousand) only for recurring expenditure during 1964 - 1965.

The above amount of Rs. 50,000 will be drawn by the Principal, Momenshahi Cadet College, on presentation of a bill signed by him and countersigned by the G.O.C., East Pakistan.

The charge will proceed against the head '63-B-Devt – K. Education – Colleges and Universities – special schools for boys – Cadet Colleges – Momenshahi Cadet College in the budget for 1964-65.'

The Accountant-General, East Pakistan, is being informed.

Your obedient servant,
Sd/-
Section Officer.

Copy forwarded to the Financial Adviser, Education for information and communication to the Accountant-General, East Pakistan.

Copy forwarded to the Accountant-General, East Pakistan for information. This has the consent of the Financial Adviser, Education.

This rigmarole looked pretty cast iron; phrases like 'will be drawn by the Principal' and 'the charge will proceed against' had about them a reassuring sound of no nonsense. I carried a bill signed by the top soldier in the Province. Nothing could possibly go wrong. I was soon to discover that the many officials with whom one had to contend had other ideas. I was met always with courtesy matched only by the determination of each and every man to do his utmost to stop me getting my money.

At the end of one breathless steamy morning, I was in sight of my target. Hours of waiting, of patience stretched to the limit, of remonstrating and pleading – at last – I had the cheque within reach. But no – that longed for loophole was spotted.

'Your college, Mr. Principal, is in Mymensingh district. We can't pay you money from Dacca.'

'But the college is only a mile over the Dacca boundary, and Mymensingh town's 120 miles away. You surely don't expect me . . .'

'Yes, I'm sorry, Mr. Principal, but the regulations say . . .'

I was back where I started with a hot wasted morning behind me. Days later, after further devious negotiation, I contrived to get a special order to the effect that, while resident in Dacca, I might draw money from there – another tiny battle won. But the Accountant-General kept his guard up and a swinging right hand always at the ready. On one occasion my Bursar, upon whose long suffering shoulders these burdens were later thrust, was denied his cheque at the very last moment because he had not got a receipt bearing the Principal's signature – his own was not considered good enough. Next day he drove the forty miles back to the Accountant-General armed with the necessary receipt.

'Where, Mr. Bursar, is the letter from the Principal authorising *you* to draw the money?' . . .

I took my grievances to a Pakistani friend. 'This,' he said with a smile, 'is a legacy of the British. You made the system, we merely carry on where you left off.'

Up to a point he was right. For a long time before the end of the British raj the Central Government in Delhi had not been as generous in its financial treatment of Bengal as her many problems had warranted. In fact the Province had been kept grievously short of money. Lord Casey, the first Australian to be Governor of Bengal, put his finger slap on it in a letter to the Viceroy, Lord Wavell:

'At some time in the past, the British administration evidently decided that Bengal – I do not know about the other provinces –

should be run on the minimum possible expenditure of public moneys, very low taxation, and no expenditure of loan moneys for developmental purposes. The result has been a pinchbeck policy under which the resources and potentialities of Bengal have not been developed. In the effort to produce checks and safeguards against spending a rupee more than the essential minimum of money a suffocating system of red tape has been developed which has throttled initiative, and has created in the minds of the services, from whom plans ought to have been forthcoming, a sense of frustration and stultification which has prevented the development of the vision necessary for the framing and working out of plans.'

Thus far my Pakistani friend may be said not to have erred. But it is worth recording that in the days of Akbar the Great, long before the British had any influence in India beyond some lucrative trading, an official obtained his salary through the following maze of complexity:

'The appointment, having been made by the Emperor personally, would first be recorded in the diary, in which all his orders were entered. The diary having been checked and passed, an extract of the order was then made, signed by three officials and handed over to the copying officer, where an abridgement was prepared, signed by four officials, and then sealed by the Ministers of State. A statement of salary was made out, and after being entered in the records of all sections of the office, was sent on to the Finance Department. There an account was drawn up, and a report submitted to the Emperor, and on an allowance being formally sanctioned, a pay certificate was drafted, and passed through the hands of the Finance Minister, the Commander-in-Chief and the Military Accountant. This last officer prepared the final document, which required six signatures from three separate departments, and would at last be accepted by the Treasury as authority for payment of the salary.'

That 'suffocating system of red tape' lived on into the 1960s; the Bengali is heart and soul a clerk, and this is a situation in which he revels. Of course, once acclimatised, one looked on it as a sort of game from which both sides must extract the maximum enjoyment. In that way sanity was preserved; one generally got one's money in the end.

In marked contrast to bureaucratic vigilance was the attitude to finance of my Governors. In my previous contact with governing bodies I had been taught to look upon the item on the agenda marked finance as one certain to tax me to the uttermost. But I was dealing then with shrewd businessmen and Yorkshiremen at that, their questions searching, their scrutiny assured. My Pakistani governors took a different view. It would be inaccurate and discourteous to describe their attitude as one of indifference; rather did they prefer to tread lightly, and to move on to the next item with as much despatch as possible. No doubt if I had chosen to help myself from the till they would have spotted it fast enough and acted with vigour. As it was, they knew their limitations and left most of the sorting out to the Principal and the auditors.

*   *   *

The man at the prison gate was reluctant to let me in. He was clearly a versatile fellow, as zealous in his aim to stop anyone getting in as to stop anyone getting out. Not that I could really blame him; the business of a tall, red faced foreigner at his gate early on a wet July morning might seem to him obscure, if not suspect. At last my official pass carried conviction, and I was, in the malefactors' jargon, inside.

My first impression on stepping into the courtyard was one of ineffable peace, for Dacca Central Gaol lives in location well up to its name. It is very central indeed. The hubbub of the old city embraces it like the coils of a boa-constrictor. High walls shut out the ebullient clamour, the sudden stillness is impressive. But there was a feast for the eye as well as the ear; trees, lawns, flower-beds, all in beautiful order, were the surprising substitutes for the 'vile prison of afflicted breath' which one had been led to expect. A warder, keys jangling, led me to an office. On the wall hung two faded group photographs. Faintly I had the feeling of being a new boy in a big alien school.

I thanked the officer behind the desk for receiving me so courteously. We exchanged cigarettes; a well-groomed young man in spotless white uniform and a red band on his arm brought bottles of mineral water. We settled into talk about the prison system in Bengal.

I was at once struck by its similarity to British methods. 'We took over a lot of your ideas after partition,' said the officer. Remission was an example; for good conduct a man could earn four, or in some cases five, days remission a month, while for special duties he could earn more. A 'trustie' for instance – another British inheritance – would be rewarded according to the extent of his responsibilities with a slice of remission. No cash payment was made to prisoners.

Basically the prison population was divided into two classes – A for a first offender or non-habitual, B for the recidivist. 'In Class A there are three divisions,' said the officer, 'which means that a division one prisoner will get better diet, better accommodation and more visits – one a month instead of one every two months – than a division three man.'

'How does a prisoner get to that grading?'

'He may go straight into it. The government decides that and takes into account the nature of the offence and the background of the prisoner. Or, of course, a man can be upgraded for good conduct and so on.'

'How do you manage to keep them occupied?'

'The prisoners maintain and run the prison under supervision. They cook and garden, do the cleaning, the laundry and all the odd jobs.'

'Do you try to teach a man any sort of trade?'

'Yes, indeed. We've quite a lot of handiwork and machine tool operations going on, such as carpentry, metal work, basketry, and we've a big blanket factory. We'll see some of the work in a few minutes.'

'I suppose you've a wide range of sentences?'

The officer smiled. 'Everything from a month to one man who's got a total of one hundred and twenty years. Of course the prison is his home for the rest of his life.'

'Do you carry out capital punishment?'

'Yes, but only for murder, and a lot of murderers get reprieved. We don't have many executions.'

Execution was by hanging, and in its gruesome details there was a striking similarity with the system as it was in Britain, except that the hangmen were volunteer prisoners – 'Two months' remission for that job,' said the officer – and the length of time between sentence and execution could stretch to many months on account of an elaborate appeal mechanism.

'Executions cast a spell over the whole prison, a nasty eerie atmosphere,' said the officer. Shades of Pentonville!

'What about food?'

'They get three meals a day, top class men four. They can choose a rice or chupatti diet. They have meat or fish at least once a day, and a lot of tea.'

'Men put on weight here,' said the doctor who had joined us in the office. 'Every man is medically examined on admission. If he's sick we've a hundred bed hospital with a T.B. and leprosy ward.'

'What size medical staff have you got, doctor?' I asked.

'I've three medical officers working full-time under me,' he replied, 'and a number of orderlies – trusties of course.'

'How do you deal with prisoners who give trouble inside the gaol?'

'In various ways,' replied the officer. 'Solitary confinement, cellular confinement, standing handcuffs and very occasionally the cane.'

'I've been here five years,' put in the doctor, 'and we've not had a beating yet.'

'Standing handcuffs?' I asked.

'Yes, a man may be handcuffed standing against a wall for a given number of hours.'

Dacca Gaol was overpopulated – two thousand four hundred and fifty was the ration strength on the day of my visit, including twenty nine women, against a sanctioned strength of a little over one thousand nine hundred.

'It's the same everywhere,' said the office. 'Now you come and I'll show you the workshops.'

We walked down a long pathway lined with lawns and flowers, a procession of three headed by the senior warder, a splendid figure in starched khaki drill, long puttees, glistening boots, the whole topped off with a white beard of Falstaffian proportions. On all sides men paused in their activities to salute, themselves not outdone sartorially in their trim white prison uniforms. The military atmosphere was obtrusive. Junior warders slammed into the salute; the men lived in 'barracks', only a few knew the solitude of a cell; a queue of prisoners squatting outside a ration store was brought to its feet by a parade-ground shout.

We watched the carpenters, the carpet-weavers, the tinsmiths ('All utensils for use in the gaol are made here,' explained the shop overseer), the basketry workers – I ordered for the college twelve beautifully made chairs – the durrie makers and the leather workers. The standard of workmanship was high, of mailbags there was no trace. Last we visited the blanket factory in full production of blankets of coarse quality for the prison, of high quality for sale outside. The great machines, on many of them the stamp *Tomlinson, Rochdale, England*, thumped and groaned; activity was intense and orderly. The pride with which the superintendent showed off his workshop was reflected in the attitude of his workers; one sensed a satisfaction in the job, the more remarkable in light of the fact that it carried no financial benefits, that it was being done by people not endowed in the main with a love of craftsmanship nor with the will to work. In the kitchens lunch was in the last stages of preparation, big vats of rice and vegetables, fish, dixies of tea. Beaming with pleasure, a white-hatted cook hefted across a thick pile of chupattis like a mound of elephants' ears. We fingered the texture and nibbled appreciatively.

The most striking impact on a visitor was the sheer brittle cleanliness of the whole area. One could have taken food off any part of the pathways without revulsion; the clinical tidiness was almost overwhelming. Much time and energy had been spent on whitewashing; there was nothing that would have offended the sensibilities of the most pernickety R.S.M., of the most house-proud suburban wife. We walked back towards the office, passing a group of prisoners having their daily bath, an outdoor exercise in the traditional Muslim style, nothing to bring a blush to the cheek of the most bashful maiden. On the other side of a tall iron fence crowds of remand prisoners littered a big yard, looking in their own clothes scrofulous and unkempt in comparison with the smartness of the convicted men.

'No work for them,' said my guide. 'Like in your country, they're innocent until they're found guilty.' As we passed a door in a wall marked 'Women', the officer grew expansive.

'There is nothing nasty here,' he said. 'Some of the men are real bad men, but there are no beatings-up and everyone is content.'

If his spectacles may have been a shade rose-coloured, there was no gainsaying the smiling faces, the erect bearing, the physical well-being of most of the scores of men I had seen in the past hour.

'They certainly look fit enough. How do you manage it?' I asked.

'It's the regular food and hours. And they have P.T. and football.'

'How many hours work do they do?'

'From 7.30 to 12. Then they have a bath and lunch. Rest for an hour and work again from 2 to 5. On Fridays and public holidays they do not work.'

Back in the office the same well-groomed young man was waiting with a pile of ledgers for the officer's signature.

'He's one of our matriculates,' explained the officer. 'We try to give the better educated ones some work suited to their abilities.' In fact education goes on within the prison walls, though as yet it had only reached Class 5 (about nine-year-old) standard.

There was a question I had to put.

'You're giving these men regular meals and work and shelter. They're getting free medical attention. Aren't many of them far better off in prison than out of it?'

'You're quite right,' replied the officer. 'This is a much higher standard of life than most of them can hope for outside. The only thing that's missing is the company of their families and womenfolk.'

Better off inside than out? As the gate clanged to and I was engulfed again by the squalor, heat and poverty of the old city, I wondered how much the two thousand odd men shut in behind me appreciated the cleanliness and orderliness of their lives. No doubt most would be glad to exchange it for the threadbare existence that was their lot in the world of the free.

*   *   *

Five morning newspapers were published daily in Dacca, two of them in English. *The Morning News* was pro-Government, giving top place to the latest utterances of the President and the Provincial Governor, *The Observer* was the opposition mouthpiece, and the interesting thing about it was that it really did oppose. Governmental inadequacies, ministerial shortcomings were exposed with a good deal of venom. This paper had to publish official hand-outs, but, apart from that, it was given remarkable freedom. It was not reluctant to spotlight the nation's faults, as this extract from a leader headed *De-littering* shows:

> Money's first use, whether it lies in private pockets or public coffers, must be to clean up the simple physical façade of life, to make it shine with civilized lustre. And that is how a citizen, a city, a country or a nation is judged, i.e. by the sort of looks it puts on, by its own sensitive inhabitants or visitors from outside.
> It is common knowledge that much filth and litter have accumulated on the façade of our cities and towns. Drains stink, roads and residential neighbourhoods wear a dismal look. Whether the public funds available for cleaning and de-littering are properly spent also remains an intriguing question.
> Perhaps less money than is required or money ill-spent coupled with chronic apathy keeps the cities and towns as unclean as ever.

The editors of English papers in Bengal – there were two published in Chittagong also – must have had the most appalling difficulties in keeping their editions free from error. Like the editors of Laurence Durrell's unforgettable *Balkan Herald*, they suffered from rough work in the composition room; the problem of keeping a deadline inhibited the careful proof-reading that the weaknesses of the compositors demanded. Occasionally a particularly shattering misprint would give delight. Whose breakfast table would not be enlivened by:

'Derbyshire lost another wicket at 98 when a good delivery from Carling flacked off Johnson's balls.'? The same match, though in a less intimate context:
'On a bull and placid wicked the crowd again witnessed to their dismay Newzeland batting in these sticky aoods to collect a mere 233 runs for 7 wicket throughout the day.'

*   *   *

Having been some weeks in Dacca, much of the time spent on a rather wild goose chase, I began to feel the urge to have a look at a machine working at full pressure with all systems at go. If I was going to launch a cadet college successfully, I had better find out, the earlier the better, how things were managed at Fauzdarhat, stronghold of Colonel Maurice Brown, whose image had appeared so formidable back in London. Having some stores to pick up in Chittagong, I took the car down, driving much of the way in torrential monsoon rain.

There I spent three active, useful days. Maurice Brown and his wife were delightfully hospitable. They had just returned from a month's holiday in their native New Zealand, and were feeling a little nostalgic for that lovely country. Into the ears of the callow, ignorant new boy was poured a welter of advice based on five years' experience of education in Bengal; I could not have been learning at the feet of a more knowledgeable pair. Everything about the college was impressive, not least the bearing and attitude of the boys. I was shown round the living-quarters by the head boy; it was hard to believe that he lived in a mud hut, that his father earned less than a hundred rupees a month; his speech, his manners suggested a background of the most genteel English middle class. At the College feast I sat at High Table with the prefects; there were speeches and the singing of the National Anthem. All the staff and their ladies were present – it was oddly impressive and very friendly.

July is the middle of the Rugby season, the game is played in late afternoon when it is just cool enough for exercise so strenuous. Only the senior boys played; for the game they seemed to show a good deal of enthusiasm and not a little skill. Conditions were all against them, for the mud was thick and spurts of water splashed up under their boots. Maurice Brown, umbrella at the ready, gave advice and encouragement from the touch-line. But I was not convinced that Rugby was the game either for Bengal with its climate so wet that it is played in a mudbath, or for the Bengali whose excitable temperament is put to severe strain by the vigour and physical contact of the game. They are, what is more, natural soccer players and have a great love for it.

I had lunch with a young master who was shortly leaving for England to do a year's teaching at one of our largest and most expensive public schools. He was short of stature and looked about twenty one. His eagerness to go and his many questions only made sadder my fears that the Sixth Form would make mincemeat of him. Events proved me right – he lasted one term.

*   *   *

I was anxious to seek out a reputable printer to get to work on college business. 'Go to Ahmed Khan,' said an American friend. 'He's intelligent and reliable. He's a young man on the way up. Here's his address.' I found Ahmed Khan in his printing works on the edge of the Old City. The approach had not been too encouraging; indeed the last lap, down a narrow lane beside which one of Dacca's few public lavatories gave off a pungent aroma into the hot morning, was forbidding.

'We can't talk in here. Let's go to my house,' shouted Mr. Khan, a suggestion to which I deferred with alacrity. His office and works were undergoing reconstruction. The noise and confusion were such that it was difficult to make oneself heard, let alone to think constructively. To my disappointment the house was less than a stone's throw away; the sense of chaos hung about it. This was a poor dwelling; we sat in a tiny room shoddily furnished. A double divan in one corner proclaimed that it was in fact the principal bedroom. The stench drifted across from the public lavatory as we sipped the pale sweet tea; the hum and sweat of an Eastern city pressed thick about us.

I found the set-up fascinating. Mr. Khan was intelligent; equally clearly he was on the way up. He spoke perfect English, about him there lurked an air of competence and determination. He was a most likeable person; so too was his wife, if for rather different reasons. Were one seeking the classical Oriental beauty, one need have looked no further. She was, to put it briefly, a stunner. Mr. Khan's conversation was urbane and confident.

'I like to go shooting near Momenshahi,' he said. 'Mostly wild boar. My father-in-law was a great shikar. He owns much land around there.'

Mrs. Khan, with little English, took no part in the conversation. She just sat there in a brilliant sari looking superb.

'We get away up country whenever we can. Last year my wife was ill. She doesn't like it here too much.'

I could hardly blame her, and herein lay the fascination. Mr. and Mrs. Khan were a bright, attractive pair with plenty of money in the bank and the prospect of plenty more to come; in the ramshackle garage I caught sight of a gleaming Mercedes; they dined out and were to be seen at the smarter parties; they were extremely well connected. Yet they were content to live their young lives in, to bring their small children up in, an atmosphere not far removed from squalor. Even a serious illness – it was in fact polio – had not driven them to a habitation more salubrious. We concluded our business most satisfactorily and parted with genial enthusiasm. As an example of a young pair on the way up, Mr. and Mrs. Khan presented a charming and enigmatic picture.

*   *   *

In the matter of selecting teachers the procedure was similar to that followed in Britain, and, I presume, in most parts of the world. One simply stuck a notice in the press and sat back to await the outcome. I decided to seek out two mathematicians, two geographers, two teachers of English, one of Bengali, one physicist, one chemist, one teacher of Urdu, one of Islamiat and one of social studies. The last three call for a little explanation. Urdu is the language of West Pakistan; it was certain that we would have at the College a few boys who had been brought up in the West and who, although speaking and understanding their Bengali tongue, would feel much happier on paper in Urdu. Someone to teach it was essential, though in terms of numbers rather uneconomic. Islamiat must be taught as part of the curriculum; this is the study of the Quoran and of the Islamic way of life. A specialist teacher would be needed here. Social studies embrace history, civics and geography, and a history/civics specialist must be found to fill this bill.

With eleven teachers, or lecturers as they preferred to be called, (a pity, for it encouraged the belief that it was their duty to lecture rather than to teach – the two are not quite the same), we should be well staffed with good specialist cover. The salaries offered were slightly higher than the approved government scale, in the hope that the best men would apply. The bottom of the ladder was four hundred rupees a month with annual increments of increasing size until the ceiling of twelve hundred was reached. No teacher could wax rich on this, but accumulation of wealth is not the teacher's lot anywhere. By comparative national standards this salary scale was reasonable, while there was the added incentive of free furnished accommodation which meant a great deal.

Judged solely by numbers, the response to the press notice was more than encouraging, totalling many hundreds, enough to stir the envy of any headmaster anywhere. But when one looked closely at the applications the situation was not quite so satisfactory. There was about them a monotonous uniformity: all were Bengali, ninety per cent Dacca University, 2nd Class Honours degrees, keen on games, loyal citizens of the regime. Open testimonials were of little or no value – they followed a stylised, almost liturgical formula:

'Mr. _____ is a man of honour, hard working and a good teacher. He has taken no part in any activities subversive to the State. I wish him success in life. Signed ....'

How to make a short-list out of such uniformity was something of a poser. It was done in the end by the only possible method, automatically selecting the tiny number of Firsts, the even smaller number who had ventured outside East Pakistan, and those personally recommended. Dr. Nafis Ahmad was particularly helpful in choosing geographers, most of whom had been his pupils. We held interviews over two days, Colonel Rahman and I. Happily we were in complete agreement on each and every case. The selection may be said to have proceeded satisfactorily . . .

As the days moved on towards the time when we must set up shop and go into serious business, the problem of labour recruitment became more pressing. Besides the important teaching appointments, a huge administrative tail had to be gathered in. In Bengal this problem was never likely to be one of quantity, the bodies were there and in profusion. It was a question of quality. We decided, the Bursar and I, that we must try to fill our key administrative posts – the mess manager, office superintendent, medical staff, estate manager, head mali – well in advance of the move out, and with men of the best calibre that the labour market could provide. In this we were singularly successful, though we had our bosh shots among the less important appointments, none wider of the mark than in the case of the sinister Mr. Malik.

Mr. Malik measured sixty three inches, and wore a black beard topped by a pair of the most crafty eyes ever bestowed on human kind. There was about him something of Scrooge, something of Fagin, a good deal of the Artful Dodger. Day after day he hung about our office in Dacca, beseeching us in a cunning squeal to give him a storeman's job. He got in our hair, he was totally indifferent to snubs of the most blatant kind. The office door would open six inches (no-one ever knocks in Bengal) and the black beard and shifty eyes would ooze into view. 'Your honour can see me –

yes?' he would pipe, his voice apologetic and deprecatory. 'Not this morning, Mr. Malik,' if I was in a good mood, 'Get out!' if the pressure was on.

One attribute he possessed in abundance, persistence, and it gained him a transient reward. As it happened we were short of a ration storeman and time was against us. We decided to engage him on a two-month basis with the promise, if he came up to the mark, which seemed improbable, of a permanent appointment. Mr. Malik subsided into the backstreets of Dacca and was seen less often about our headquarters. As soon as we were operative, Mr. Malik's qualities quickly became apparent; he was a confirmed absentee, and a classic exponent of the art of taking a mile when given an inch. He would be allowed by his immediate boss, the mess manager, to have a Sunday off in Dacca in order to 'attend to urgent business', and would turn up again on Tuesday. When reprimanded, his air of injured innocence was a histrionic masterpiece. At last, after a particularly outrageous bit of absenteeism, due to a bout of 'terrible sickness', we gave him two hours to pack his scanty belongings and be gone.

Mr. Malik was not the man to express his feelings openly; he was too surprised by the curtness of the dismissal to voice a protest, but his demeanour, as the meaning of the fateful words became clear, betrayed a keen sense of outrage. As I watched his wizened form disappearing down the drive – even from the back view he inspired distrust – I felt that we had not heard the last of him. I was right; about a month later, I received this letter from a Mr. B. Hossain, M.A. LL.B. (Cal.) Advocate High Court (Formerly of Calcutta):

Dear Sir,
    Under instructions and on behalf of my client Mr. A. Malik of Dacca I am to address you as follows:
1. That my client was appointed by you as a Ration Storekeeper Clerk on a starting salary of Rs. 140 a month from December 1st 1964.
2. That since the date of his appointment he has been doing his duty regularly and with due diligent.
3. That on the last 9.2.65 he was seriously ill and could not report to his duty as usual and he sent an application at your office praying for leave of that day i.e. 9.2.65 M.C. may be produced if required.
4. That on 10.2.65 he did his duty as usual and on 11.2.65 you suddenly prevented him to do his duty and told him orally that his

services has been dispensed with without assigning any reason
violating E.B.S.R. Parts I and II.
5. That you did not pay salary to my client for the month of
February and house rent @ Rs. 60 for December '64 to February
1965, as he was not provided with any family quarter which was
made available to other staffs.
6. That my client is also entitled to conveyance allowance @ Rs
4 per days for 31 days of January and 3 days of February 1965.

In the circumstances you are hereby requested to pay to my
client his salary for the month of February '65, house rent @ Rs
60 per month for three months amounting to Rs. 180 and conveyance allowance @ Rs. 4 per diem for 34 days amounting to Rs.
136 within 7 days from the date of receipt here of and also
reinstate him in his service with immediate effect failing which
necessary legal action will be taken against you without further
reference to you which please note.

Yours faithfully,

To this notable piece of fiction, we replied thus:-

I am in receipt of your letter of the 9th instant on behalf of your
client, Mr. Malik.
1. Mr. Malik was appointed on a temporary trial basis. A copy of
the appointment letter is attached.
2. Mr. Malik's work at the College was thoroughly unsatisfactory. He frequently absented himself from duty without permission, and his time-keeping was most irregular. Both my Mess
Manager and the College Bursar were so dissatisfied with his
work that they recommended to me that his temporary appointment should be discontinued.
3. No agreement was made with Mr. Malik regarding accommodation (see appointment letter). As a goodwill gesture Mr. Malik
was provided with free single accommodation as soon as he took
up his duties at the College.
In the circumstances I am unable to accede to your Client's requests.

We omitted at this stage any mention of the debts which the aggrieved
fellow had left behind him, or of the fact that he had on one occasion

extorted money from the wife of one of our havildars under threats. These titbits we reserved for the courtroom should the sinister Mr. Malik be foolish enough to press his case. Anyway, this was the last we heard of him. Perhaps some gleam in those tell-tale eyes warned the legal gentleman that he was unlikely either to win his case or to recover so much as a rupee in fees from a client so unreliable.

The engagement of supernumerary, as opposed to key staff, presented problems of a different kind. From early on I was inundated with written applications for posts, none of which commanded more than a hundred rupees a month – chowkidhars, gate-keepers, peons, buglers and the like. These were written – in most cases no doubt by a pavement scribe hiring out his inadequate skill for a few annas – to a set formula, and were almost pathetic in their optimism. They invariably started with a false premise: Your Honour, Hearing from a reliable source that some posts of gate-keeper are wanted etc. etc. These requests came in a steady flow week by week, and bore no relation whatever to our labour requirements.

The Bursar and I decided that we must recruit on the spot without regard to these shoals of written applications, and a gathering of the clans was therefore convened outside the College office on a bright December morning. From this assembly I chose to absent myself, leaving to the Bursar and his staff the task of dividing the sheep from the goats, the able-bodied from the halt. The outcome was a labour force numerically impressive, though not, I was assured, superfluous by local standards. For the benefit of those fascinated by the minutiae of administration, here is the payroll – excluding lecturers – which remained constant throughout our first six months –

Office	No. employed	Average wage per month.
Accountant	1	270
Office Superintendent	1	230
Chief store-keeper	1	250
Plumber	1	150
Pump operators	3	150
Head driver	1	180
Driver	1	140
Estate Superintendent	1	300
Compounder	1	175
Hospital attendant	1	118
Peons	4	85
Mess Manager	1	250

Office	No. employed	Average wage per month.
Ration Storeman	1	150
Head cook	1	115
Cooks	4	85
Table boys	6	85
Cooks' mates	4	85
Chowkidhars	6	85
Dormitory bearers	4	85
Clerk to Principal	1	200
Junior clerk	1	150
Head gardener	1	108
Gardeners	11	85
Head sweeper	1	86
Sweepers	9	76

There are, of course, always more behind the line of battle than in it; to this we were certainly no exception with sixty-five bodies, excluding teachers who totalled eleven, to look after the interests of one hundred and twenty boys. Some features of this list never ceased to puzzle me; I could not understand the distinction between cooks and cooks' mates in light of the fact that they were all paid the same (catering staffs, in my experience, like to be thick on the ground, a tendency to which this establishment was no exception). I was perplexed by the need for so many gardeners until I had had the opportunity of watching them at work. To have six chowkidhars also seemed excessive, but in fact these night watchmen were essential, and six was not too many in an area spreading over seventy five acres. Our total wage bill for the month, including my own salary, came to approximately fifteen and a half thousand rupees, averaging out at 198 rupees a month per head, a shade over £15. These figures go some way to explaining, if not quite justifying, the numbers we employed.

I have suggested that we were lucky with most of our key appointments, and never more so than in the case of our Mr. Barbhuyan, the mess manager. A trim little man, he had a military past and was forever springing to attention. He was also a father. 'Sir, I am blessed with seven daughters,' he cried, clicking his heels and looking as if he meant every word of it. 'Well with my four, Mr. Barbhuyan, we'll field a football team between us.' Which heavy jest kept the kitchens in fits of mirth for a week. He exercised some sort of control over our cooks, and was anxious for the financial solvency of his department. During the whole of our first term, in spite of difficulties which would have defeated all but the most resolute, he did not fail to produce a meal on time. I never ceased to be thankful to whatever fates had brought us together.

And what of sweepers? Here was a little problem in itself. One of the reasons why East Bengal was not as clean as it might have been was that the Muslim regarded sweeping a floor as something not quite in his line of business. 'Drudgery divine' finds a low place in Islamic philosophy. This was all very well for the Muslim in his private home, but it was hardly an acceptable situation for a school. We were no doubt fortunate in having around us a number of Hindu villages, and it was from these that we recruited our sweepers (Hindus have slightly different views on this subject which make provision in their ideology for a sweeper caste). On the whole they gave us good service, and I was often grateful for their presence. Such troubles as they generated sprung more from the Muslims than from the sweepers themselves – objections to having to live near them, objections to their spasmodic habit of imbibing a cheap alcoholic mixture which reduced them for a few happy hours to a state of inebriation. With instinctive sympathy for the underdog, I rather liked our sweepers.

*   *   *

President Ayub Khan laid the foundation stone of a new university, and to the ceremony Harry Forster, British Council representative in East Pakistan, and I repaired on a roasting September morning. The site was little more than a clearing in scrub jungle some twenty miles from the centre of Dacca. Access was not easy, and, along with all but V.I.Ps, we had to leave our car some half a mile from the centre of operations. With a vast throng we tramped along a track cut through the paddy, tropical suits like curbstones on our perspiring backs.

In the clearing a big marquee had been erected, gaily striped and devoid of side walls to catch the fitful breeze. Seats in here were reserved for those with the pink tickets; outside at a discreet distance the country people stood six deep, silent and curious. There was no dearth of police. Punctual to the minute the helicopter touched down, words of command, salutes, and the great man was mounting the tastefully decorated rostrum at the business end of the marquee.

It was my first sight of him, a burly figure, dressed in a well cut London suit, seemingly younger than his fifty seven years (I was told that he smacked his drives a good 250 yards; he looked as if the effort would not tax him). The proceedings began with a reading of the Holy Qoran, an affair which is likely to take the stranger by surprise; traditionally this is intoned in a sing-song voice, alarmingly nasal. After a brief speech, not too well read, from a Minister, the President purred into the microphone. Had I closed my eyes, I might have been listening to a company chairman giving the annual report at a City meeting, so perfect was his English in accent and emphasis; it was an excellent speech, brief and to the point, military in its precision.

The foundation stone well and truly laid, the President moved to the side and spoke to the patient, gaping crowd in a language which not one of them could understand; his words were interpreted by the Governor. There was little acclamation. From a loud speaker, mechanical and disembodied, shouts of 'Ayubkhan! Ayubkhan! Ayubkhan!' were trumpeted forth; the multitude showed little inclination to take up the refrain. The helicopter took off, and we made our thirsty way back to the transport. It had been an oddly impressive affair – quiet, dignified, effortless; it had lacked only a spontaneous enthusiasm.

From time to time rumour would suggest that the President was about to visit the College again (he had, it may be recalled, laid the foundation stone). I found this a useful gambit when trying to spur C. & B. into livelier activity. In fact, I never saw him again.

Towards the end of September, I became involved in an incident which might have cost me the loss of a valuable piece of machinery with a sore head into the bargain. Now and then the opposition parties in Bengal sank their differences and banded together, the better to take disruptive action against the government of the day. Hence the hartal of this September Tuesday. This was akin to a general strike, and lasted for as long as the authorities would tolerate it, the organisers organise it and the participants take part in it. Now we were to have one timed to last one day, or rather the better part of one day, ending at 4 p.m.; the excuse put forward on this occasion was 'the government's oppressive rule', a suitably vague and attractive spotlight on which to focus discontent.

It so happened that on this morning I was due to visit the G.O.C. at nine o'clock, necessitating a journey of about ten miles from my home to the military cantonments. This being an appointment I was anxious not to miss, I drove the Zephyr out of my garage and along the main road towards the airport and my target beyond. All was quite exceptionally quiet, not another vehicle in sight, few people abroad. This was driving *de luxe*; I pressed hard on the accelerator, foot loose and fancy free. Oh, if only all motoring were like this! I was early for my appointment.

About ten o'clock, the interview over, I headed back towards the city and home. At first the ride was again care free, but, just beyond the airport which marks the boundary of the cantonment area, a change came over the scene recently so relaxing. At the first big road junction a large crowd had gathered; a few lorries full of tin-hatted police were parked in expectant idleness like huntsmen at a meet. Of other vehicles – cars, buses, rickshaws, bullock carts, the usual bric-à-brac of the city streets – there was no sign at all. I began to feel naked and unwanted. The attitude of the crowd enhanced this impression; there were boos and catcalls, delivered, in view of the posses of police, in tones slightly subdued.

I was now about half a mile from home, and the sensible course was obviously to get there with a minimum of delay. I therefore pressed on down the empty dual carriageway with no sense of alarm, with no presentiment of unease. I was not to be left long in such detachment. From a level-crossing about a furlong ahead, a crowd debouched with startling speed and in considerable strength; they carried long staves and made rude angry noises. They surged up the road towards me; considering the rate at which the two parties were converging, a meeting was imminent and full of explosive possibilities.

I trod hard on the brake, and paused for an instant to take stock, to make what the military delight to call an appreciation of the situation. I remembered two things – one, that fifty yards behind me was a gap giving access to the other lane of the carriageway; two, that a quarter of a mile back a number of policemen sat inert in lorries, anxious, maybe, to give proof of their tutelary powers. By now the mob was a hundred yards away and closing fast; their intentions were manifestly clear – they were after me or my car or both. I shot into reverse – one would have preferred a quieter operation of the gear-box – backed fifty yards, swung into the down lane and moved off back whence I had come. My antics had been ridiculous and therefore risible. Elated by the experience of mild personal danger, I laughed and waved at the crowds lining the road. They, catching the comedy, laughed and waved back. Suddenly humour had restored the situation to its rightful proportions. I pulled up beside a police lorry. 'Officer, would you very kindly give me an escort to my home just down the road?'

I have always loved policemen, never more than now. The officer was charming and decisive. Within a minute I was heading back along the homeward road, a lorry in front, a lorry behind, a jeep in the van. I felt more than ordinarily foolish, absurdly akin to the filling in an outsize sandwich. We sailed sedately along, such bellicosity as possessed the crowd being thwarted by the spectacle of so much fire-power. Far down the road, a red mini careered towards us. A shower of bricks successfully halted its progress; police rushed from nowhere to rescue the occupants.

I turned down my quiet side lane with much waving and shouting of thanks to my protectors. A few minutes later I was out again, this time on foot, to the home of friends. Ahead of me in the peaceful backroad strolled three men chatting and seemingly at ease with the world; a youth drew abreast of them on a bicycle. Out shot a foot, fists swung. The unlucky lad was somersaulted into the road, whence he rose with a yell and fled. Violence, erupting so suddenly out of the quiet morning, was shocking. But this was a hartal, and anything on wheels was fair game.

By mid-afternoon the roads were filling with rickshaws, then with cars, emerging from their lairs like animals cautiously sniffing the air. At five o'clock the situation was back to normal; no-one had been injured and all had had a pleasant day off. A few had worked off their inhibitions by bunging bricks. That any political advantage had been gained did not seem remotely likely. But one person had learnt his lesson the hard way. I was undeservedly lucky to be the possessor of a car intact, a body unbruised. On hartal occasions, if you must go abroad to keep appointments, you leave expensive machinery in the garage and try out the quality of your shoe leather.

*   *   *

One of the things that had to be decided was the question of an opening date. Here it seemed I might come into conflict with my masters. I was determined to delay the start of the college until the buildings were reasonably complete, the drains in order, furniture in place and essential staff appointed. This may seem so obvious as not to be worthy of mention. But a young emergent nation is a nation in a hurry; understandably she wants to get on, to make up for the time which she feels she has lost. Hence the tendency to open up office buildings while the plasterers are still at work, to start up schools with the plumbing scarcely begun. My case was not strengthened by the fact that another Cadet College was neck-and-neck building-wise with Momenshahi; the Principal there, a Pakistani Army Colonel, was quite prepared to take in his first pupils in June, and did so. He faced successfully the most appalling difficulties; I was not prepared to accept the risks involved. In the end the General agreed to an October start, but at this point prominent and influential educationists entered the lists.

'It is madness,' they said, 'to start in October, almost at the end of the academic year. You'll get a much stronger intake at the beginning of the year. From the educational standpoint, you should start in January.' Alarmed by the sharp brake which the rains had put on the building programme, and not forgetting the delays in starting my own house, I welcomed this point of view; it had about it the sturdy ring of common-sense. Finally the General saw it that way too, and January 9th became the appointed day.

By the original scheme I was to open with sixty boys, all of Class 7, which meant in the main, eleven-year-olds. This seemed a sound basis, the group small enough to receive the individual attention which I felt might be needed. In August, however, a new chairman was at the helm – Major-General Moqeem Khan, a big sturdy man, who had been Commandant of the Pakistan Military Academy. He differed from his predecessor in that he was prepared, over and above extensive military duties, to give time and thought to a Principal's problems. I accompanied him on his first visit to Momenshahi. At the end of our tour of the buildings, he took me on one side. 'This place is too big for sixty boys. I want you to take in three classes, 7, 8 and 9. We can't afford not to use so much space.' Here was something of a bombshell; all my planning for staff, furniture and equipment had been based on an entry of sixty. There was nothing for it but rapid readjustment and rethinking. 'Can you do it?' he asked. I made a lightning calculation, gulped and replied, 'Yes, sir.'

A word of explanation about the school class system in Pakistan. These classes range right through from Kindergarten to Class 12, the latter being the equivalent in time to the English second year sixth. Matriculation – or G.C.S.E. – is taken at the end of the class 10 year.

It was now time to think about getting boys. The method of selection was carefully laid down – a written examination followed by interview and medical tests. Only if a boy passed all three stages could he be admitted. A chunk of space was hired in all the newspapers.

The call went out – 'Momenshahi Cadet College will open on January 9th next with three classes 7, 8 and 9. Written examinations Sunday November 10th. Application forms may be obtained from . . .' We were all set to go to work on the raw material.

I was scarcely prepared for what followed. The demand for application forms swamped my shabby little office, and left the admin. staff tottering but game. The latter at this stage was rather thin on the ground, one stenographer and one clerk. We engaged temporary help, despatched forms and catalogued the final entries. The total was over nine hundred. Inexorably events were moving towards the Battle of Curzon Hall. There was no indoor space big enough in Dacca to take such a number at one sitting. The problem was further complicated by geography. Many applications came from the area of Mymensingh, the capital of the district in which the college was located. There were entries, rather fewer, from Chittagong and Comilla in the South. This represented a spread of over 250 miles, and one had to take into account the fact that a number of parents would lack the means to send their sons on long journeys. We decided to hold two tests simultaneously in Dacca and in Mymensingh, 120 miles to the North. Further fragmentation I would not, and could not, accept, for my resources were stretched to the limit.

It was necessary to journey to Mymensingh to make arrangements at that end. The early morning drive took us – I had my twins with me – through typical Bengal countryside, so flat, so green, so intensely beautiful and intensely monotonous, with everywhere people and more people. We repaired at once to a school in the centre of the town. I stopped the car in the parking lot which happened to be slap in front of a line of classrooms, thereby inflicting on the twins a somewhat traumatic experience. The arrival of a foreigner in a car with two blonde young girls was altogether too much for the boys at their studies; they simply broke ranks and crowded to the windows and to the verandah to feast their eyes on so unusual a spectacle. Their stares were accompanied by nudges, chattering, giggling and pointing, what time the teachers sat helpless at their desks. I hurriedly drove to a quieter spot, and made for the headmaster's office. This was a large square room with a number of doors and windows.

News of my coming had spread through the school like measles; the fact that I was sitting in conversation with the headmaster was no bar to curiosity. Every aperture was quickly filled with eager dark faces, three deep, peering, jabbering, jostling. The headmaster, a gentle person of great courtesy, found nothing unusual in this, and we continued our talk as if we were the star performers in a circus ring. After this we looked at a Teachers' Training College, which turned out to be ideally suited to my needs, modern, spacious and set in grounds of considerable beauty. It had once been the country seat of a wealthy rajah; the gardens had lost little of their former grandeur. Here too, the Principal was the essence of courtesy and helpfulness; business was proceeding very smoothly until we struck an unexpected snag. Mymensingh, it appeared, did not observe Sunday as a holiday, and he could not accommodate my candidates until two in the afternoon. I had already made multiple arrangements in Dacca for a

Sunday morning exam, to change them was a prospect not to be contemplated. The risks were obvious, but I pinned my faith on the eccentricities of the trunk call service, and accepted the inevitable.

Our plans for the examination had to be most carefully laid. In the bazaars, a brisk trade was carried on in the sale of examination papers. Many a printer supplemented his income by slipping a few copies to an accomplice who in turn had the right contacts to multiply these copies a thousandfold and to place them within reach of the candidates at a useful price. It is a transaction bringing in a handsome return, and therefore very sound business. Healthy too, for it bestows ineffable benefits on the purchaser, and all parties are the better for it. The story goes that one year the University authorities grew wise overnight, and changed the papers at the eleventh hour. Hot with indignation, the candidates, their rupees wasted, flounced out of the hall, and refused point blank to take any further part in the examination. Nor, it should be added, is this guileful traffic confined to the subcontinent; it is not unheard of in the Western hemisphere.

Against such sturdy practices, precautions had to be taken. The printing of our exam papers I decided not to entrust to a commercial printer. I preferred to spend a somewhat exhausting afternoon in a dark corner of the British Council auditorium churning out papers on a duplicating machine. The English I had set myself; the mathematics was in the hands of two of my staff, carefully briefed on the security angle. Two thousand odd papers were borne off in triumph to my house, there to remain under lock and key until required. As far as I could judge we had defeated the hosts of Midian, but I could not be sure. At least we had tried.

To each of the candidates we sent a card, giving him brief instructions and a number. This he was supposed to produce before being admitted to the exam. The day before, we toured the halls, positioning desks, checking on drinking water, locating lavatories; arrangements were finalised for the despatch of one of my staff to Mymensingh complete with papers and stationery; everything it seemed had been done that could be done. It was now up to the freaks of chance and the machinations of the local citizenry to put into the works the largest possible spanners.

*   *   *

The Bengali does not take readily to discipline; this is due not so much to inherent prejudices as to sheer lack of practice. He so seldom hears the terse direction, the curt word of command, that his unaccustomed ear reacts sluggishly on the occasions they are applied.

This worked unfavourably for us in our endeavour to organise large numbers into tidy groups. Perforce I had to split the Dacca contingent – some 700 strong – into two sections, the one to Curzon Hall, the other to Dacca College; the latter in turn had to be subdivided into two halls adjacent to one another. Here I placed the Bursar in charge with a reasonable number of assistants and a most elaborate plan guaranteed to cover all emergencies. This plan did not, of course, work. The direction signs were ignored, the requests (an order is seldom given) of guides and supervisors became the mainspring for vigorous argument. Pandemonium resulted, and it is much to the Bursar's credit that the exam started only half an hour late, and passed off with no bones broken, all papers safely gathered in.

Meanwhile, happily ignorant of events half a mile away, I was conducting operations in the Battle of Curzon Hall. This is a vast, uncouth structure put up by Curzon as a viceregal pied-à-terre at the turn of the century. It is now used as an examination centre by the University, and I had hired the big hall in the middle of the building for the four hundred youngest candidates, class 7. Desks had been arranged – rather too closely for my liking, but space was short – on the ground floor, the overspill being housed in galleries which circled the hall in tiered ranks almost to the lofty ceiling. For candidates bent on skullduggery, the situation could hardly have been more propitious.

I arrived at the hall on D Day just before nine, in good time, or so I thought, to get things under way for a ten o'clock start. The precincts were already thronged, each candidate being accompanied by not less than one relative, whose self-imposed task it was to ensure that his charge's interests were protected to the full. I forced my way through to the main door, knocked stentoriously and vanished into the cool interior to marshal my forces for the fray.

Napoleon's dictum that you cannot have too many men on a battlefield was one with which I on that day wholly sympathised. Unfortunately, like many generals before me, I had inadequate resources at my command – four invigilators (one turned up late), my stenographer, whose usefulness was offset by his extreme excitability, and a handful of peons borrowed for the occasion from the British Council. The final check-up, briefing and pep talk was conducted against an alarming crescendo of noise from outside. The hands of the clock stood at 9.20 and it was time to address the multitude. Feeling like one of the minor prophets, I stepped out into the bright sunlight and was at once aware of a vast throng.

'Gentlemen!' I roared . . . Three minutes later silence of a sort fell, and in a few well chosen words I gave preliminary instructions. The impact of these was to a large extent nullified by the fact that only about half of my audience understood a word of what I was saying. For this we were prepared. 'Translate, please,' I said to my assistant, trying to keep the anxiety out of my voice. Alas! his lungs lacked carrying power, and the translation reached no further than the front rank a good two feet away. We dodged back into the hall and slammed the door.

Phase one, I felt, had misfired, an impression strengthened a minute or two later. Ye gods! Someone was making a speech, and moreover he was clearly in a great rage. His comments – against me? Against the foreigners? Against the government? I had no idea – were interrupted at intervals by a noise which suggested that the crowd was working itself up into a fine old fervour. I thought of the police, of my family, of the splendid end of a Principal done to death on the stage of the Curzon Hall, question papers still clasped to a blood-stained breast.

It was clearly time for action. 'Open up!' I cried. The peons, hiding their reluctance with difficulty, flung wide the great wooden doors. The mob surged in, men and boys rushing forward in a mad scramble for desks. Battle was joined.

Before anything useful could be done, before anything remotely like an examination started, it was necessary first to remove the parents. This they resisted, it being evidently their intention to camp out beside their sons' desks rendering whatever assistance the moment demanded. I had never till that hour kicked a parent, however strong the temptation. To this expedient, all others failing, I was now reduced. At the toe of my shoe, the last reluctant body was driven from the hall, the doors made fast, and the peons posted to their stations on guard. Meanwhile the four hundred small boys had shown little inclination to be tamed by disciplinary methods which nothing in their previous upbringing had taught them to expect. However, the young are more impressionable than the old, and at ten forty a stage had been reached which made possible the distribution of the papers.

I then had difficulties with those whom in the army we used to call 'own troops'. In spite of much preliminary sermonising, I had obviously failed to make the point clear that the invigilator's duty is, in the main, to keep silent. To my horror hands were shooting up all over the vast hall, and invigilators were busy answering questions clearly of a pointed nature. Even a peon, fancying himself one of the literati, was hard at it with advice and explanation. My stenographer was in his element, spreading his wisdom with glee and animation. This had to be stopped; matters then proceeded with some degree of quietness.

Unhappily the bladders of the little Bengalis proved to be uncommonly weak; there was a steady procession to the lavatory, where, no doubt, books were scanned, even accomplices met for hurried conference. Lacking the ability to be in more than one place at a time, I could do nothing about it; to some extent, I must swim with the tide.

There were two papers, one in English, one in Mathematics, both of ninety minutes. Half an hour's interval was allowed, and, if a critical commentary on the Battle of Curzon Hall is ever written, this will be recognised as a serious tactical blunder which might have had disastrous results. On the reopening of the doors, the mob surging in clashed with the mob surging out. The noise was catastrophic, the situation back to normal. Many of the parents brought in bananas, bowls of cold rice, sweet cakes, bottles of lemonade; picnics were spread all over the floor, the better to sustain junior through his next ordeal. Once again the unexpected had reared its uncouth head. All too soon it was time to attempt to re-establish some sort of control. By loud voice and pointed toe the elders, now in a mood best described as Ugly, were once again despatched. That they had another card up their sleeves was made plain shortly after mathematics had got into first gear.

There was a thunderous hammering at the main door. The nervous peon with infinite caution opened it a fraction. A dark hand shot through, grasping a piece of paper. This was extracted and brought to my desk.

'Principal Sir,' it read, 'We the guardians of the boys now being examined under your care protest strongly that there are IMPOSTORS in the hall. We protest strongly and wish for something to be done for this great injustice to our sons. Action take AT ONCE please. Signed Mohammed _____ _____, Chief Magistrate.'

This was something of a poser. I had been warned well in advance that the insertion of talented substitutes was a long-established tradition in exam rooms thereabouts. Against this threat I had armed myself with a huge bundle of photographs purporting to show the likenesses of the four hundred children now facing me in the hall. But it was one thing to hold the weapon, another to use it with effect. No doubt a quicker, more subtle brain than mine might have come up with an answer. I did not know the school solution, for the very good reason that there wasn't one.

I took refuge in shameless subterfuge. I paced the hall with beady gaze, photographs held aloft, stopping, staring fixedly at dusky heads bent low in mathematical concentration, obviously *checking up*. If a youthful eye met mine without flinching, he was clearly no impostor. If he flinched, he clearly was, and what to do next was anyone's guess. It was all a meaningless charade, but it served to justify the reply posted to the outside world that I did indeed Action take AT ONCE.

The long, long morning – or rather afternoon, for we were now well behind schedule – wore on; with sweet relief I watched the hands of the clock move on towards closing time. But all was not quite done. Curzon Hall boasts a battalion of rather splendid chandeliers, each with its burden of bulbs. With a sudden sharp report one of these burst, showering tiny particles of glass over the little candidates beneath. Here was a situation dear to the Bengali heart. He was as anxious to play it up as I was to play it down. One boy, and one only, had sustained a tiny cut on the cheek; from the hullabaloo he might have been struck a mortal blow. Others, imagining themselves wounded, wailed in unison. All adults within reach rushed to the scene of carnage, the better to succour the little ones, the better to savour the drama. Once again my voice had to assume its cutting edge . . .

Just before three, the last boy disappeared through the door. The strife was over, both sides in retreat with feathers ruffled. We now had the considerable problem of correction, and of selecting those out of the nine hundred whom we felt merited interview. It had to be done quickly; within twenty four hours of the end of the exam the phone started ringing. 'Allo, this is the guardian of number 786. What is the result, please?' In the end I left my phone off the hook. Bengal is a land of paradoxes, here was yet another. People, many of them highly intelligent, were painfully surprised that the laborious operation of marking 1800 scripts was not completed, signed and sealed within a matter of hours; the same people would think nothing of taking three months to answer a letter. In ten days the list was finalised, checked and cross-checked a dozen times – the smallest slip might be disastrous – and despatched to the press for publication.

Interview cards were sent to the two hundred boys chosen for the next hurdle. Meanwhile I endeavoured, as far as was consistent with normal business, to make myself scarce. Again the phone was disconnected; to all callers other than known friends, I was firmly out. There were some seven hundred failures, a good proportion of whom wanted to know the reason why, and, more important, to bring pressure to bear to have the situation put right.

One good lady, having unsuccessfully attempted to lobby the G.O.C., proceeded to camp out on my verandah, firmly refusing all the attempts of my household to dislodge her. At last, threatened with the police, she made off, to resume the attack by letters which became progressively more vitriolic. My good friend Major Rashid, who had warned me at all costs to stay away from the office, bore the brunt of all this, contriving by stonewall tactics to fend off the besiegers.

The interviews took place over three days at the Combined Military Hospital; the candidates passed straight from the interview room into the clutches of the military doctors. We – Colonel Rahman, the Bursar and I – sat in a small Nissen hut while a seemingly endless procession of boys marched in and out.

'What is your age?' was invariably the first question, and for good reason. There is no such thing as a birth certificate in Bengal; some fathers, themselves almost illiterate and possessed of vast families, have only a vague idea of little Abdul's birthday. The situation, too, is ripe for skullduggery. If the maximum permissible age is, say, 13.9, and I want my son to gain entry, then 13.8 he will be and who is to say different? The biochemistry of growing up sometimes defeated these schemes. Into the room would walk a boy, moustached, five foot nine and thick of thigh. 'What is your age?' 'Twelve,' he would reply in a bass that rocked the rafters. Not much time would be wasted on him. If in doubt we would ask the doctors to make an age check; this, with their access to parts of the body into which we could hardly pry, they were in a position to do.

The interviews fined the numbers down to one hundred and twenty. For those who find fascination in such things, it might be of interest to enlarge a little on the methods employed to arrive at the final figure.

The written papers were graded A, B+, B, B-, C+, C, C-, D. Each grade carried a ration of points, eight for an A and so on down to one for a D. Thus a boy gaining A for English and C- for Maths would achieve a total of ten points. The interview was graded in exactly the same way, thus giving a potential maximum of 24 points. It worked out that 12-13 was the doubtful zone, those above it were in, those below out. The answer papers of the doubtfuls were then exhumed and reassessed; it was impossible to re-interview, much as I should have liked to have done so in some cases. The medical tests ruled out a small number, about 4 per cent, mostly with eye troubles. The X-ray plates in three instances revealed the middle stages of pulmonary tuberculosis.

I cannot pretend to claim that the system was foolproof. With such large numbers and with time against us, combined with the inexperience of all of us in selection on such a scale, mistakes were undoubtedly made. But not, I think, many.

Before we could post off the final letters, there was one complexity still to be overcome, the important matter of scholarships. The government maintained with much justifiable pride that the Cadet Colleges were not the prerogatives of the wealthier classes – a taunt frequently levelled at them from the opposition benches. No man's son could be denied a place through lack of family resources; if he satisfied the entry requirements, he must enter, with a full scholarship should the circumstances warrant it. This was a quite splendid concept, it was indeed one of the factors that decided me to accept the appointment in the first place. Unfortunately the Treasury department had taken a hand with the result that in fact the number of scholarships was restricted. Of this the government spokesmen made no mention in their public utterances.

The scheme was basically simple, too simple as I shall shortly make clear. Any boy whose father's income was less than 200 rupees a month would get a free place; less than 600, a grant of 100 rupees a month; less than 1,000, 50 rupees a month. If the earnings were above this last figure, the full fees of 150 a month must be paid. In small letters at the bottom, so to speak, came the rider. The governors could only allot a fixed number of awards in each grade each year with the result that in the final count less than fifty per cent of the boys could receive any grant at all. Apart from this clause, which was to cause a good deal of embarrassment all round, the scheme had two basic weaknesses – it took no account of a man's family commitments (I was to hear many tales of hardship on this score, six other children of school age etcetera); secondly there was no satisfactory method of checking the parents' statement of income. This would be a problem anywhere, but in Bengal, where the truth is on occasions twisted to suit individual requirements, it was a situation giving rise to some unease.

The system was responsible for one remarkable case which illustrated the common reluctance to face up to facts, and to accept a decision without making the most tortuous efforts to get it altered. A few days after the College had opened a rickshaw drew up outside my office and in walked a gentleman clearly not of the more affluent classes. His name was Mr. Shamsul. He had no English at all and we conversed through an interpreter. Shamsul junior, it transpired, had got as far as the interview, but no further. Since he had done extremely well in his papers – this was news to me, the results were supposed to be confidential and subsequent events proved that this assertion was a hopeful shot in the dark – since he had done so well, he must have failed the medical. What could be wrong with the poor lad? I hurriedly consulted my records. 'Your son,

Mr. Shamsul, did not do outstandingly well in the papers. Nor did he
impress the interview board. There's nothing wrong with his health.'
    Mr. Shamsul seemed not a whit abashed by this, but returned to the
attack from another flank. Would your honour be pleased to see the boy
again? He had not eaten, he had not slept since the results were known. He
was broken hearted . . . Shamsul junior had in fact been a borderline case;
I agreed to have another look at him. Father hastened to the rickshaw and
produced him, spruced for the occasion. We talked for ten minutes, and I
decided to 'give him a chance'. Father was called in and informed; fore-
seeing trouble, I had the Bursar with me.
    'Will you please explain to Mr. Shamsul, Bursar, that I am not in a
position to offer him a scholarship? If Mr. Shamsul can afford the fees,
there will be no problem.' Much talk and nodding of heads.
    'Yes, sir,' said the Bursar. 'He understands.'
    'How can he afford to pay?' I persisted. 'Are you absolutely sure,
Bursar, that he's got the position right?' More talk.
    'Yes, sir. He says he is poor man but he has got land which he can sell.
There will be no problem.' On which happy note the interview ended,
papers were signed; the boy would join the College in a fortnight's times.
    A few days later, Mr. Shamsul turned up again bringing with him a
gentleman of polished and well dressed appearance. It was he who came
into the office leaving Mr. Shamsul outside. He had, he told me in excellent English, been footing the bill for young Shamsul's education for
some years past. Now he could help no longer.
    'Are you a relative of the family?' I asked.
    'No, but I have interest in the boy. I like to help but the fees here are too
high.' I began to see daylight; obviously our Mr. Shamsul had pinned his
hopes on the family benefactor, but the cupboard was now bare. I explained that all scholarships had been awarded, that I could offer a place
but nothing more. This he accepted, and we parted amicably.
    But Mr. Shamsul was far from done. He resorted to telegrams request-
ing details of the boy's exam performance, none of which I answered; I
then had a request from one of my governors, a military man, for the
details of the case. These I sent with a firm rider that I was not prepared to
budge an inch. Many weeks later I was tackled after a set of tennis by a fat
and prosperous-looking gentleman at the wheel of his Mercedes car. He
produced a card. 'Dr _____ _____' with a string of degrees, and,
prominent in one corner, the words 'Member of the National Assembly'.
Could I spare a few minutes to show him the College? I was pleased to do
so. We talked among other things of London which he knew rather better

than I. As he was leaving he said, 'You will not mind my mentioning it, Mr. Principal, but there is Mr. Shamsul's son. Can you perhaps give him a scholarship?' I was astonished, but growing experience was forging me an armour.

'I've made my position clear, Doctor. I'm afraid there's nothing I can do.' Just before I went on holiday, I was told that 'a man' had been looking for me to ask about Mr. Shamul's son. One must give the Bengali full marks for persistence.

On December 10th the final notices to the successful candidates – rather elaborate notices, nothing must be left to chance – were sealed and posted. We were now on the home straight, the end of the beginning in sight.

*   *   *

We decided to spend our Christmas in East Pakistan's one seaside resort called, quizzically, Cox's Bazar. This is down in the South near the Burma border, accessible from Dacca either by car – a good twelve hour journey – or by air.

Who was Cox and how did he contrive to have a bazar on this remote coastal region washed by the waters of the Bay of Bengal? It seems that Cox was a captain in the employment of the East Indian Company; in 1798, after a Burmese invasion of the kingdom of Arakan, he was sent to help refugees. He picked a delectable spot where the Bakkali river flows into the sea, founded a colony and, before departing, handed it over to an Arakanese tribe. Presumably in gratitude, the tribe named the village after their benefactor.

The better to celebrate the festival, we mustered a party, laid plans, wrote letters to the Assistant District Commissioner seeking accommodation, all of which, as is customary, remained unanswered. Eventually we ran him to ground on the telephone and got confirmation that we had in fact been allotted two furnished bungalows. There was, however, a snag. If, it was explained, a government official should at the last moment arrive at Cox's Bazar seeking accommodation, we were liable to be thrown out neck and crop. Although this seemed a one-sided arrangement we elected to risk it.

In the dawn of 23 December two cars made away from Dacca encumbered with baggage, food, bedding, cots and assorted bric-à-brac. Nestling somewhere in the mêlée was a 15 lb. turkey, a cook, a bearer and a houseboy. The women and children took to the air, leaving the commissariat firmly in the hands of the men.

The official guidebook begins with unexpected candour: 'Right in the beginning, a splash of cold water – do not expect too much of Cox's Bazar. Too many tourists expect a replica of St. Tropez, San Remo or, at the least, good old Brighton, and they are disappointed'.

We knew our Bengal and we knew good old Brighton; we were not, therefore, to be counted among those who expected Cox's Bazar to bear the remotest resemblance to the latter. Nevertheless, approaching in the twilight from inland, we found the place somewhat uninviting; sight of the beach would come later to restore morale. Nor was the first glimpse of our 'Sea View' and 'Ocean Breezes' encouraging. The position was agreeable – slap behind sand-dunes within, no doubt about it this time, 'two minutes walk from the sea'. But the cottages, two in a line of six, wore a cracked and dingy air like so many chipped teacups. It was the old bugbear, lack of paint. Inside they were clean enough, though they might have drawn criticism from the fastidious.

As always privacy was at a discount. We had not been in the bungalow ten minutes before men were at the door selling shell necklaces, baskets and 'rubies' at ten rupees a time. Small children stood about, thumbs in mouth, round expectant bellies pushed out in silent wonder. They were joined now and then by their elders anxious not to miss any details of our life within doors.

The party was too large for the bungalows, two had to resort to a motel half a mile away. Here there were setbacks, dozens of cockroaches, jealous in possession, resented the intrusion, and drove the intruders to uneasy sleep – one in the back of the car and the other on a kitchen table. Next day they surrendered and sought refuge in our bungalows.

The sea and the tremendous beach soon routed resentment. I have seabathed in many parts of the world, none better than here on this long sandy seashore stretching seventy miles down into Burma. A warm sea, free of oil and sharks, clean firm sand and, above all, solitude made this a bathing paradise.

For our solitude we had to work a little. On the first morning we sunbathed near the bungalows and drew inevitably a crowd of gawpers, squatting immovable fifty yards away and decorating the sweet air with noisy expectorations. The four-wheel drive of one of our vehicles got us over the sand-dunes and we sped away from the multitude to peace and privacy. Before our wheels a million tiny crabs dived, panic stricken beneath the sand, like red lights dying one by one at the flick of a switch. Later a crab, bolder than his fellows, rose beside my wife, nipped her in the behind and was gone in a trice. Her yell was a bombshell on the drowsy afternoon.

Christmas Day morning had about it an unusual aura; at 7 a.m. we were in the sea. It was a hot day, full of sunshine; the Christmas tree and coloured wrappings looked incongruous, hard put to compete with such brilliance outdoors. We lounged and swam and lounged again. After dark we ate turkey and plum pudding, drank champagne – a bizarre, invigorating day.

We observed with interest the Bengali attitude to a seaside holiday. Mostly he seemed to take his ease with little enthusiasm; fully clad, he wandered along the edge of the sea, disdaining to get even his toes wet. A few, bolder than the rest, took hurried bathes; once, even a gaggle of begums, voluminously clad in saris, gingerly entered the water amid a chorus of giggles. It was all very Victorian. On the open space outside our bungalows buses pulled up, discharging streams of humanity who wandered about looking lost, pausing now and then to urinate or take stock of the horizon. From the roofs of the buses loudspeakers belched out an incessant roar of Oriental song. One busload, more venturesome than the rest, produced cooking pots and lit fires. These were the day trippers. In common with day trippers the world over, they left behind signs of their passing. For four days we exploited leisure unashamedly; then, sunsoaked, we headed back northwards and to work.

Time was running out; we were now less than a fortnight away from the opening day. There was much to be done – a family move from our temporary home in Dacca, a new house to be possessed, the final details of college administration to be settled. After six months in the city, frequently chasing my own shadow and getting nowhere with a great deal of effort, I was glad to be off to the country, glad to be immersing myself once again in school life. On 1 January, a lorry drew up outside the house, crates, trunks, suitcases, multiple odds and ends were loaded up; everyone got very cross, very overheated; the portly Isnahjuddin – still with us – was finding the upheaval altogether too much for him; at last the caravan was ready. We were off to a new life in the wide Bengal countryside.

5.30 on a summer morning; the whole college limbers up for the day ahead.

Shopping in our village High Street. Arrival of this entourage always brought out the crowds.

Lamming into the curry – a business repeated twice a day, every day.

Prelude to a very eventful football match – see page 177

Our second Adjutant, the splendid Capt. Wasim Khan. In attendance: UNCLE.

Hanging the jute out to dry beside one of the great jheels near the college.

Baby Nickler leads the way. Bengalis of all ages love little children.

In the Geography Room. Note the globe – courtesy of BOAC.

*A little quasi-military activity. The boys appeared
to enjoy this aspect of the Soldier's Art.*

*Judging from the pomp and circumstance on the roof, this was Pakistan Day, '65.
Note: gardens taking shape.*

Flowers of the Forest – in a jungle clearing near our garden fence.

Spotting the birds – twins and week-end visitors.

Principal's House – built in about fourteen weeks – wife, daughters and week-end visitors.

"The silver, snarling trumpets" – *a salvo from the college roof.*

Founder and first pupil – *the village school just outside the college boundary.*

We lacked gymnasium and swimming pool, but sports facilities were way ahead of other schools in Bengal.

Part Three

The First Term

Disasters of the opening day

Bengali Boys

Rules and routine

A long way from Lord's

Hazards of the road

A case of kidnap?

Pakistan Day, '65

Matters clerical and medical

More financial worries

The Helen Pitt School

End of term

The arrival of Gertie and Gilbert

Calcutta – social life – a wedding

Golf in Bengal

All aboard the 'Skylark'

'Mr Hamid and all his family are vomitting . . .'

So many people . . .

The First Term

If nothing was more remarkable in the life of Charles the First than its ending, nothing in the life of our college could have been more remarkable than its beginning. Not that we were without plans. With my two housemasters I sat for hours preparing the minutiae of The Arrival, how the boys were to be met, how conducted to their quarters; how parents were to be cossetted, how cleared off the premises, and a dozen other fussy details. The housemasters were stalwart fellows, but, in common with the rest of the staff, they had no experience whatever of life in a residential school. One walked with cautious tread, leaving no avenue unexplored. In the event, it was scarcely our fault that our hopeful plans were turned to emptiness.

In the best circles, the important day always dawns bright and clear; we were no exception. This was 9 January, 1965, our opening day. Main anxiety centred round the College kitchen. Against the advice of everyone who knew what they were talking about, the government contractors had installed in the kitchen three enormous tullahs – the vernacular for stove – fashioned at Allah-knows-what expense out of bricks and mortar. They were perfectly splendid affairs save only for the fact that no power of man could get them to work. They stood four feet high, and would have taxed the strength of giants in the lifting up and down of the big rice dixies; our cooks were built in the regional mould, short and wiry. The holes into which the fuel was fed were so tiny that a spoon rather than a shovel seemed to be the proper implement. The tullahs were coal burning in a land where coal was about as easy to come by as lipstick in a monastery. Above all, the tullahs simply would not work; if, after a monumental struggle, one got them to light, they, with massive ineptitude, quietly went out.

93

We had temporary recourse to oil stoves; eight of them smoked and blazed – it was quite beyond the wit of our cooks to maintain a blue flame – flinging dollops of smut on to walls and ceilings. A fig for our fine new paint! Should there be a kitchen in Hell, ours was its big brother. Not for nothing did we nickname our cooks the Furies.

If, as seemed more than likely, something blew up and started a fire, we had no water with which to put it out. At eleven o'clock in the morning of this, our big day, the water pump spluttered, coughed and died. This of course was nonsense. Bedded down in a neat, brand-new house, the pump itself was new. It looked, and was, expensive. Nestling below a fifty foot concrete tower, there was no obvious reason why it should not be discharging water from the tube well beneath at whatever rate these machines are presumed to operate. The fault was less mechanical than human; plainly the three simple fellows who laboured under the name of pump operators were defeated by the very size and complexity of the engine they were charged to control. The answer, a makeshift one, was the water cart. Driven by two cheerful rogues, whose company on a dark night one would have striven to avoid, this vehicle careered around the compound filling every available receptacle with water. The rogues sensed the emergency, and in the importance of the role they had been so suddenly called upon to fill, that day they were my best friends.

Throughout the warm January afternoon the Furies laboured to prepare the First Meal. I fussed about checking furniture, lists, timetables; like the motor mechanic on the day of the big race, I was obsessed with last minute preparations. The admin. block was abuzz with activity. At about five o'clock the boys began to arrive, accompanied in the main by hordes of relations – fathers, mothers, brothers, sisters, grandparents, uncles, aunts, cousins – all parties in a state of near collapse at the prospect of imminent farewells. They milled about in the gathering dusk, their numbers multiplying each minute. Being winter it was dark by half past five. At six o'clock the lights went out.

To describe what followed as chaos is a masterpiece of understatement. What should have been a dignified and orderly operation was reduced in a trice to a rout of panic-stricken humanity. One can in retrospect sympathise with the multitude; we were, don't forget, forty miles out in the country; many of them had only the vaguest idea where they were; town-dwellers mostly, they were all too well aware of the proximity of unfamiliar jungle.

At the time one could only deplore the disinclination to show a stiff upper lip. Women and girls took refuge in screaming, men and boys in moaning – the din was cataclysmic. There was one torch – mine – and this I lent to a housemaster whose morale seemed to be sagging under the pressure of events. I groped about seeking whom to succour, whom to pacify. The thing into which I bumped was a well rounded parent.

'Mr. Principal,' he wailed, clutching me by the lapels, 'this is terrible! What is to be done? What are we to do?'

What indeed!

I had in my pocket – for what purpose I cannot imagine – a whistle, and this I blew repeatedly in the futile hope that it would do something to restore the status quo. All it did was to add to the confusion.

A car was despatched to the nearest village, the driver charged to milk the bazaar of every candle it possessed. We had three Tilley lamps and these were pressed into service in the dining hall. They proved our salvation, they and the splendid havildars, who with raucous shouts at last managed to herd the boys together and marshal them into the oasis of light where by some miracle a meal was ready. The boys came in looking bewildered and blinking in the unfamiliar glare, as well they might, poor creatures. Not without difficulty the army of relatives was dissuaded from following them into the hall. By the time the meal was over, most had departed, and candles stood sentinel in the dormitories.

At eight o'clock the lights came on. A huge peace enveloped us like a blessing. The natal pangs were over; a new infant was born.

That the same occasion, important in the lives of two people, can be seen by those two people in a very different light is borne out by this extract from the College magazine:

At last my dream came true. My long cherished desire was going to be fulfilled. I still remember the exact date, it was the ninth of January . . .

From my very childhood a little trace of hope though little but very much determined was in the depth of my mind to make my career as an officer in the Pakistan army. A soldier in full uniform was an ideal for me. I made up my mind that I would have to join the Pakistan army.

To speak frankly, in those days opportunity was not as plenty as to-day because institution like that of our cadet college was rare here. So when one day through newspaper I came to know about the inception of a few more institutions including my one, I thought chances are at my door. I decided to seek admission and sat for the admission test which was on purely competitive basis. A few days of tension what might have happened to me ended with the happy news of me being selected as one of the fresh cadets for the newly established college.

One fine morning I started for my college where I will have to start a new chapter of my life, a life full of promise and preparation, a life full of daylight and discipline. It was the cold days of January. I parted from my parents and relations with a warm heart full of mixed emotions as it was the first time I was going far off my sweet residence leaving everybody behind. The state of excitement prevailing in my mind at the time of my arrival near the Adamjee school, our starting point, is still as alive as before in me. Gradually by four-thirty all the cadets arrived at the spot. Two big buses were ready for the journey. The Adjutant, our beloved Captain Ansar, was there to receive us. Unlike the cold afternoon of January the broad smile in the face of our captain was very warm and he received us with a very warm and affectionate heart. I liked our captain at the first sight.

After saying 'good-bye' to the guardians who were there to see us off we boarded the bus which started next moment. In the bus primary orientation among the cadets took place. Within moments we became friends. On the way we saw the daylight was fading with the arrival of dusk. I was very eager about the sight of my college, how it looks like? On the way we saw a replica with the inscription 'Welcome to Mymensingh'. I could understand the college was not far off. Within moments we reached our destination. I was charmed to see the scenic beauty of the surroundings within which our college was situated. The college building is a nice piece of oriental architecture. The whole area was plunged in darkness as there was no light. Our beloved Principal was standing with a broad smile in his face to receive us. For moments we forgot about the darkness around, as we were listening to our beloved Principal. The Principal left us as he was busy in arranging our dinner. Next moment we were standing in que and we were alloted our respective rooms. The moment I entered my room, the place where I will have to stay for many days, a new chapter of my life started. I entered a great institution, my beloved alma mater, where I will continue until I build myself as a perfect citizen, an efficient personality by the grace of Almighty and with the help of my efficient and affectionate teachers who are gallant in this profession.

*   *   *

There was nothing very unusual about the postcard itself – a coloured picture of terraced cultivation in the Hunza valley. It was the written matter that caused wonder.

'Dear Uncle,' it ran, 'My best regards on this happy day. I hope you'll not mind at all, for the salutation of this note. I, in fact, take you as the one next my father. I would be thankful if you would let me know next time I meet you, whether you have any boy of my age to be my friend. With anticipations. Yours – Ziauddin.'

Nothing in my previous experience had let me to suspect that I would one day be addressed as 'Uncle' by one of my future pupils, but here it was in black and white: our relationship, it seemed, would blossom rapidly, if, on such slender acquaintance, he was prepared to place me 'next my father'. Indeed, postcards apart, we had already established a rapport.

'Uncle', as he was thereafter known to us, was a gangling child rising six foot with a lugubrious expression and a pair of dominant steel spectacles that caused the trouble and made him the first boy with whom I established perceptible contact. Uncle did very well in his written papers, and pleased us on interview. The sight of those formidable glasses, however, frightened the doctors out of their wits. 'Failed on medical grounds' was the verdict that threatened to send Uncle out of my life.

This was a situation under which he was not prepared to lie down. I received from him a letter, eulogising his ability at work and games, pouring scorn on the medical profession, and declaring his undying wish to enter the College. Would I see him that I might the better judge the truth of his remarks for myself?

I was aware that to tinker with official decisions could land one in all sorts of trouble, but I thought the risk was acceptable. A messenger was despatched, and within half an hour Uncle loomed up before me, spectacles flashing fire and determination. I shot questions at him about himself and his eyesight; the better to prove his assertion that he could see like a lighthouse, I hurled a tennis ball at him, first with specs on, then off. He caught the ball each time, his air almost contemptuous. There was no doubt about it, Uncle was a winner. Quietly I shelved the medical report, and wrote the glad tidings to him next day.

I never had cause to regret this decision. If Uncle was not quite the cricketer nor the centre-half he said he was, there was no denying his sharpness and all-round ability. He was a natural leader, exercising the little authority we gave him with tact and good sense; it was no surprise to me to find that, when we came to form a military band, Uncle was to be seen out in front, wielding the baton with a minimum of skill and a maximum of assurance. He was another example of the old saw that you can't keep a good man down. Half way through the first long vacation, we received yet another postcard, this time a coloured picture of the Khyber Pass. The message was succinct, and added a further dimension to our relationship. 'With best wishes,' he wrote, 'to you, aunt, baby Nickler and other respectedly, faithfully yours as ever, Ahmed Z.'

In dealing with the boys, one of the early difficulties was getting to know their names. Unless you have a gift for it, this is not easy in a Western school. In Bengal the problem was aggravated firstly by the fact that all the boys were dark-haired, secondly by the fact that the Bengalis have a very, very limited range of names. They have their Smiths, Joneses and Browns, but precious little else. To make confusion doubly confused, the same limitations applied to first and second names (if they had them which was not always the case). Of the one hundred and twenty boys in our first intake, we had ten Ahmeds, three Ahmads, eight Chaudhuris, nine Rahmans, five Haques and nine Hussains (variously spelt Hasan and Hassain). Sixty boys had an M among their initials which meant Mohammed as like as not. Sorting all this out was quite a headache, and confusions in the early days arose not infrequently. The boys themselves treated the whole business with the utmost good humour, clearly enjoying the opportunity it afforded of making their elders feel slightly ridiculous. In desperation one day I called *all* the Rahmans to my office, where I paced up and down trying to distinguish Rahman M. from Rahman M.N., Rahman A.S.M. (i) from Rahman A.S.M. (ii). What time the boys stood in a line suffused with mirth, anxious to be both helpful and iconoclastic.

The teachers had an easy method of coping: they simply did not try. I would go into a class and find, as late as six weeks after we had started, the teacher pointing at boys and getting nowhere near a name. When I suggested that it was his business to know the names of the boys he was teaching, he would react with apologies and not a little bewilderment. No one, I suppose, had ever made this point to him before, and the simple logic of it took him unawares. Once he had grasped it, he was eager to make amends.

Finally, to make the whole thing just a shade more complex, fathers and sons did not always share the same surname. 'I shall not call my son

Haque,' said Mr. Haque, a friend of mine in Dacca. 'It is too common a name.'

Of parents, we saw little. They turned up in shoals at the entrance exams, as I have already told, but that was in the city, and junior's interests on that occasion had to be most carefully protected. Some had been in evidence on our opening day. Otherwise there was little to remind us that parents existed. The reasons puzzled me: certainly it was not due to lack of interest or affection – children in Asia, especially sons, are cherished. At last I put it down to two things: firstly, very few people owned cars, and public transport was chancy (although we were only forty miles from Dacca, where most of our pupils lived, the road and the buses were such that a journey could take anything up to three hours). Secondly, the child's destiny had been temporarily settled, and he was in the hands of a thoroughly reputable institution – Allah would surely take good care of him. Though it had certain advantages, lack of contact with parents was something we regretted. As any educationist recognises, to know the child without knowing the parent means that important links are missing.

Mr. Grimwig, it may be recalled, knew 'only two sorts of boys – mealy boys and beef-faced boys'. My experience had been entirely with English boys – mealy, beef-faced and other varieties. Of the Bengali boy, I was none too sure what to expect. Any misgivings I may have had were quickly put to rout. He was polite, with a brisk sense of humour, temperamental and emotional.

'Oh how beautiful the sunset is! How pleasant the scenery is! Ahh! I won't be able to forget it in my life. How beautiful sight is created in the seashore. I can find half the beauty of nature in it. The men who had not enjoyed this charming scenery has failed to see the half the beauty of the nature.' This was an extract from a fourteen-year-old's essay.

The Bengali boy was quick to tears and to anger; he painted well and enjoyed music. Physically he was well-shaped and good-looking. One of the things from which he suffered was excessive spoiling by his parents; he therefore expected to be constantly cosseted and comforted. Typical was the case of Ali Hussain. For some no doubt justifiable reason, the Adjutant was sharp with him, whereupon I received a letter of complaint, a quite scurrilous document full of accusations and unsigned. Although in many respects an excellent boy, he was, like a host of others, ready to complain at the smallest provocation. This was the more surprising in that the facilities we provided – food, space, cleanliness, to mention but a few – were of a far higher standard than most of them would have met in other schools, or, indeed, in their own homes.

Later, the same boy was to break his arm at football; the fussation of his family was almost beyond belief. It reached a climax when the time came to transfer him from the local hospital to one nearer his home. No fewer than six able-bodied men (father plus five uncles/brothers/cousins) came in two cars to fetch him in the middle of a working week, taking a whole day over the performance. They were all of junior executive status; I began to see why, when one called during working hours at business houses in the city, the manager was so often 'not available'. Was it really the boys' fault that they seemed at times to lack backbone?

Nevertheless, the Bengali boy in the main took his work very seriously indeed, believing, rather sadly, that he had only to pass exams to become – favourite phrase – a 'great man'. In matters of discipline, he presented fewer problems than his Western counterpart; there was, for instance, no tendency to slip behind the gymnasium with a dormitory maid, nor to celebrate a house match victory by getting sloshed on a bottle of whisky. Most of the 'crime' he committed could be put down to negligence or sheer stupidity, rather than deliberate wrongdoing.

What for want of a better word I will call 'the schoolboys' code' did not appear to operate. This code is rigid, respected by both management and labour; simply, it vilifies the tell-tale. No such ethic existed in our establishment, a fact of which I was made keenly aware when the first serious case of indiscipline was brought to my attention. Half a dozen boys ran minor riot in the College building during a rest period, doing a little superficial damage, including, horror of horrors, tearing the pages out of the Black Mark register lodged for safe keeping in the Staff room. An attempt was made to damage the electrical circuit. One of the six was a good deal bigger than the others, something of a bully and in this instance clearly the ringleader. Which latter fact the other five, interviewed one by one, were eager to underline, while belittling their own parts in the enterprise. Positively no pressure did I have to apply in order to extract the information I wanted. Much as one might deplore such wholesale surrender to the doctrine of self-preservation, there was no denying that it made the task of the judiciary a great deal easier.

The Bengali excels at soccer; in light of the fact that ninety per cent of the boys had received no coaching and very little practice on inadequate grounds, the standard of ball-control and general know-how about the game astonished me. At hockey and cricket, he was less skilful than the West Pakistani. But there was a tremendous enthusiasm for all games. In the College's first weeks, we were short of playing space and had to improvise by using little patches of ground anywhere. On minute hockey pitches, on a dust-choked soccer-cum-cricket ground, on pitiful basketball and volleyball courts, they showed limitless zest.

Just as the playing-fields were completed, the rains came. We blessed them for carpeting the ground with a rich layer of grass; we cursed them for periodically turning the whole area into a morass. One could not but admire the Bengali boy's refusal to be daunted by the weather – his enthusiasm for football was too strong for that.

I recall an afternoon in mid-July. A lull in the rains had brought out our full labour force in an attempt to drain off some of the wetter patches. A final trial game was to be held at five o'clock in preparation for two matches the following week. By one o'clock the field was in fair shape, and, with four hours to go before kick-off, prospects were good. At three, the rain returned in full force, setting at nought the hours of morning labour. By five, the field was a lake and it was still raining. 'Do you want to play?' I shouted to a damp phalanx of about a hundred boys. Within a couple of minutes, four games were under way. I watched the final trial under an umbrella, and was impressed at the players' ability both to enjoy themselves in such conditions and to demonstrate some considerable skills.

If at times the Bengali boy behaved, like all boys, irrationally and with scant thought for others, if at times he showed lack of resilience and a tendency to crumple under pressure, if at times he was querulous and vindictive, he had, nonetheless, much to offer to anyone inclined to help him along the perplexing path of adolescence. In short, he was a thoroughly worthwhile character on which to work.

*   *   *

One of the questions asked in the entrance examination required the candidates to write their reasons for wanting to go to a Cadet College. Their answers to this were of great help to me in deciding what line to adopt in matters of discipline.

All too clearly there emerged from these answers a theme – they wanted a school life that was well ordered and an atmosphere in which they could study with some degree of method and concentration. With this went a good deal of implied or direct criticism of the schools the candidates were attending. This I found depressing, but it recurred too frequently to be ignored. Here are some extracts from answers chosen at random and reproduced in their original form (most of them are from candidates who fell by the wayside):

'I intent to read in the cadet college as it is the only best type of institution in the province to get better education, discipline and good prospect in life.'

'The school in which I study is not a good school. In cadet college higher education is taught and also behaviour.'

'I think the rule of the school will be very strict.'

'I want to go to a cadet college because to bring up my life with good behaviour good manners and well disciplined.'

'The next thing is that I want to learn discipline, in our other schools we only go and study and come back.'

'This school will give good Educations and strict discipline. (Not that I am an unruly sort of fellow but such things do help in the long run.)'

'I want to go to cadet college because I don't like my school. The education of my school is not good. We cannot read well because it is too noise in the outside of our school. It is situated in a bad noise and dirty place.'

'There is a diceplen in Cadet College but some schools have no diceplen.'

'There will be very good disipline in this college. Disipline is the most important things in our life. Men cannot run exept disipline. Our Qued-i-Azam Mohammed Ali Jinnah has gone with disipline.'

'There is a system of playing, studying and feeding. Everything is done in appointed time. The boys are always under control. They are not allowed to fight or abuse.'

'The cadet college's boys are teach very good the discipline. It is much used for the human life. This is also a very hard thing to teach in the common schools of East Pakistan.'

'I want to go to cadet college to become a great man' was a theme that persisted; indeed one boy saw his future in so rosy a light that he had only to gain admission to the College to be assured in the end of the Presidency. Alas! he failed – another village Hampden gone? To serve Pakistan to the best of one's ability was another sentiment frequently expressed. Indeed these three themes – discipline, ambition, patriotism – occurred time and again among the nine hundred odd scripts we examined.

It seemed to me essential that, if from the start we were to have some sort of order in the place, much use must be made of our havildars. Accordingly boys were paraded before all meals, before morning school and before games; gradually this was thinned down as they became accustomed to the new way of life. They played games compulsorily four times a week, voluntarily on Friday – which day is the Muslim Sunday – while on Mondays they played at soldiers, this being mostly foot drill and a little gentle messing about on a vaguely military basis.

I enjoyed sitting down to frame a set of School Rules right from the start. I purposely kept the initial issue very brief; there were in fact only five:

1) BOUNDS. a) All areas outside the wire fence are out of bounds.
   b) The following areas inside the College are out of bounds –
   i) Kitchens
   ii) Dining hall except at meal times
   iii) Staff Quarters
   iv) Class rooms except in work hours.
2) SMOKING is forbidden.
3) SILENCE will be observed after lights out.
4) Cadets in classrooms will stand up when a Lecturer enters the room and remain so until told to sit.
5) Cadets will enter and leave the College building by the side door and NOT by the main entrance.

The brevity of this legislation rather shocked some of my Army friends. When I pointed out that schoolboys are no more capable than private soldiers of swallowing volumes of written instruction at one gulp, they began to see the point. We added to these rules as expediency dictated. We would publish from time to time things somewhat pompously called 'Cadet Orders', of which the following is a sample selection:

Fans:
Cadets are reminded that fans consume electricity which costs money. Cadets in charge of classrooms and hostel rooms will ensure that fans are switched off when there is no-one in the room.
Windows:
Cadets are forbidden to jump through the windows of their hostels.
Dress:
Cadets should not walk about the College with the blue shirt hanging outside the trousers.
Shower:
Cadets should have a shower bath after games in the afternoon.
Blankets:
It is understood that a few cadets are feeling too cold at night. Those who wish to draw a third blanket should report to the Adjutant at the clothing store at 1745 to-morrow.
Morning P.T.:
Cadets who are late on parade at 0630 hours will have their names taken and will be reported to the Principal.
Letter Writing:
Every cadet is expected to write a letter to his parents once a week and time is allotted on Sunday for this purpose.
College Flag:
The College flag will be hoisted for the first time at sunrise tomorrow.
Blackboards:
Cadets are forbidden to scribble on blackboards in the classrooms.
Discipline:
Cadets are reminded that term does not end until 0900 hrs tomorrow and that discipline must be maintained right to the end.

In parenthesis it should be explained that the windows referred to above were on the ground floor; happily we were not a breeding ground for suicides. I reproduce this selection of rules, many of them quite trivial, to show that school administration in Bengal was much the same as it is in Balham or Baltimore.

After a short period of trial and error, we arrived at a routine which, with minor modifications to suit the seasons, remained the same during my tour of office.

At 6.00 a.m. a bugle brought to their senses those boys who had not already got up to greet the dawn with prayer. Although the Bengali is fond of his bed, the business of routing the boys out was not a difficult one, rather different to the English boy who normally regards one and a half minutes as sufficient time to wash, dress and make his somewhat unwholesome appearance at the first concourse of the day. At 6.25 a.m. the havildars had appeared on the scene, and, with much blowing of whistles and military injunctions to haste, the college was assembled for a roll-call and fifteen minutes P.T. or drill. On most mornings I turned out for this myself, though in a strictly passive role; it was good to be out in the freshness of the morning before the sun had mustered its withering strength. Breakfast was eaten at 7.15 a.m., a meal very similar to that taken in the West – cereal, an egg in some guise, bread and jam, tea – and eaten, too, with a rather sullen resignation which was not unfamiliar; 8.00 a.m. and everyone was in class, the day's teaching under way. The morning was broken into seven periods each of forty minutes with a break of half an hour, when the staff drank tea, the boys a generous glass of milk.

This made a long morning and by midday a certain weariness was perceptible on both sides of the classroom. But it was quite the most satisfactory way of coping with the climatic difficulties inseparable from the tropics, and it was an agreeable sensation to feel the day's teaching over by early afternoon, and the day free for other activities.

At 1.30 p.m. the boys trooped in for lunch, setting about huge piles of rice and curry with a zest which only a growing boy can achieve. I was at first a little appalled by the sheer monotony of the diet; twice a day, every day, they ate curry and rice. Admittedly the curry might be meat, fish, chicken or vegetable, and on these we rang the changes in an attempt to achieve variety. Sometimes, instead of rice, we put on chupattis, but the Bengali is a rice eater, and at first the boys did not take too kindly to this effort to widen their tastes. For a second course we gave them either fruit – usually a banana which is the one fruit easily acquired in East Bengal – or a rather insipid sweet dish which they appeared to enjoy.

After lunch the whole place was supposed to be enveloped in a great slumber for a ninety-minute rest period. While I personally always set a signal example in this, the boys, in the cool season, were inclined to wander and had to be restrained; in the hot humid summer the problem did not arise. At 3.30 p.m. havildars and whistles were at it again, the boys paraded and parcelled out to whatever was to be their game for the day – soccer, hockey, tennis, softball, volleyball or basketball. This was organised by the Adjutant, and right well he did it. The games were taken mostly by the havildars. The boys had a little over an hour to themselves after games during which they could drink tea, clean up, make purchases from the little canteen – boiled sweets, chocolate, biscuits, toothpaste, the usual merchandise of a school shop on a rather small scale – or racket around in the style common to boys everywhere.

Prep was meant to start at six, an occasion which frequently found the College not quite at its best. It will be understood that we had in the early days no boys of the age and experience to assume effective control of their fellows. One therefore had to rely exclusively on the lecturers, or, in the case of the prep periods, on the housemaster and house tutor, for the work was done in the boys' dormitories. The Bengali is not a particularly punctual person, so I would frequently go up to prep a little after six, and find the situation, broadly speaking, unsatisfactory. To put a little ginger into the master concerned and to harangue such boys as were obviously more clamorous than the rest were tasks speedily accomplished. After quite a short time people began to get the hang of things, and a calmer atmosphere prevailed. After prep came the evening meal, which was, as I have already indicated, a repeat performance of lunch. Lights-out for the younger boys was at 8.30 p.m., others at 9.00 p.m., though under pressure from the older boys who complained of lack of time to work, we altered this to a later hour.

By and large, the boys may be said to have had a reasonably full day; it was interspersed with five or ten minute periods for prayer. The problem of religious observance was one which proved a bit of a headache. The strict Muslim will pray five times a day, each session taking about ten minutes; the exact timings vary according to the position of the sun. To do this his requirements are simple – a good wash, a little white skull cap and a prayer mat; the place itself matters not a whit; he can, and does, pray anywhere. Once we perceived, a few feet from our garage, a fellow gazing with statuesque attention at the back of our car. A sudden genuflexion revealed that he was in fact at prayer. It should be stressed that by no means all professed Muslims observe this prayer routine – like human beings everywhere, some are more devout than others.

From certain quarters I was under pressure to introduce communal prayer throughout the college according to the strict Muslim rule. On a postcard a parent wrote:

'I like to suggest that every boy should be compelled, forced and beaten if necessary, to go to the prayer hall early in the morning and just before going to bed at night. The defaulter should never be given the meal even. You will never find any guardian who will turn down my suggestion.'

Sturdy religious injunctions here – John Knox would surely have approved. (I cherished the thought of the reaction on my native heath had I driven a boy into chapel at the point of a stick.) The effect of this rule of prayer on a school time-table, remembering that the prayer times were constantly shifting, can be readily imagined; I resorted to compromise which put no compulsion on the individual but made it possible for him to pray if he so wished. The times were carefully arranged in order not to disrupt the working day. On Fridays, we ended school a little early, at five to twelve, and, in line with Muslim custom, held a short communal prayer session in the Assembly Hall. The authorities had not quite made up their minds what to do about Sundays; most observed it as a holiday, and to this we were no exception. Once a month we held – disastrous term – a 'visiting day', when parents and relatives could satisfy themselves that Junior was still alive and kicking, but very few turned up.

Again by trial and error, we evolved a method of dealing with defaulters. As I have suggested elsewhere, the sins were more often of omission; it was not so much what the boy had done as what he had failed to do. We eschewed those traditional stand-bys, detention and punishment drill, and relied substantially on a black mark system which, we flattered ourselves, worked as well as any punitive method can hope to work. One aspect of this I considered shrewd; we recorded on the end-of-term report the number of black marks 'awarded' in the course of the term. The Bengali boy, in common with the English boy, likes to keep his parents in ignorance of any misdemeanours he may have committed at school. Of this I was vividly reminded in the one and only case of a serious nature which was brought to my notice during the first term. A boy was reported to me by his housemaster for a rather nasty little case of sexual exhibitionism. He was in many respects a sad child, overgrown and something of an introvert. His offence merited expulsion and he knew it. However I chose to give him a second chance, but insisted that his father must be informed of what had happened. Understandably this filled him with horror, but it had to be done. As to other punishments, we imposed fines for wilful damage, and on very rare occasions resorted to the cane. But only one person was authorised to use it – the Principal.

Punishment in schools is a controversial question the world over. Anyone who claims to have found the whole answer is kidding himself. The fact is indisputable that, if an institution is to function effectively, a system of bringing to heel those members who are bent on putting a spanner in the works must be worked out. Some sort of action has to be taken – but what action? Between the two extremes – the method, now outmoded, of corporal punishment and the frequently derided 'modern' method of letting the child go its own way unchecked – between these two perhaps the best course lies. In the final analysis, common sense and humanity are probably the best yardsticks.

*   *   *

Some three weeks after we had opened the College, the boys decided that it would be a good thing to play a cricket match against the Staff. To this I could see no reasonable objection though I had secret misgivings. Nothing in the attitude of my colleagues had given any indication that they knew of the game's existence. In their interviews they had declared to a man their devotion to all games, but when it came to the pinch they were showing some reluctance to capitalise on this devotion. I had a clear impression that the staff side would comprise the Adjutant, perhaps two of the younger lecturers, myself and an assortment of A.N. Others from among the boys. In the event I was proved gloriously wrong.

I drove up to the scene of combat where a large crowd had assembled. I at once had two surprises. Firstly, I was greeted with a fervent burst of applause; apparently I had acquired a Fan Club. Secondly, every member of the staff had turned out, all of them in white; we were in fact in the astonishing position of owning a twelfth man, a situation for which our selectors had made no provision. This could lead to some unseemly and highly embarrassing argument. The boys rejected my suggestion to play 12-a-side as unorthodox and therefore suspect. Tact was needed.

I addressed the last man to arrive.

'Mr. Ahmed, would you mind very much . . . there's been a slight mistake, we are twelve. I should be so grateful if – er – perhaps . . .'

'Not at all, Principal. I will not after all play.'

'Thank you. You are most kind.'

'It is a pleasure, sir.' With smiles and bows the danger was averted.

I won the toss and decided to bat. Being totally ignorant of the virtues of my own side, I found myself in difficulties with the batting order. It was in fact as much a hit and miss affair as most of the batting subsequently turned out to be. I sent in two of my more athletic-looking colleagues, and it was apparent from the first over that a straight ball would prove their undoing. Happily for us this was a rare commodity, and with the help of snicks and byes our score reached eight without loss.

Things then began to happen; with sickening speed our fortunes declined to a score of fifteen for six wickets. Unless something was done about it, the prestige of the staff would receive a devastating blow and the match would be over within the hour.

I had put myself in about number five. I do not claim to be much of a cricketer, but it is a sad fact that in this company I stood out like Geoff Boycott on the village green. By good luck – I was badly missed twice – and some juicy long hops outside the leg stump, I began to find the hitherto untroubled boundary. I collected, perhaps, thirty-five runs before banging a full-toss into the hands of mid-on. But our face was saved; the score had reached fifty to perfervid cheers from the onlookers who appeared, oddly, to be on the side of authority on this occasion. Myself was cheered to the ropes as if I had won a Test Match off my own bat. Our numbers ten and eleven offered little resistance – both in fact had to be shown how to hold the bat and where to put it in relation to the wicket. We mustered a grand total of fifty eight.

A word about the spectators. My experience of schoolboys watching cricket *en masse* had led me to believe that the game induced torpor rather than enthusiasm. A tense finish to a House match would hold their attention, but little else; for the most part compulsory cricket watching was looked upon as a bore. Not so in Bengal, here spectator participation was total. They cheered, yelled, groaned, exhorted, laughed, prayed, chattered, clapped; I have heard boys applaud a maiden over in the third hour of a game. It was all a little like a Hospitals cup-tie. The goings on at Test Matches in tropical areas became totally understandable.

Any shortcomings the staff may have shown individually at the wicket were multiplied by eleven once we had taken the field. For the captain, management of bowling was simplified by the fact that only two members of the side appeared able to raise an arm above shoulder height in the manner prescribed by the M.C.C. It was perhaps fortunate for us that occasionally one of these maestros threw up a lob of respectable length. Avid for runs the boys pounced on these, charging down the wicket the better to execute the onslaught. Sometimes they missed, and, mid a tumult of shouting, I was given ample time to administer justice from behind the wicket, which position I had adopted in a determination to prevent extras figuring as prominently in the opponents' tally as they had in ours. In this manner we removed some five batsmen, but meantime runs were garnered. Our bowling received no support whatever from the fielders, most of whom were clearly of the opinion that the foot was a better instrument for stopping the ball than the hand. In this malpractice they were encouraged by the spectators, still loyal to their masters, who cheered each stop to the echo, while moaning in sympathy when, as more often happened, the ball sped through to the boundary. Such catches as were offered fell to the ground untouched, what time the fielder ran round in small circles to a chorus of conflicting advice from his team mates.

At fifty four for five, the battle lost and won, we sustained a further misfortune. The senior geographer, who had in the words of the pundits 'kept one end going', elected to use his shin in an attempt to check a sizzling straight drive. He retired, not without honour; twelfth man was awoken from a deep siesta, and I decided that the chemistry master must by virtue of his position in the batting order – number eleven – be given a bowl.

This was a mistake. Rating economy of movement a virtue, Mr. Hamid eschewed a run-up; he simply stood at the wicket and plugged. It was the most flagrant case of throwing yet seen on a cricket field. The boy umpires remained silent, whether out of politeness or because they were all too keenly aware of the nectar now being proffered to their own side, I was not sure. Nevertheless, with the collaboration of his beloved Principal, Mr. Hamid took a wicket. His fourth ball, which he delivered underarm, rose never an inch above the turf. The batsman rushed out, missed and fell flat on his face. A leisurely stumping was achieved, to the accompaniment of gales of cheering from the Fan Club on the boundary. It was all a long way from Lord's . . .

The game ended as most games end, handshakes, back slapping, smiles all round. On record was a win for the College by four wickets, but we had salvaged out of the wreckage enough honour for us to be able to resume normal relationships with our pupils in the classroom next morning.

*   *   *

The forty mile drive between the College and the centre of Dacca was one which I came to know uncommonly well; for me it never quite lost its fascination, in spite of the heat which often made driving something of an ordeal. It varied enormously according to the season of the year. At all times it called for intense concentration; other vehicles one met far less often than on English roads, but, when met, they seldom failed to register personality and a leaven of unpredictability. These vehicles were mainly buses and lorries, very few cars. It was the buses that provided the most colour and excitement. They ranged from the sleek modern State Mail bus to the far more numerous ramshackle conveyances which seemed to get along the road by a combination of vehicular will-power and bits of string.

They were invariably full, and, as anyone who has been in Asia knows, the word 'full' has quite a different meaning there to what the European understands by the word. 'Full' means passengers standing so tight that breathing is barely possible, 'full' means passengers on the running-boards, half out of windows, on the roof, on the back bumper clinging on by ten bare toes. The whole is topped up by an assortment of baggage, livestock and freight of varying shapes and sizes. The vehicle sags and snorts and groans; it seizes every opportunity to boil over; it has long since lost its paint; it has aged indifferently. No doubt, as for so many of its passengers, life has been hard with too little sustenance and too much toil.

The method of passing one of these boneshakers was a ritual, bringing into prominence not so much the driver as the conductor. The former was too busily engaged in steering, too deafened by the snorts and groans to pay heed to so unimportant a factor as a vehicle approaching from behind. No, this is the chance for the conductor to show himself a man of mettle and significance. One hoots and keeps one's hand on the button – the bus of course is slap on the crown of the road. At last a figure hangs from the back door, anger in its face, and waves frantically. This means 'Why all the hurry? Wait a minute, you impatient so-and-so, until I can bring myself to attract my driver's attention,' which he proceeds to do by shouting or banging on the tin flanks of the vehicle – usually both. The bus would slow down, pull slowly left; the driver's hand lolls from his window, an index finger waggling imperceptibly – exertion must be avoided – and the stage is now set for a safe passage.

Much the same drill was employed with the lorries that plied the highways in varying degrees of decrepitude. Standing in the back would be four or more mistris in head cloths and dirty vests, one of whom would be the eyes in the back of the driver's head. Here, too, a flurry of hooting, shouting, waving and banging – much ado in fact about nothing. Buses and lorries were often to be found abandoned by the road-side, the ghost having been given up.

Other hazards there were in plenty; the bullock cart, propelled by oxen or water buffalo, creaking in a way that only a bullock cart can, the driver, if one may so misuse the term, often asleep at the reins; the assorted livestock, cows, sheep, chicken, goats, dogs; last, but not least, the people, shambling along the roadside in their unending thousands, alive mentally to nothing but the half-dazed cloud-cuckooland in which most of them existed. Dangerous above others to the driver were the old men who had clearly never come to terms with the motor age, and who might, at the sound of a horn, perform any one of a number of erratic fandangoes, calculated to test brakes to the limit. Driving in Bengal had its peculiar fascinations.

The drive from Dacca was divided in my mind into a number of distinct phases. First the busy dual-carriageway to the Airport, then past the East Pakistan Flying Club and into the army cantonment. Here all was order and tidiness, the colourful signs – Garrison Cinema, H.Q. Military Police, Regimental Road, Flagstaff House – it might be Tidworth or Catterick. Out past the golf course to the Tongi toll bridge, the operation of which showed up the local lads at their best.

The toll part of the bridge was not impressive – a kutcha hut of mud and corrugated iron, the gate itself nothing but a bamboo pole. The enthusiasm of the toll-keepers for their task was governed entirely by the zeal of their superiors. If in some government office the great panjandrum of toll fees exerted an inquisitive interest, then the front line troops stood to their guns. If not, they slept the livelong day, leaving the bamboo pole upright and the wayfarer unmolested. The latter situation applied for fifty odd weeks in the year.

Early one evening, hurrying to the city, bound, I seem to remember, for a cocktail party, we found the gate closed. About the kutcha hut there hung an unusual atmosphere of purpose. Clearly the great panjandrum had been exerting himself, but I was unperturbed. The nature of my work had secured for me a government permit allowing me at all times to pass the toll without charge. My position was impregnable. The toll-keeper had other ideas.

Before the closed gate, Driver Nazir entered into a lively discussion with the master of the bridge. The flow of words was clamorous, the gestures explosive. Frequently both men were talking at one and the same time. 'What's all this about, Nazir?' I shouted impatiently. 'Tell him to open the gate, and let's get on.'

'No, sah. He say you pay. He no good,' replied Nazir with a meaningful shrug.

By now the traffic was building up behind us, and advertising its presence by prodigious honking. There was nothing for it but to pull into the side, alight, and continue negotiations within the confines of the kutcha hut. Followed by Nazir, I strode into the holy of holies, my brow dark with righteous indignation.

The interior of the hut was neither more nor less impressive than the exterior. On a rough wooden table a hurricane lamp lit up the dark faces of the toll-keeper and his clerks. The furnishings were strictly utility. With natural courtesy, he offered me a chair.

We had by now attracted a large crowd. An altercation was always worth a gawp; when one of the disputants happened to be a large red-faced foreigner, the temptation to get in on the act was too strong to be resisted. The throng, six deep, pressed thick behind me, their naked torsos lightly flecked with beads of sweat. In this tight aromatic atmosphere, we got down to business.

The toll-keeper was not easily shaken. The language barrier put paid to the subtleties of negotiation, one could only be blunt. Did I unashamedly invoke my close friendship with the prime minister himself? I rather think I did. Such mendacity got me nowhere. I had no permit, he averred, and what is more had no business to be arguing otherwise – I must pay my toll. The crowd, appreciative of the keeper's unswerving attitude, murmured approval; only my one ally, Nazir, showed hostility by a contemptuous scowl. I had a card up my sleeve; whether it was an ace of spades or a two of clubs, we would soon know.

'Alright, I will pay,' I said, producing a rupee from my pocket. Again the crowd murmured. The foreigner was bowing to the inevitable, another victory for good sense was being won. The toll-keeper and his staff beamed with satisfaction, Nazir alone registering disgust; plainly the Principal Sahib was losing his grip.

'A receipt, please?'

'Yes, yes, a receipt, of course,' said the tollkeeper, nudging a clerk into activity with pencil, official forms and carbon paper. I waited until the scribe had completed his lengthy task.

'And now, Mr. Tollkeeper, I should like to see your government permits, please,' I said, pointing to a stack of forms hanging from the ceiling on a piece of wire. With some reluctance he handed me the bundle and I bent to my task. The crowd, sensing a new development, fell quiet. As I riffled through the pile, the tension rose.

It was a thick pile. As it shrank beneath hurrying fingers, my anxiety mounted. All the cars in the country seemed to have been granted exemption, all save mine. If my permit were not there, defeat would be total. But ah! here it was, three from the bottom. My name, car number, even my job were all down in black and white; in cold and uncompromising typescript, it was written that I was entitled to free passage.

'Look at that,' I cried, thrusting the permit across the table. 'Now, I want my money back, please!' A low, keening sound, something between a sob and a moan, arose from the multitude. It was a moment of fierce pleasure. The toll-keeper and his staff were aghast; they were faced with a situation for which there was no precedent. A sum of money had changed hands; worse still, a receipt had been made out in triplicate, and here was irrefutable evidence that the whole transaction was null and void. How to explain this to the great panjandrum in the government office? How would they avoid the stigma of officialdom made to look ridiculous, how indeed would they keep their jobs against proof of such incompetence? Over their tired, hungry faces, there spread the aura of despair. Suddenly I began to feel despicable.

'All right,' I said, 'keep your money and your receipts, but don't forget me next time.' The despair evaporated to be replaced by smiles; I shook hands all round amid much commendation of each others' ancestors. The crowd, sensing the victor, applauded me to the car, Nazir, pride in his gait, clearing a way through with imperious shouts.

I was late for the party, but it mattered not. Never again was I stopped on the toll bridge with its kutcha hut of mud and corrugated iron, the gate itself nothing but a bamboo pole.

On then a couple of furlongs to the hoarding 'Welcome to Bata Tongi the Town of Good Shoes'. This was a sprawl of new and half-finished factories, no prettier than industrial development areas the world over. One was glad to leave the Town of Good Shoes behind, and press on down a long road cut straight through the paddy. On each side tattered, rusting signs proclaimed a better age. 'Site for Metal Industries and Foundries Ltd.' or, less categorically, 'Site for New Project.' Especially we enjoyed 'Ark Construction Ltd.' the more so as it first appeared in the middle of the rainy season. How many, one wondered, would ever mature beyond the drawing board, beyond the pipe-dream of some petty tycoon with rosy ideas of future riches? Next the roundabout, the purpose of which was not quite plain, there being only one metal road – ours – branching off it.

Swing left and the scene changes. Free of the planners and their rusty signs, the countryside is on terms with itself, now the villages and rural economy come into their own. Soon we are crossing, by bridges and banked carriageway, the first of the jheels, great wide expanses which change in character so markedly with the seasons. In summer they are vast stretches of water like the Norfolk Broads on a grander scale; traffic is all by boat, the thin graceful punt, or broad beamed barge propelled by sail and oar. Of power boats there is no sign. It is a cool, gracious scene, indescribably leisured. In winter the water has gone; bullock carts, even lorries, ply along dusty tracks not long before submerged; the earth enriched by soil deposit, yields a bounteous rice crop; brick kilns fashioned out of dried mud belch smoke as if in a hurry to be done before the waters return. Here is a transformation as total as one can find anywhere in the world, a transformation above all of colour. In summer the infinite richness and varieties of green; in winter the broad acres subdued in parched subfusc browns and yellows.

Somewhere beside the way one will pass a country market, its position pinpointed by the stream of humanity pouring along the road, on their heads baskets, sacks of rice, bundles of firewood, melons, jack fruit, trussed chickens – the fruits of a thousand small holdings for miles around. Or one might pass a posse of villagers on their way to fishing; better still to catch them on the way home, a half-naked chattering throng, their smiles in direct proportion to the size of the catch nestling in the round baskets. The bigger the fish, the lesser the hunger ache.

We drive on past the Mouchak Boy Scout Centre, twelve neat bungalows ranged around a grassy campus, on which, rather seldom, tents would spring up, and the whole area be transformed into a lively kaleidoscope of youth. Through the Chundra Forest, too populous now for the wilder beasts, another jheel, and we are abreast with the road sign 'Welcome to Mymensingh,' on its reverse, 'Thank you. Come again.' A furlong further and we swing left off the road on to the broad driveway leading to the College.

One was glad to reach home, not only because it was home but also because of the nagging anxiety always in the back of the mind that one might have a breakdown. This could have awkward, even serious, consequences. It happened one weekend to Driver Nazir in the big Chevrolet; the poor fellow was stuck by his vehicle, the cynosure of a thousand eyes, for twenty hours before we could locate him and marshal the necessary assistance. No such thing as a breakdown service existed; telephones were a bit of a joke; garages lay few and far between, being in any case no more than filling stations staffed by men whose range of mechanical dexterity extended little further than the pealing of a banana. One could only wait by the roadside for a sufficiently powerful vehicle to stop, take compassion and agree to tow. If one was alone, there was always the difficulty of the language barrier; again, if alone, one could not leave the vehicle and walk off in search of help. On return, one would find every extractable part of the car extracted. On the whole it was better not to have a breakdown . . .

*   *   *

That life during term time was seldom dull is illustrated by this remarkable document which I found neatly typed out on my desk at the end of a long hot morning:

To the Principal.
Momenshahi Cadet College.
　Subject: Forceful confinment of my daughters by
　　Mr. and Mrs. Ziaur Rahman

Most respectfully I beg to draw your kind attention to the following facts for favour of your kind immediate necessary action:-
To-day the 18th June 1965 at about 1 p.m. when I was in Dacca on official duty my daughter Miss Shely about seven years old went to see a mad-woman from top floor of the building while mad-woman passing through the road.

When she was getting down from the top floor of the building wife of Mr. Z. Rahman caught hold her by hand take her into her own room forcively by order of Mr. Z. Rahman. He used rough and offensive words to my daughter Shely. He threaten her that he will slaughter her. Wife of Mr. Z. Rahman bent my daughters hand with rope and asked the maidservant to beat her. The maid-servant did accordingly. My daughter was weeping for fear of death and beaten by Mrs. Z. Rahman and the maidservant. She was in a position to felt heart.

As soon as the news reached my wife she sent my eldest daughter Miss Lily about ten years old for her rescue(sic). On reaching in front of the quarter of Mr. Z. Rahman knocked the door. Mrs. Z. Rahman opened the door and caught hold her hands as she did in case of my daughter Miss Shely. When again my wife get information from sister in law of Mr. Abdul Hamid and other babies that Mr. and Mrs. Z. Rahman beating my daughters inhumanly, my wife went to Mrs. Abul Hassain for their rescue.

When both of my daughters are not returning in a reasonable time finding no other alternative my wife went to Mr. Abdul Hossain and others present for their rescue. I heard that getting information from my wife Mr. Abul Hossain, Mr. Shah Ashrafuddin Ahmed, Mr. Farhad Ali, Mr. Abdul Hamid, Hav. Haninuzzaman and others went to the resident of Mr. Ziaur Rahman and knocked the door to see the incidents. But he refused to open the door at first. At last Mr. Ziaur Rahman came out. from the room after some 15 minutes and began to exchange hot conversation with the presents members. Inspite of repeated request he showed attitude not to get them free. But at last he freed them after about 30 minutes.

Then I reached at my residence at about 4.30 p.m. I found my daughters still weeping and trembling like anything.

The truth of my statement may kindly be confirmed from the persons present on the spot.

I believe all those were intentional and pray to your kind honour legal action and justice immediately in this regard.

Yours faithfully,

A.M. Ghulam Rahman.

Dated: 19th June 1965

I got signed statements from persons concerned, set in train a committee of enquiry – one was careful to avoid the word 'court' – and sat back to await events. Throughout the weekend the squabble seethed and bubbled with futile fervour. Information reached me piecemeal; Mr. Z. Rahman, it seemed, had been busy forming a party from among the lower paid of our community – malis, peons and so on – to what purpose it was by no means clear, unless it was to line his own pocket, for he extracted from each member an entrance fee of one rupee. One had to admire his resourceful cheek, though his motives were almost certainly sinister; he was up to his eyes, one would guess, in some sort of petty intrigue.

The committee of enquiry comprised the Bursar, the Adjutant and myself; we duly met to try to sort out the tangle. It was apparent early on that this was a storm in a teacup. The maidservant, far from being the strapping wench suggested by the original complaint, was a puny child of about eight, no bigger in fact than the alleged victim of the outrage. In the role of flagellator she cut an improbable figure. We spent a couple of hours listening to evidence conflicting at every point, much of it hearsay and all of it as reliable as a paper hat in a deluge.

Our findings were inconclusive, in the circumstances they could hardly be anything else; it would have taken the combined efforts of Sherlock Holmes, Sir Patrick Hastings and Judge Jeffries to have prised out the truth. 'A squabble of over-excited women and children' was one of the phrases in the brief communiqué issued to all parties concerned, together with a warning that 'male employees are responsible for the behaviour of their womenfolk and children, and further outbreaks of this kind will not be tolerated.' Fine words – one could only hope they might have some effect.

There was still the little matter of the party-making to be sorted out. When the hubbub over the first incident died down, I sent for Mr. Rahman. He readily admitted to taking money off the least affluent, but all, he argued, in a very good cause. Our Mr. Rahman, it seemed, was combining in his person the role of welfare officer, banker and the man who calls every week for the insurance contribution.

'They are very poor men,' he explained. 'They approach me to keep their money so that they will not spend it too soon.' The idea that this was any sort of trade union, any sort of co-operative venture for the protection of Mr. Rahman, he indignantly denied. 'It is my enemies, sir. They want to get me away from this place.' Though I was aware that extortion of money from the lowest paid is by no means uncommon – on most road gangs the sweating coolie must pay his dues to the foreman, or he will not long hold down his job – I was prepared to give him the benefit of the doubt. After pointing out that I could not quite accept him as paterfamilias to the under-privileged, especially when it meant that he would become the repository of the under-privileged's hard earned cash, I sent him about his business with a flea in his ear.

*   *   *

Of Pakistan Day – March 23rd. – we felt obliged to make something of a splash. The Bengali enjoys a chance for patriotic display; although not of martial disposition, the gaudier trappings of militarism delight him; a little colour, a little pomp and circumstance, the swing of a marching tune – in these he revels. We therefore laid on a parade. In spite of the earliness of the hour, seven in the morning, a large crowd of spectators forsook their beds and turned out to watch the fun. It was a glorious morning, cool and sunny, and the cadets performed their evolutions with skill and aplomb. I felt that the occasion warranted from the Principal a few Well Chosen Words. These, with apologies, I reproduce, for they afford a clue to the character not so much of the speaker but of those to whom they were spoken:

> To-day is Pakistan National Day; you must all feel very proud of the development of your beloved country in the short space of eighteen years. Much has been achieved, and among those achievements of which you should feel especially proud is the foundation, at the express wish of your President, of the Cadet Colleges. I hope that your pride and love for your own College grows day by day. We want to make this the best College in Pakistan; with our motto of Faith, Unity and Discipline to guide us, I believe we can do this.

Let me on this National Day remind you once again of your duty to your family, to your College and to your Nation. You are the future citizens of Pakistan; some of you will be its leaders. Now is the time for you to train yourselves for the life ahead of you; now is the time for you to acquire those habits of hard work, loyalty and discipline which can equip you to carry forward the banner of Pakistan to new heights of achievement and world renown. Good luck to you all, and may this – the first Pakistan Day to be celebrated here at Momenshahi – may this day be for each one of you an occasion of joy, of prayer and of dedication for the days that lie ahead.'

This is a shade more fulsome, more sentimental than anything one would dare put over to a more phlegmatic race. However, I flattered myself that this was the Stuff to Give the Troops; the boys appeared to listen without flinching, nor did they dissolve into laughter . . .

*   *   *

The school I left behind me in England had as its motto *res non verba*. Not so keen on *res*, the Bengali is a great chap for *verba*. I went into a Dacca Post Office for stamps. Behind the counter there was the usual assortment of operatives in various attitudes of inertia. But not for long; a conversation broke out, everyone talking at once, gesticulations of a Gallic ferocity, the noise was stupefying.

'What on earth was all that about?' asked my wife, when I got back to the car.

'Just a little chat about the storm last night,' I replied. It is always that way. In a country where there are so many people, it is necessary to raise one's voice in order to be heard; what begins as a cosy tête-à-tête quickly swells into a ten man debate of heroic proportions. The natural inquisitiveness of the Bengali puts a severe limit on private conversation. After all, a man's problems are the lighter for being shared, the more the merrier.

I never schooled myself to exert the same patience or to show the same relish for conversation in my own office as one was accustomed to meet in the offices of Dacca. I was the Westerner, the hustler, not, I hope, discourteous, but always anxious not to prolong an interview beyond its useful limits. In this way I fear I may have offended my visitors who sometimes showed in their eyes a pained surprise as I rose from my chair with extended hand. A visit to a Bengali office is invariably a leisurely business – the courteous bestowal of a chair, the elaborate small talk like a very slow waltz, the cups of pale sweet tea, the final, oh so regrettable moment when business can no longer be postponed. Even when this climax is achieved, momentum is perpetually deflated by a flow of incomers – the peon with a file or message, the colleague with a question, the visitor seeking a favour – all walk through the piece of curtain, which does duty as door in most offices; as if by right, all claim – and get – the immediate attention of the man behind the desk. This can be maddening to whoever is in the driving seat. There is nothing he can do about it; he can only surrender to the accepted condition that the one who enters *last* has the right of way. When finally business is done, the farewells are as devious as the overtures. This, of course, is not a Bengali custom, it belongs to the East. No doubt fewer Asian officials die of thrombosis.

Neither government nor business could get very far without the services of the peon. All day he sits – or lies if it is hot – outside the office awaiting the ting of the desk bell; he runs errands, carries messages, brings tea, collects files, keeps out (or admits, if the bucksheesh is good enough) unwanted visitors, posts letters, switches on fans, explains his master's absences. He is a man not without importance; apart from his onerous responsibilities, he is in himself a status symbol. To command the services of a peon is to have arrived. Of this he is well aware, and it allows him to adopt an air of superiority in the face of office visitors. Unless, of course, the office visitor happens to be his boss's boss in which event his demeanour is reshaped to suit the circumstances. He may command a salary of less than eighty rupees a month, but his is a job much sought after, for without him the wheels of government and commerce would come to a sharp halt. A man with a real pride in his job . . . enviable peon!

The astonishing fussiness of office administration was something which at first was hard to stomach at the College. The chief architect of this was a character graced with the name of Office Superintendent. In his own eyes he was a man of consequence which in a large office he might well have been. Here with a staff, including himself, of three, he had to struggle to justify his position. As an example of his ingenuity in this respect I cannot do better than cite the Case of the Dropped Cadet.

One morning late in the term, I found on my desk yet another file, scrupulously neat and tied with the usual pink ribbon. I opened it to unearth a sheet of foolscap on which was written the following:

'82. No. 1. 6.4.65. This is a letter from the guardian of Cadet No. 3 with a request to drop his ward from the bus which is carrying

the cadets to Dacca on the way near his qr. As the bus will pass by the side of his qr, there is no harm to drop the cadet there. This may be permitted. Passed to Bursar. Signed xxxxxx, Office Superintendent.
Principal's attention, please
    As desired by his guardian Cadet No. 3 may be dropped at Awlad Hossain Market stoppage. Capt. Ansar may kindly be directed accordingly. M.A.C. Bursar.'

Beneath this highly explicit nonsense was the Letter, twenty words and written on very dirty notepaper. In such ways did our office staff kill the idle moments thrown up in the course of the day.

    It would have been futile to point out to the Office Superintendent that his methods could benefit from streamlining (though one did have a word with the Bursar on this particular one!). His English was poor and it is doubtful if we could have achieved a real understanding. He was good at his job, such as it was, and an agreeable person. At least once I caught him bending. He was found to be indulging in a little mild skullduggery over the sale of firewood. I had him in to receive an Imperial Rocket which he took with much mopping, mowing and gnashing of teeth. But he was a resilient character. Next day he was back in my office, his mien as deprecatory as ever. 'Sir,' he piped, 'the accountant he has a desk. I only have a table. Should not I too a desk have like he?' One could not help liking the man.

    It was towards the end of our first term that we acquired a tailor. English boarding schools are blessed with a universal aunt in the guise of Matron, who, apart from looking after the health of the boys, supervises – or in many cases undertakes herself – the patching and mending of clothes knocked about in the hurly-burly of school life. Such splendid ladies we could not possess; there was no accommodation for them nor has there yet evolved out of the Islamic state that social class of womanhood from which school matrons are usually to be found. For making and mending, a tailor was essential. We found the right man; he simply arrived one day out of the blue asking for a job – a cheerful rogue with a ready smile and enough skill in his trade to satisfy our needs.

    He early gave evidence that he understood the nature of his position. He had not been with us a week before he produced, entirely on his own initiative, a quite splendid signboard in red and white which he nailed outside his shop –

Mr. Shaftkur Rahman
Tailor Shop
All Best Tailoring

There was however one feature which gave it real distinction. In big letters across the top he proclaimed to the world, 'Momenshahi Credit College'. In view of our straitened circumstances the Bursar and I saw both humour and irony in this announcement.

The health of the boys was an altogether more persistent and complex problem. Rightly or wrongly I had refused to enrol on our strength during the first year a full-time doctor, seeing no justification for such an appointment in an establishment of one hundred and twenty boys in a country chronically short of medical practitioners. This may have been an altruistic viewpoint; it certainly did not make our lives any easier.

I soon learnt that the Bengali is much preoccupied with matters of health. This is not to be wondered at; for many hundreds of years he has been exposed to, and the victim of, a rich variety of tropical diseases – I was told that even to this day as many as 90% of the East Bengal peasantry suffer permanently from amoebic dysentery to which malnutrition in his childhood years made him the easiest prey. In the absence of doctors he had recourse to the hakim or local witch doctor with results generally more harmful than otherwise. Small wonder that when modern drugs became available in large quantities, as they have done since the last war, he should be eager to make as much use of them as his pocket would allow. In every town and most villages of Bengal the chemist's shop brings its owner a tidy little income; he does not have to wait long for customers.

The boys were temperamentally volatile and much given to dramatisation. Moreover they tended to lack the fibre which enables most people to treat a headache as a headache and not the onset of some fell disease.

'What's the matter with this boy, compounder?' I asked, looking down at a small figure groaning on the bed and to all appearances edging towards the D.I. list.

'Ah, sir, he has a fever.'

'What is his temperature?'

'Sir, he has no temperature.'

'Well, he can't possibly have a fever then. What are you talking about?'

The compounder looked at me with a sad and puzzled frown. 'Sir, he has a fever.'

There was of course nothing wrong with the boy that an aspirin tablet or a dose of mild laxative would not have put right (he was in fact playing football next day), but I began to see how these people's minds worked under the stress of illness.

In the early days the sick-list was a good deal longer than I thought proper. We held two sick parades each day, one at 6.15 in the morning – an old army dodge this to discourage malingerers – and at 5.30 in the evening. Over these musters there presided a young man known as the compounder.

The Shorter Oxford English Dictionary defines a compounder as one who 'compounds in the various senses of the verb, historically a title for those who wished for the restoration of James II on conditions.' It has become, I think, an almost exclusively Anglo-Indian word for a man who combines roughly the offices of dispenser and male nurse. He holds a position which is officially recognised and for which he can gain qualifications through examination. In our case the compounder filled the role normally taken in the West by the school matron. We gave him a little surgery well stocked with medicines and containing a couple of beds for patients mildly ill.

Hospitals in the Dacca District were scarce, crowded, under-staffed and ill-equipped. We were fortunate to have four miles from the College at Mirzapur, a hospital rather better than the average.

Early one Saturday evening there appeared on our doorstep an unusual figure. A portly man, he was clad in a red Norwegian sweater and a red knitted bobble cap. His air was jaunty; he might have been on his way home from Highbury to fish tea in a North London terrace. We sat him down. 'I am Shaha. You come see my hospital?' he asked, adding with an appreciative glance at the blonde hair-dos around him, 'you and your so beautiful daughters?'

We thanked him. 'To-morrow you come. You have lunch with me. You like vegetable dishes?'

Mr. Shaha was immensely rich and in his old age a considerable philanthropist. He had built, equipped and maintained out of his own pocket a hospital of one thousand beds. To complete the unusual picture, he was a Hindu.

By the standards of London and New York, the hospital was no great shakes. There was the usual tendency to overcrowding, beds on verandahs, beds too close together: there was the usual lack of interior decoration, the usual oppressiveness of jaded plasterwork. No patient in a Bengal hospital wears pyjamas; he lies in bed in his workaday clothes thus contributing in no way to the sense of hygienic orderliness which one normally associates with hospitals.

Nevertheless, this was a splendid place. The patients were treated free of charge, itself remarkable in a country which knows no health service; equipment in the operating theatres and labour wards – all scrupulously clean – was modern; the kitchens would have satisfied the most exacting food inspector (to feed the patients was in itself remarkable. In most local hospitals, relatives brought in sustenance from outside). The nurses lived in a spacious hostel, the doctors in trim houses. Above all there was an atmosphere of purposeful healing, of a job being well done.

After our tour we crossed a river by punt to sample the hospitality of Mr. R.P. Shaha. He had, we were told, a fine house near Dacca, but every Saturday he repaired to the Hindu village of his birth, to this primitive dwelling, the largest in the area and fitted with electricity, but still essentially a kutcha building of mud walls and tin roof. For the week-end retreat of a millionaire it was distinctly unusual. We nibbled a vegetable curry and sweetmeats, Mr. Shaha eating little but talking a lot. 'I can get no good doctors,' he lamented. 'Soon I build new hospital and school for boys.'

A remarkable person, Mr Shaha. Until such time as we became medically more self-sufficient, we were grateful to him and to the people of Mirzapur Hospital for opening their doors to our sick and lame.

A word on witch doctors. That their influence still counted we discovered within the four walls of our own kitchen. Rummaging in the fridge ice-box, my wife was horrified to find the beaked and feathered corpse of a sparrow.

'Cyprian!' she yelled, 'What on earth's this doing in here?'

'Ah, memsahib, I have trouble, I not well.'

Cyprian studied his shoes, content, apparently, to let matters rest there.

'What's that got to do with it?'

'I not well. I go to hakim. He say me put sparrow in ice-box one day . . . er . . .'

'Well, go on!'

'Memsahib, he say me eat sparrow raw, me well again.'

There was a speedy burial; Cyprian, fortified with two digestive pills, soon forgot about his ailment.

*   *   *

In the course of the term, we held our first Governors' meeting at the College. The turnout was decidedly disappointing, three out of a possible seven. The General in the chair shot us through the business at breakneck speed, and a formidable agenda was disposed of in a little over an hour. It was, of course, all too fast. My suspicion had now become certainty – a Governing body which does not control the sources of financial income is a cypher, a mere rubber stamp. How, for instance, could we make constructive plans for future development without knowing if we were going to get any money with which to develop? No, we were not autonomous at all; even our expenditure would be vetted by auditors answerable to the Government. To give some substance to the existence of a governing body, some justification for the assemblage of busy men, recourse was had to detail – the ratification of College rules, furniture scales, salary scales already in force, appointments already long taken up.

We were by now in serious financial straits; the Treasury was refusing to ante up. I put the situation as succinctly as I knew how in a letter to the Governors prior to the meeting:

'I have so far received this financial year the sum of rupees 4 laks (about £30,000) with which to equip the College with all items including furniture, transport, clothing (I must remind Governors that every boy is provided with a full wardrobe free of charge, including towels, handkerchiefs and linen), laboratory equipment, mess utensils, medical stores, sports gear etc. and with which to meet running costs before and during this current term now about to end. The College is heavily in debt to the tune of about 2 laks; we have 8,000 rupees in the Bank with which to carry on day to day running. The Bank is reluctant to allow an overdraft. I am told by the Accountant-General's officials that I may get another two laks, but of this they cannot be certain, nor will they give any indication as to when we shall get it. The matter is serious and I must respectfully request the Governors to consider it as such.'

This produced a calm and ponderous reaction. Would Colonel X write a letter to Mr. Y in the right department asking him to speed things up? Since letters are commonly ignored I was not hopeful of the outcome. Two months later, apart from a pittance of 25,000 rupees – enough to pay the wages and food bills for one month – we had received nothing. Meanwhile I was besieged with creditors begging for money. Fabian tactics were the order of the day: 'I am sorry. The government won't give me my money. Come in a fortnight and you may be lucky.' Many of them had themselves experienced bureaucratic reluctance to honour bills, and they seemed to understand. Eventually they were paid and all was well, but one reflected ruefully on the anxiety unnecessarily caused.

Later, when crisis again bit deep into our financial affairs, the Bursar was to put his finger on what was perhaps at the root of the whole problem. He had spent five days of his leave in Dacca in and out of offices in futile pursuit of money we urgently needed; it was even doubtful if we would be able to meet our next wages bill. He wrote to me almost in despair:

'I think Colonel Rahman delivered to you the Bill for 25,000 rupees duly countersigned by the G.O.C. But even then I am afraid the Bill is not going to be cashed shortly. The government has issued a new order that all payments due to the College will be done by Tongail sub-treasury. But the said treasury won't make any payment unless authority for the same is issued by the Accountant-General, East Pakistan. I have been to the A.G.'s office consecutively on two days and to my utter surprise they told me they had not yet received the govt. order and therefore they could not authorise Tongail to make payment. I ran to Mr. Irfan Ali. But as he had nothing to do in the matter, his part in the matter having been done, I went to the Finance department from whom the order will pass on to the A.G. Yesterday the document was detected from heaps of paper and as the officer under whose signature it should be sent was not available, I shall again try to-day to take personal delivery of the same and carry it to the A.G. who in his turn will then send a letter of authority to Tongail treasury. I am to go either to A.G.'s office or Secretariat every day and run to pillar to post and post to pillar. This is the way I have been enjoying my holidays you were kind enough to grant me.

I have had a sad experience out of these irrelevant formalities, which seem to me ridiculous and sometimes disgraceful as more than often I find the clerks both in the Secretariat and in the A.G.s office unsympathetic and non-cooperative.'

* * *

We had from the very beginning suffered a little mild embarrassment from the presence in one corner of the College of a decidedly ramshackle bazaar. This had been established, long before I arrived on the scene, to serve the needs of the large gangs of contractors' men who littered the premises. This bazaar was, we felt, something of an eyesore and hardly in keeping with surroundings dignified and, on the whole, clean. Once we had established a grocery shop of our own, we sent forth an edict that the half dozen or so merchants must up and be gone. They asked for a short stay of execution that they might collect in their debts; this was granted, and on the day the ultimatum expired the rickety bamboo stalls had disappeared.

But not for long. Within a week they rose again, bloody and unbowed, this time just outside the compound fence, where no edict of mine nor my governors could touch them. This, in a sense, we welcomed. Mrs. Ahmed differs not a whit from Mrs. Smith or Mrs. Brown – she likes to be selective in her shopping; in her eyes it is better to have three shoe shops in a row rather than two. Moreover, a little competition would do our own shopkeepers no harm. We acquiesced silently in this new situation until the day they elected to hold a market. This happened to be a Sunday at the very end of the long summer break. I was horrified to look out of our windows towards the College to see it a seething mass of people, men, women and children, most of them carrying on their heads baskets of varying shapes and sizes. Clearly we were the focal point of interest for the population from miles about; equally clearly, this was a thing up with which we could not put. Next morning the enraged lecturers, whose gardens had suffered grievously under a thousand feet, left me in no doubt on this score. There was nothing for it but to hold a meeting of elders and to confront them with our troubles.

To this meeting the Adjutant and I made tracks one red hot morning. In the middle of the little bazaar an awning had been erected, under it tables and chairs arranged. Superfluous to add, a very large crowd had assembled to witness a spectacle from which some hoped to derive benefit, from which all would derive entertainment. So far, so good; I sat down, the Adjutant beside me and we were quickly joined by a little gaggle of elders, courteous and diffident. As soon as we were all seated the crowd closed in, making what I felt must be a colourful and not unattractive picture.

'Will you please say, Captain, that the College welcomes the establishment of a bazaar which will be of use to its members?' I was set on establishing good relations from the start, and evidently succeeded for my opening gambit was received with a loud burst of applause. Sensing an advantage we moved at once to the difficult item on the agenda. Explanations of our privations were greeted with sighs, aahs and noddings of grey heads. 'What,' I asked through my excellent interpreter, 'did the elders think they could do about it?' We had reached the climax of the meeting, the point where the reporters stop filling in their pools and start taking notes. The spokesman was an elderly man of beautiful and kindly countenance. He spoke at length in a tone quiet and dignified.

I was, I reflected, the latest in the long, long line of my countrymen who had sat thus in the shade with a similar concourse of bearded worthies judging a dispute or debating a point of possession. But they would have been better equipped than I – they would have had the language. Seldom had I regretted more my lack of Bengali. 'He says,' interpreted the Adjutant, 'that next week it will be all right. They will send round the word.' We established a few details, and I felt that the moment of departure was nigh. But another item appeared unheralded on the agenda. 'They want you to go and see the site they have chosen for their school.'

'Of course I'll go. But tell me – who builds the school?'

'They will build and furnish the school with wood and materials from their villages.'

'What about a teacher?' I asked.

'They will form a committee to run the school and will find a teacher. When that is done, they will tell the government who will then pay the teacher.'

'We shall benefit from this school. How can we help them?'

'Perhaps one or two of our staff whose children will go to the school could be on the committee?'

'Good,' I said, now feeling more sure of my ground. 'Will you please say that the College will help with the setting up of the school in every way possible?'

Another burst of applause and we were off round the corner to look at the site. It was ideal; I shook hands with each of the elders, and with grunts of satisfaction the gathering dispersed about its several ways.

I came away feeling elated, yet wishing that one could do more to help these simple, kindly people; if only one could do something to break down the tangled skeins of procrastination and intrigue which I knew they must meet before their attempts to help themselves could ever reach fruition . . . On this occasion, however, my fears were groundless.

The elders lost positively no time in getting down to work. The next morning I was writing letters in my house when I was handed the following message:

'Sir – Some local people want to see you regarding their primary school. The main object is that they want to name the school after your wife's name. Instruction solicited whether they will see you at your residence or at office. ____ Office Superintendent.'

Four men were awaiting me at the office, one of them the spokesman of the day before. They produced a minute book written in faultless English, the outcome of a meeting held the previous afternoon. A committee had been formed, business was already in train. I wrote in the book: 'We consider it an honour that the school should be named after my wife, and thank the Committee for the suggestion. It should be called the Helen Pitt School.'

I volunteered a small private donation towards the building costs, and we dispersed once again with smiles all round. Not without anxiety, we watched developments at the next market held the following Sunday. Things were peaceful and orderly enough. Whether this was due to the vigilance of the elders, the light rain that fell throughout the afternoon or the fact that the novelty was wearing off, I do not know; probably it was a combination of all three.

Meanwhile no time was lost on the school – words were very speedily transferred into deeds. A collecting team moved from door to door, and within a week one thousand rupees had been garnered, and generous dollops of building materials given free. Exactly seven days after the first meeting, the foundation trenches had been dug, and my wife was ladling concrete with the words: 'I declare this foundation stone well and truly laid'. It was an abnegation of Noel Coward's famous jibe that 'in Bengal to move at all is seldom if ever done.'

At the end of our tour, we received this undeserved tribute:

FAREWELL
To
Mr. M. W. PITT, M.A. (OXON)
Founder-President, Moin Nagar School, Rajbari
in the District of Mymensingh.

Sir,

It is with a heavy heart that we have assembled here this afternoon to bid you farewell on the eve of your departure from this place. It is a sad occasion for us and words can hardly do justice to our feelings.

Sir,

We shall ever recall with gratitude your untiring efforts and able guidance to establish this institution. It is you who visualised the idea of an institution here to serve the cause of education of

this place and, to your great credit, you implemented the idea within a short span of time.
Sir,
    This school is in fact a monument of your love towards humanity. It is not too much to say that the Institution itself is a glaring proof of your genuine anxiety towards humanity. It is not too much to say that the Institution itself is a glaring proof of your genuine anxiety to solve the educational problems of the people of the locality.
    To day, on the roll of the school we have two hundred and fifty boys and girls who are receiving free education under the care of your qualified teachers in a moderately well-built house. This is no mean achievement and the credit goes to you.
Sir,
    With you let us remember Mrs. Pitt in whom we found a great Patron of learning. She honoured us by laying the foundation on the thirtieth May, nineteen hundred and sixty five. This will shine as a golden chapter in the annals of this Institution.
Sir,
    With all humanity we can say that this assembly of ours is not just an observance of a mere formality, but a venue to express our real love and affection for you. Indeed, we are very sorry at your departure.
    May God grant you the best of health and spirit in the years to come.

We remain
Sir,
Yours affectionately,
The students, staff and members of the Managing
Committee, Moin Nagar School.

*   *   *

I approached the end of term with some misgivings. Like the Persian nobleman who never departed from the Sultan's presence without satisfying himself that his head was still on his shoulders, I was on the alert for disaster. Not that I was unfamiliar with the atmosphere which pervades a school – especially a boarding school – as the last few days are ticked off on multiple grubby calendars. With these boys, more excitable than most, there was no knowing what might happen: the prospect of once more setting eyes on the beloved father, mother, brothers, sisters, uncles, aunts and cousins, might well prove too overwhelming to leave room for rational conduct. Clearly, I felt, a firm hand would have to be kept on the pulse, even if I allowed a more avuncular spirit to spread itself about the Principal's person. Little Ahmed, in fact, must be patted on the head rather than clipped on the ear, while being kept aware of the horny fist within the velvet glove.

The proceedings may be said to have begun with the end of term exams. These are approached in a Bengal school with a feverish intensity bordering on the hysterical. On the first morning of the exams, I went up to early P.T. To my practised eye the parade looked on the thin side. The Adjutant, after calling the troops to attention (yes, we were often very military), turned to me with a quizzical expression, '84 cadets on parade, Sir.'

'84?' I let my voice be heard in all corners. 'This needs investigating, Captain,' and we duly set off to investigate. In no time we ran the thirty missing boys to earth, and it was difficult to be cross with them. There they were in two of the classrooms, their heads bent low over books, from their lips came the murmurings of passages being learnt by heart for verbatim transfer later in the morning to their exam papers.

A night or two earlier, being sleepless, I was startled when taking a 2 a.m. cooler on the verandah, to see lights on in many of the dormitories. The explanation was prosaic, merely boys getting up to put in some small-hours study; *that* had to be stopped for I feared nervous breakdowns. I need not have worried; this was merely routine to them in their hectic struggle to keep ahead of the Jones's.

I had with intention placed the exams as near to the end of term as possible in order to avoid anticlimactic conditions which tend to breed disturbance. The boys had two idle evenings, one idle day, and then away. I endeavoured to fill the first of these evenings with a recorded programme of Western music. My choice of programme laid heavy emphasis on the Beat – the records were shrewdly chosen by the twins who understood about these things – with three Classics for good measure – the opening bars of the Tchaikovsky B Flat Minor, the opening chorus of Bach's Christmas Oratorio, and the third movement of the Trout quintet. My selection was severely limited by the number of records available, but I was not too dissatisfied with this choice. Attendance was voluntary, but all turned up; they appeared to enjoy themselves.

As I was leaving the dining hall after the recital, Mr. Abdullah-al-Amin, who was producing the following night's variety show, asked if the boys might rehearse there after the late meal (lacking an assembly hall we

were in those days compelled to use the same room for eating and entertainment). I readily agreed and went home. Ten minutes later there was a
devilish hammering on the front door, punctuated by what sounded like
human groans. Dashing outside, I found, collapsed across the bonnet of
my car, our Mr. Barbhuyan, the mess manager. 'Hell's bells,' I thought, 'a
coronary. How does one cope with this one?' Not a bit of it; our Mr.
Barbhuyan was suffering from an acute attack of Wounded Pride.

'Sir,' he gasped, 'I have been insulted. Mr al-Amin he call me a- a-
bastard in front of the cadets.' More groans, tears began to flow. 'I cannot
do it, sir. My men are exhausted. He tell me to clear the hall, I say no, he
abuse me . . .' A crescendo of sobs.

'Yes, yes. Now calm down, Mr. Barbhuyan. Get into the car and we'll
go and see what this is all about.' I helped him to a seat, and drove back to
the hall. The boys, sensing drama, had gathered in groups to watch us pass
in silent curiosity; I felt like the driver of a V.I.P.'s hearse.

This was, of course, another of those storms in a teacup which erupted
with such startling frequency. Mr. Barbhuyan – the poor little man was
overworked – had reacted violently to the producer's announcement that
he would rehearse in the dining hall. Tempers had flared, hard words were
spoken. Next morning all was peace, both parties apologising to me, and,
more important, to each other.

In spite of my misgivings, this appeared to be the only untoward incident in the end of term proceedings. We all dutifully put in an appearance
at the variety show which turned out to be mostly a sequence of native
folk-songs, some of them very sweet to the ear. The few items involving
the spoken word showed up the Bengali gift for mime. My family was
referred to by the compere as 'distinguished guests'. 'For the first and last
time in our lives,' was my wife's comment. Next morning the boys piled
into special buses which had arrived only half an hour late – good going,
that – and with much waving and cheering, disappeared down the drive in
the hot morning sunlight. The first term was over; I headed home for a
long whisky and soda.

*   *   *

Now that we had been *in situ* for over three months, our domestic life had
assumed a pattern that many would consider intolerably monotonous.
Which in a sense it was, yet we failed to find it so. We were without
benefit of wireless or television, and missed neither. Abetted by the excellent Council library we recaptured the pleasure of extensive reading,

and, in my own case, of writing. Newspapers came, through the kindness of the British Information Services, in thick bundles, a week or more late; thus what at home had become a habit grew in Bengal into something of an occasion, something to which we looked forward. We may at times have felt ourselves a little out of touch with the news of the world, but it must be said that we hardly seemed the worse for that; we caught up with it in the end, including the League tables and cricket scores. It was much the same with the mail which arrived, not in a daily trickle, but in solid weekly packets, and so became a focus of excitement. Friends who came out to see us did so because they really wanted to see us; on our visits to the big city we looked up those friends whom we really wanted to see.

These visits took place on my day off, Tuesday. Soon after breakfast we would bundle into the car for Nazir to drive us into Dacca. First port of call, the British Council compound where we would do the round of our friends' offices – Jim Chaffey, Jim Mulholland, David Bradley, David Brown – to catch up with the news and local gossip. I would certainly lay my burdens at the feet of Harry Forster, the boss (later in our tour, he was succeeded by John Mitchell, whose guidance of my faltering footsteps was no less shrewd and kindly). Library books would be changed, shopping done, perhaps a little College business negotiated, a call at the British Information Services to pick up newspapers. Then it would be time to drive out to a friends' house for lunch – often a lengthy business, taking us well into the afternoon. As, with darkness drawing in, the car turned into the last leg of the journey back – the driveway up to the house – Deenat and Daniel would be waiting at the front door – smiles and cries of welcome – to offload Baby Nickler and the day's purchases. Baths would be running upstairs, clean towels laid out, ice on the drinks tray, Cyprian busy about the dinner; home seemed, at that moment, an uncommonly good place.

With electricity and running water, the house had many of the mod cons nowadays considered essential; we were in no way irked by physical discomfort. The furniture – not our own, we enjoyed 'free furnished accommodation' – we designed ourselves. When the College was in session, I was much preoccupied, and the burden of a somewhat uneventful life fell more heavily on my wife (during their nine-month stay with us the twins were busy with examination preparations) but she bore it all well, finding time for pursuits which domestic chores at home had hitherto denied her.

She had hard tussles with the basic problem of getting food, which, in our jungle fastness, was not always easy. The markets that flourished around us hardly catered for English tastes and stomachs. Meat and fish were often difficult, so were some groceries. Milk not so, for Dacca possessed, thanks to the initiative of a local businessman, the only pasteurising plant in the province, if not in the whole country. Thus we could drink our milk ice-cold from the fridge without boiling it. Somewhat scrawny chickens, bought alive and slaughtered out of sight of the sensitive English ladies, were not difficult to come by.

We felt most acutely the lack of fruit and vegetables which in East Bengal was chronic. For fruit there was always the banana but little else – a very short season, no more than three weeks, of the delicious lychee, and a rather longer season of the mango. In the early summer one had pineapples, in the winter oranges and lemons. Fruit imported to fill the big gaps was of poor quality and ruinously expensive. Vegetables were plentiful in winter and practically non-existent in summer, when one missed especially the ingredients for green salads. Many a week-end visitor to Calcutta would come back with big baskets full of cabbages, lettuces, tomatoes and the like. Why East Bengal had not yet tackled the business of fruit and vegetable farming on a sensible scale was something we were never able to discover.

Occasionally we received presents. These were invariably in the form of food – 'they must think I'm starving you' was my wife's understandable comment. When a Bengali family hits the jackpot, an animal, usually a goat, is slain and the portions are distributed among the relatives, friends and the deserving poor. They were never given direct, a child or servant would arrive at our back door bearing a leg of goat or some hideous impossible lump of guts hacked steaming from a bullock's flank. News of the windfalls would reach us via Deenat or Cyprian. These coming more often than not from people of humble station (a pineapple from my office peon was a case in point) we were put to some embarrassment. Many would argue that we should have returned all such gifts with a polite note on the grounds that the donor's intentions would often be aimed at putting one under an obligation. Rightly or wrongly, we felt that the risk of giving offence, of hurting someone whose motives were purely beneficent, was too great, and so we took what was coming to us with expressions of thanks. To this rule we made one exception; from contractors or prospective contractors we refused all presents, the donor's intentions here leaving little scope for speculation.

Our most cherished gift without doubt was Gertie. One afternoon the Bursar, coy and alight with smiles, said: 'I bring two gooses from Dacca.

I send one to you with much pleasure'. Thoughts of goose for dinner were quickly abandoned when, a few minutes later, Gertie arrived full of protest and very much alive. What is more, in spite of Deenat's frenzied shooings, she waddled straight into our living-room, where she announced her intention of making a home with us for as long as it suited her convenience by delicately depositing her visiting card on the carpet and waddling out again, head held high.

That we had never given serious thought to a career in farming was due in some degree to my family's hopelessness about animals; our farm would have been a sanctuary for ageing livestock, an old folk's home for cattle, pigs and poultry. No beast would have been allowed within miles of nasty things like abattoirs. That Gertie should be slaughtered and eaten was unthinkable; she was at once taken on the ration strength and housed in some style. Even a pond was made in the garden for her express enjoyment. More important she was provided with a husband. The veneration bestowed upon Gertie and Gilbert ('they're marvellous watchdogs, and they'll be so good for Nicola,' said my wife without enlarging on the second point), was another example of the eccentricity expected of foreigners, though it must be admitted that our servants entered wholeheartedly into the spirit of the enterprise. Daniel the sweeper was made keeper of the geese, having had it carefully explained to him that his neck would be wrung should misadventure befall Gertie or Gilbert or both. These responsibilities he accepted with gravity and discharged faithfully. The appointment gave him status, raising him for the nonce above the station in life which fate had decreed for him.

Gertie and Gilbert prospered and multiplied; the offspring, of course, were even more adorable than the parents. I could see the day approaching when we would become goosebound, hedged in by anserine clamour; it was an alarming prospect for there seemed to be no end to it. A more resolute person would no doubt have hired assassins, but I was content to let things drift. At least I knew when I was beaten.

*   *   *

India and Pakistan lived side by side in a state of permanent suspicion and mutual distrust. This situation would erupt periodically into crisis, and frontiers would be closed. Normally, however, we foreigners were not prevented from making the journey – usually by air, a mere 35 minutes – from Dacca to Calcutta. We were going from Bengal to Bengal, but it was an international flight involving passport regulations and customs. Well worth it, nevertheless, for a change of scene and for advantages mainly of a mercenary nature. As I have suggested above, such a visit helped to restock the larder, especially with fruit and vegetables.

'Shopping in Calcutta? Give this chap a ring, he'll help you out,' said a friend who knew his way around, handing us a rather grubby card. From our hotel, we rang. Within five minutes a lad was banging on the door: we were whisked into a taxi for a journey all of three hundred yards.

'No, HE pay,' said the lad, pointing to the gaudy silks and clothes in a shop at the other side of the narrow street. HE was fat; a dozen wrinkles sprang to life across his face in a smile of welcome. A child was despatched for beer and coke. For nigh on three hours we sat, chatting, laughing, bargaining; we chose the sari at eighty rupees, not the one at two hundred which HE said was the only one to do justice to my daughter. Half-way through a meal appeared.

'You not mind me. I eat breakfast,' HE cried, tucking into bananas and cakes, cross-legged on the floor amid the litter of silks and stuffs we had rejected. On his chunky fingers rings twinkled in the morning light, ridiculing the poverty so frequently pleaded.

'You want fruits? I send you!' Another boy was whistled up, and we were escorted to the great indoor market. The fruit vendor would have us buy up his ample stock. With swift strokes of the knife he peeled oranges, grapefruit, mangoes, begging us to sample there and then their matchless flavour.

We went in search of cosmetics, and found ourselves momentarily lost in the labyrinth. But not for long; a voice from behind and HE was there. 'Scents, leepsticks? He my brother, all good and cheap.' By now, threatened with insolvency, our sales resistance had hardened. We refused offers of gold bangles, ivory elephants, monumental brassware, cornucopias of edible delicacies. HE bid us sad farewell, protesting his love and beseeching us to worship again at his altars when next we visited the city. No doubt about it, we had been helped out!

One face of Calcutta is alert, brimful of business, smiling; it is busy in smart, well-ordered restaurants, hotels and clubs; busy in driving hard bargains, and giving service in pursuit of every rupee it can suck out of tourist and wealthy customer. The other face is very different – a city of unimaginable slums, of millions living in bestial squalor. How many live on the pavements? They have never been, could never be, counted. As we strolled back to our hotel that night, well dined and aglow with the euphoria of an evening's luxury at the Blue Fox, we paused an instant to take stock of the spindly manchild asleep in the doorway of a shop, homeless, parentless, hopeless. This we knew was the real face of the metropolis once called the second city of an Empire.

The social life of Dacca was lively enough; most entertainment took place in the home, there being no restaurants – save for two Chinese places of moderate quality – no night-clubs. In the matter of eating and drinking out, things did take an upward turn half-way through my tour when the Hotel Intercontinental opened its doors, providing facilities of a standard hitherto undreamt of in the area. Receptions, dinner parties, cocktail parties and the like – there was usually something going on of an evening. 'Official entertainment' was centred for us on the British Residency, a very beautiful house in Ghulshan, Dacca's most spacious residential area. We were lucky in that, during the whole of our time in Bengal, the king and queen bees of the Residency were Roy and Freda Crook, which meant that a party at their house, however official and stuffy it might threaten to be, was always a delight.

Social life on the College campus did not exactly hum; the Principal held occasional tea-parties to which the Bursar, the Adjutant and all Lecturers would be invited. Weak tea, sticky cakes, bananas – this was standard fare: conversation was formal and the atmosphere a little tense – if one attempted a joke, it would be greeted by a nervous gale of wholly undeserved laughter. Alcohol was taboo, likewise ladies – the two ingredients considered in some societies most necessary to make a party go with a swing. In fact, the whole of my time at the College, I never set eyes on one of the wives of the teaching staff. The ladies, if not exactly in purdah, lived in a state not very far removed from it. My wife would make occasional bold sallies into domestic areas, surfacing with tales of darkened rooms, of sweet tea, of quiet women with whom it was well nigh impossible to find topics of conversation. No, social life within the College was of a somewhat restricted nature . . .

Of the arts, drama seemed to flourish, though cinema, as is suggested elsewhere, was a strictly indigenous occupation. Joint Anglo-American groups produced either plays acted on stage with all the paraphernalia of the amateur dramatic society, or play-readings in members' homes. The dramatic highlight of our tour was the visit of the Royal Shakespeare Company with three plays –*The Tempest*, *Richard II* and *The Taming of the Shrew*. (Tremendous demand, tickets hard to come by, packed houses). Emlyn Williams also pulled them in with his wonderful Charles Dickens readings – the latter is very highly regarded among the literati of Bengal.

There was little musical activity. Jim Chaffey made a noble attempt to stir up interest, organising presentations by different people of recorded programmes at the British Council. These drew a mild response from Pakistanis, virtually none from Westerners. In this context my own attempt to win friends for Benjamin Britten's Spring Symphony was a flop. Indeed, those bent on organising entertainment for others had to withstand a certain apathy. People lamented the lack of opportunities for dancing (I speak of the Western variety), yet when the U.K. Association tried to launch a ball on St. George's night it had to be cancelled – nobody wanted to come.

One of the problems facing a foreign resident in Dacca was the lack of rural amenities within reasonable reach of the city. Almost every inch of the countryside around was either cultivated or under water; it was also, as I have already indicated, massively overpopulated, so if you did set up a picnic from your car in an apparently quiet spot, you were immediately engulfed by a fascinated populace. In this respect those in Dacca were at a disadvantage compared with their opposite numbers in Chittagong who had, within easy reach, the sea, the Hill Tracts and the great lake at Kaptai. So, to get away from Dacca, one had to take a holiday – to the Sundabans, to Khulna by river steamer, to the tea plantations in Sylhet, to Cox's Bazar for sea bathing.

We, the possessors of a 'country residence', were in a position to benefit from this situation. Friends seemed pleased to be asked, not so much for lunch or dinner (after dark travel was not undertaken lightly) as for a weekend. For them it was a positive relief to forget town life for a night or two. We had a spacious home and plenty of servants (houseguests meant tips – Deenat and Co. thoroughly approved). There wasn't a great deal to do: country walks in the jungle, to the astonishment of the locals who appeared from the most improbable places to gaze on the weird white folk actually walking for pleasure; tennis on one of the College courts; a Sunday morning stroll round the boys' houses where our visitors would be greeted with enthusiasm and delightful manners; a very mini-golf course laid out in the garden; bridge; talking, eating and drinking. The weekends passed quickly; one got to know one's friends really well.

On occasions we were asked to weddings, or rather to parts of weddings, for in Bengal the marriage ceremony is a lengthy affair lasting the better part of a week. The invitations would commonly arrive a day or two before the event – occasionally the date after.

We had a vivid impression of our first Muleema dinner. (This is given at the house of the bridegroom's parents, and marks the climax of the long ritual.) At the dinner in question our host was a very distinguished person; his house and spacious garden were ablaze with coloured lights, the effect was inviting. By the time we arrived the party was already in full swing, and the garden was thronged with guests. Not a drink of any kind was to be seen, for the very good reason that there wasn't any. People stood around in desultory groups, youngsters scrambled and played around their knees. Under a strip of awning sat a gaggle of V.I.P.s, most of them staring into space, none of them looking too happy. My wife was at once firmly but politely detached from my side and led away into a secret sanctum where the ladies were having their fun.

Punctually at eight the host and the V.I.P.s processed solemnly into a marquee, where we all sat down at trestle tables. Decorations and table linen were somewhat threadbare; notices stuck on the tent poles advertised the name of the caterer at whose hands we were to suffer. The meal was appalling, and eaten almost in silence save for the gobbling of the hungry multitude. Twenty minutes later we got up again and trooped out. I was joined by my wife who had eaten on the other side of the partition in the marquee. We were not long left in doubt as to what was to happen next – everyone prepared to depart. We had drunk a glass of warm water, eaten a little tepid curry, seen neither the bride nor bridegroom, listened to no speeches. These jollifications we had shared with a gathering of not less than five hundred people; it was all over in well under the hour. In parenthesis, most of the marriages in Bengal were arranged; divorce, though permitted, was very rare.

$$* \quad * \quad *$$

Whenever opportunity offered, I played golf. Readers who look upon that game as a pleasant country walk marred by unnecessary pauses should skip the following pages. My golf in the subcontinent was restricted both by lack of time and by my location. But in the first six months of my tour I managed to play a good deal in Dacca, Calcutta and Chittagong.

Dacca had two courses, one within the race course in the heart of the city, the other some five miles out in the military cantonment area. Except that they were both dead flat, they could hardly have been more different. The hazards on the city course were almost entirely human, for this was a public right of way, and the public knew it. They walked about with a fearlessness born of ignorance. Foolish the golfer who did not take out a third party insurance before driving off the first tee. Additional hazards were cattle and a smattering of water.

On the cantonment course one was up against problems of a more familiar order, for this was the countryside. It was in fact a fiendishly difficult course constructed by the Army with advice on lay-out from P.K. Cassels and Michael Heald, two low handicap players with a nice eye for country. Out of a piece of flat, low scrub jungle, they had hacked eighteen fairways, the narrowness of which called for accurate striking and an alarming straightness. The length was 6,400 yards and the S.S.S. 73, with four short holes and five par fives. Trees gave shade and graciousness to the surroundings. By any standard, this was a fine test of golf.

A great deal depended on the season of the year. During the monsoon the hours of play were limited – dawn to about 11 a.m. after which it was too steamy for even the most dedicated. The course itself became very soft – at times some holes were flooded from tee to green and so unplayable – while the thick moist air cut fifty yards off the most perfect drive. Even playing from forward summer tees, the course was a long, hard grind, one's shirt black with sweat and a towel constantly in use to keep the hands dry enough to grip the club.

In winter one could play all day in conditions akin to perfect June weather at home. The atmosphere had thinned, the ground was bone hard, and to pitch full on to the green could land you in deep jungle no matter how much backspin you contrived to put on the ball. The winter tees were well back, and called for some terrifying carries. It is not easy to convey in writing the full horror of the rough on this course. There was about it an obduracy, a bestiality that made one at times feel that to dislodge the ball a spade would be of better service than a wedge.

Playing in the Ayub Cup one year, a friend of mine failed to negotiate one of those terrifying carries, and disappeared into the undergrowth. Minutes later the ball popped out on to the fairway closely followed by the player. His face was working strangely. 'Ten,' he muttered, 'b——it!' Dacca was that sort of course. Summer or winter, a good player had to be on top form to keep a seven or worse off his card.

As a cure for snakeophobia, I recommend a round of golf on the Dacca cantonment course. Arriving on the seventh tee with three lost balls and a score in the late thirties, one is seized with a Miltonian desperation and dismay. The next drive, teeth clenched and to hell with it, is an ugly mixture of overpress and head-up; it pitches first bounce into a thicket a good twenty yards off line. 'Give me a wedge, caddy,' is the despairing cry. Clean out of temper, one plunges about in the jungle hacking and swearing; if one were to meet a serpent now, his head would be off in a trice, and the search resumed without a second thought. Moreover, if the player has any misgivings about crawling things, these are quickly put to shame by the appalling courage of his aghi wallah, an infant of about nine. The job of this tattered mite is to stand ahead of your shot and to mark the ball; the extent of his labours is in direct ratio to his master's skill. In my case the aghi wallah's lot was closely akin to slavery. Near naked he would burrow into the densest undergrowth – at all costs he *must* find the ball – entirely regardless of anything that might lurk therein. To him a cobra would seem to portend no more harm than an earth worm. Splendid child – let's find that damned ball and retrieve something out of the wreckage!

Golf had not yet caught on in East Pakistan; apart from Army officers very few local people played. This was certainly not the case in Calcutta which has two splendid, long established courses. Arriving to play at the Royal at six o'clock on a weekday morning, I found the car park nearly full and the course crowded. The Club had a very big membership – the vast majority Indian – and a long waiting list. This is hardly surprising, for the course is one of the finest in Asia, of great natural beauty – heavily treed parkland – and a very fair test of golf. The facilities were exceptional by any standards – club house, service, bars dotted about the course, greens, all were of the highest order. There was too a wonderfully friendly atmosphere which made a nonsense of racialism. Visitors were made welcome, stuffiness was not tolerated. An invitation to play there was one to be sought after and accepted without hesitation, all business commitments giving way. Not for nothing does the Royal Calcutta Golf Club have its own marquee at the British Open.

One could not play the Royal without being conscious of tanks – the Indian word for ponds. The thirteenth, par five, was a case in point. A quick hook off the tee was gobbled up by a tank, slightly left and eighty yards ahead. The well struck ball had to finish short of a much bigger tank which bestrode the fairway at about a furlong. The second shot called for a clean hit to clear this wide greedy hazard, while one was all the time conscious of an out-of-bounds wall running the length of the hole on the left. Beside each one of the tanks squatted a club employee clad only in a loincloth, his job to descend into the waters and retrieve the precious ball – a thing he did with surprising skill and success. As he surfaced from his dive gasping, with the ball triumphant in his dusky palm, one was momentarily conscious of the small ways in which India's overpopulation made easier the lot of those fortunate enough to have been born into the ranks of the few.

A bad slice from the Royal's first tee would pitch across the main road on to the thirteenth fairway of Tollygunge. This was a rather easier course (if the word easy can ever be applied to golf), but no less beautiful. The name of every one of its magnificent trees was recorded on a big chart in the club house. For many reasons Tollygunge was popular with the ladies and lent itself to family golf. It was, moreover, a country club, offering tennis, squash, swimming and horse racing in immaculate surroundings. The patriarch could go out to his four-ball with easy conscience, leaving his non-golfing family in happy pursuit of pleasures more to their taste: as Hamlet put it, a consummation much to be desired.

I played one highly enjoyable round on a remarkable little course at Chittagong, five minutes drive from the centre of the town. It was nine holes, and a perfect example of the Anglo-Saxon genius for fashioning a golf course out of nothing. But for a really astounding nine-hole course, the one in the famous West Pakistan hill station, Murree, took some beating; it added a new dimension to one's golfing experience. To start with, it was higher than most – 6,500 feet; secondly, the scenery was simply magnificent. To take a 20,000 foot Himalayan peak as one's line off the tee was invigorating. The course was decidedly primitive (the cynics suggested that only the proximity of one of the President's houses kept the course in existence). It was extremely difficult. The suspicion of a hook on one's tee-shot was liable to send the ball to kingdom come in the valley two thousand feet below. The longest hole was 225 yards, but every shot had to be played with unerring accuracy. You were forever climbing up or down; you needed the agility of a mountain goat. Huge boulders and rocky outcrops begot freakish, monumental bounces; there was scarcely any fairway in the accepted sense of the term. Tiny rock hard greens boasted a few blades of grass and a surface like a crazy ice-rink. If this was hardly a place for serious golf, it was wonderful fun.

*   *   *

'You will have very fine boat, sir,' said the agent. The better to drum local atmosphere into our week-end guest, we had decided that water transport must be hired, and a voyage over the great flooded plains set in train.

For this it was necessary first to commission an agent. We were thousands of miles east of Suez, we were in Bengal, than which no country appreciates more keenly the importance – nay, the vital necessity – of this ubiquitous official. So I sought out a likely fellow, put my proposition and left the matter in his hands. Mr. Mondiad was equal to the task. Our boat was indeed 'very fine' – thirty feet long, made of wood, painted black, with two sharp ends gracefully tapering; broad too in the beam, a good six

feet amidships. But what unquestionably earned her superlative grading
was the semi-circular bamboo superstructure, which denied standing
room but gave shelter against sun and storm, and a desirable residence to
the owner and his family; a chatti, two hurricane lamps, scraps of clothing
bore witness to its domestic function. Three cotton sheets, none too clean,
covered the decking, out of deference, one presumed, to the fastidious
requirements of foreigners.

From the river bank we stepped aboard – Bernard, alert with camera,
my wife, 'baby Nickler', and I. The agent stood sentinel on the river bank,
trying to reassure us, by nervous grins and laudative comment, of the
seaworthiness of our craft and the reliability of the crew. The latter were
lads of mettle. The skipper, a greybeard with bushy eyebrows and skin the
texture of a very old Gladstone bag, took the helm; sartorially he would
have cut a poor figure on the bridge of a steam yacht, here he was clad
exactly right – a grubby headcloth and a piece of coloured cotton round
his middle. Ahmed, the first mate, perhaps twenty years old, eschewed
headgear, and did all the work. The deck-cum-cabin boy, a fledgling, did
little save grin and add ballast. We were in the hands, we suspected, of a
family business.

We cast off, not without difficulty. The presence aboard of so much
protein-fed Western weight put us lower in the water than our skipper had
anticipated. We crowded in the bows, the naked greybeard and his motley
complement of passengers, what time the crew heaved and grunted and
sweated to get us afloat. From the bank the agent, now supported by a
large crowd, lent vocal encouragement, but no more, to the sweaty operation. It was the Volga boatmen in a tropical, more incoherent setting. At
last we were off; the first mate wielded with a high degree of competence
a long bamboo pole while the skipper gave terse, guttural commands from
the wooden tiller. I had nursed the hope that I might take the pole myself –
on the Cherwell years ago I had messed about in punts – but the size of
our boat and the need for the closest liaison with the skipper soon put an
end to such aspirations. In the field of international co-operation we
would have made a sorry pair; to capsize a boat is no way to foster racial
relationships.

Across tracks and meadows over which we had so often walked dryshod
in winter, we now made watery progress. It was early evening, and the sun
gilded the wide wet plains with shades of pale pink and yellow; clumps of
trees sprouted from the water; we threaded our way through acres of jute
and paddy; clusters of huts, ten feet above flood level and shaded by
mango and banyan, bulged with humanity, much of which erupted from

homesteads to gaze at the bizarre spectacle. If we were not the first whites to pass this way on foot, we might with more certainty claim to be the first to negotiate it by water – as such we were freaks. We passed stout junks, propelled by four punters and piled high with bales of jute on their way to the world's markets. At all points the light was an enchantment – the reflection of sky on water and every shade of green upon which the eye could hope to feast. Bernard, artist and photographer, shouted with pleasure; 'baby Nickler', aged two, used a more limited vocabulary to no less effect; Ahmed, clearly an addict, was busy soliciting tobacco from the male passengers; the cabin boy sat and grinned; we were a happy ship.

But not for long. Ahead of us to the south a huge phalanx of cloud was building up. To those who know Bengal in the monsoon season such portents are not lightly ignored. I began to grow anxious, our skipper seemed not to be keeping a weather eye. Placidly we sailed due south, the big nubiferous battalions marched towards us. 'Bernard, what is the Bengali for going about?' I asked without much hope. At last by gestures overemphatic we prevailed upon our lord and master to give best to the elements and run for shelter. By the time we had executed this manoeuvre, the skies had assumed a terrible aspect; a vast wall of blackness, flecked with dark greys and angry whites, covered the southern horizon. Out of it, lightning stabbed. Somewhere in the west the sun continued to throw shafts of light, a last defiant gesture before the holocaust.

The storm hit us with homeric fury. Waters placid and glacial were whipped in a second from inertia to boiling point; the temperature dropped perceptibly; little white horses whistled over the surface of the jheel. Rain was not long in coming, suddenly we were in an elemental stewpot. The skipper and the first mate, shoulder to shoulder, clung to the tiller with all their strength, impervious to the rain which cascaded down their brown bodies in so many rivulets. They were too preoccupied in keeping our stern to the wind; to swing side on to the weather would have had us swimming in a trice. Meanwhile, without aid of sail or any pro-pulsive agent, we ran before the storm at a spanking pace. The cabin boy busied himself with the weather-proofing of the bamboo shelter; we hud-dled in its protection, silent in the main. Off and on, to bolster the morale of women and children, we shouted encouraging news of our progress. There was, it should be added, no vestige of panic; passengers and all hands behaved with laudable sang-froid.

True to the best maritime traditions we made landfall at our point of embarkation. The fury of the storm had by now slackened though it was still raining. I pressed five rupees into the skipper's damp hand, removed my sandals and bolted barefoot in the wake of my scurrying shipmates. Obeying Stevenson's dictum that it is better to travel hopefully than to arrive, Ahmed followed me some distance inshore on the off chance of another cigarette. Difficult to explain to him in Bengali, and in the rain, that he had smoked my last.

We got home damp but invigorated. As one might have expected of Bengal, it had all been a touch more dramatic, somehow, than a trip round the lighthouse in the *Skylark*.

*   *   *

With the punctual arrival of the rains on the last day of May, we became the targets of a nightly attack, pernicious and unnerving. None of us being of an entomological turn of mind, the great insect invasion made no appeal to our instincts inquisitive or acquisitive. Least popular were the cockroaches, of which two varieties we found the flying species the greater trial – two inches long and as stout as a fat man's thumb, perfectly harmless and utterly repulsive. They were the heavy bombers and lacked not for escort. Millions of flying things, basing themselves on the lights, buzzed about our ears, got down our necks, up our legs, into our hair, landed on our dinner plates or, worse still, into our soup with a splash. From the big parade only mosquitoes strangely were absent. 'Where the hell do they all get in?' was the despairing cry.

We sprang to the counter-attack, sitting in semi-darkness, making frenetic lunges with blunt instruments, sealing up holes, shutting all windows (the fans counteracted the potential fug), flitting with death spray, enjoining the servants to show a like-minded determination (their efforts were half-hearted; I feel sure they thought us unbalanced in our phobias). We burnt insecticide coils which emitted thin vapour clouds like incense; I smoked my pipe with urgent puffs. The success of our counter-attack was limited, the insect world showed a resilience, a penetrative power, a disdain for heavy casualties, which was almost admirable. None of the great captains deployed troops of more dauntless pertinacity.

The house was supposed to be fly-proof, shutters of wire netting having been provided at all windows and doors. But so poor was the workmanship that big gaps were evident where no gaps should have been, a defect which was underlined when the monsoon downpours revealed that we were in no sense waterproof; the house leaked like a Budget secret. The rain seeped in everywhere, at more tempestuous moments pouring down the stairs in a stream. Monumental wet patches appeared in unlikely places; everything began to smell rather damp. The time had come to take all clothing out of drawers and wardrobes once a week, inspect, brush, and hang it out in the fitful sunshine lest mildew take a grip. Having longed for rain, we now hated it with infinite wrath and despair. For a time we considered ourselves unsuited to life in the tropics. This state of mind was reinforced when, on going to bed one night, my wife surprised a beetle in her bra.

Even in the depths of the school holidays, seldom a day went by without incident. At 10.30 in the evening of Easter Saturday, there came a thunderous knocking at the front door. Pyjama-clad, I investigated. The Adjutant and one of the housemasters were standing there, faces as long as jutesticks.

'Something serious has happened, sir. Mr. Hamid and all his family are vomiting. We think it's cholera.'

'Have they seen a doctor?'

'No, sir. He has been to Mirzapur Hospital, but no doctor was available. He fainted in the vehicle on the way back, and now he is vomiting with all his family.'

The prospect appalled. 'If they've got cholera, will they take them in at Mirzapur?'

'Yes, but there is a special cholera ward in Dacca. That is better.'

'How do we get them to Dacca? By ambulance?'

'No, sir. I don't think so. The ambulance will only work in the town.'

'But, good heavens, what happens if a villager gets cholera?'

'Perhaps he has treatment at home and most probably he dies.'

'Well, we must get them to a doctor and find out if this is cholera. It may only be food poisoning. Captain Ansar, will you please go to the hospital yourself, see the Superintendent and explain the situation. Then let me know what happens.'

Half an hour later the Adjutant was back bringing with him little Dr. Shaha, our part-time medico from the Mirzapur Hospital. I was delighted to see him. In spite of the language difficulty – his English was almost as hair-raising as my Bengali – we soon struck up a rapprochement.

'Mr. Hamid, he must to hospital go for test,' said the doctor.

'All right,' I replied. 'Get him ready and we'll take him in the wagonette.'

We stopped outside a long single storied building. 'Cholera ward,' said the doctor. It had glassless windows as big as shop fronts; from outside everything that went on inside was all too plainly visible. Sitting in the car, I felt like a playgoer in the middle of the stalls. For the next forty five minutes, I had ample opportunity to observe the drama within.

There were three nurses at work, two wearing face masks, the third by her raucous chatter proclaimed herself the ward sister. She denied the hygienic precepts of her profession by stepping every so often to the door and spitting into the night. Two scruffy creatures clad in dirty shirts and longhis – ward orderlies, I presume – mooned about arguing with the nurses and each other. It all seemed a long way from the National Health Service.

In light of the veneration accorded to doctors in hospitals at home, it was interesting to see what scant respect was paid to little Dr. Shaha. He fussed about and did his best, but the sad fact was that no-one from the chowkidhars to the ward sister took the slightest notice of anything he said. It was another example of the sorry truth that only the burra sahib counts, only he can command instant obedience. His lieutenants, vital cogs in the machine though they may be, do not hold ultimate powers of promotion and dismissal; they can therefore be treated by underlings with impunity. It takes a man of strong personality to overcome this.

The first problem was to get our patient out of his cramped position in the back of the car and down the short pathway into the ward; not, one might think, a very complex operation for a hospital to tackle. Events proved otherwise. To bring a sick man in at such a late hour was clearly something of an indiscretion. After a lengthy argument in the ward, what time poor Mr. Hamid again vomited into the luggage boot, Dr. Shaha emerged empty-handed.

'A stretcher,' I implored. 'Can't we find a stretcher somewhere?'

The doctor looked doubtful, and whispered into the patient's ear in an attempt to urge him to his feet. In vain – he collapsed in a heap before he touched ground. The doctor disappeared, this time into the bowels of the hospital, returning some ten minutes later with a small ladder and a brace of reluctant assistants. Thus Mr. Hamid made his uncomfortable entry into the ward.

I prepared to pack up and go. The stuffy midnight air was having its soporific effect. 'Wait, please,' said the doctor. 'He has loose motion in car. Doctor come, take sample. Please you will wait?' There seemed no alternative; I resumed my seat in the stalls.

Mr. Hamid was at first the object of lively attention. A needle was applied, how blunt one could only gauge from the screams of the patient. Treatment was, however, made perfunctory by the claims of others. Each patient seemed to be attended by a familiar – female in the main, wife?

sister? aunt? – who sat huddled by the bed lackadaisically waving a bamboo fan over the prostrate body. Off and on, there was an outburst of wailing which would bring the entire medical staff running to the bedside. Our poor Mr. Hamid was left to vomit unassisted . . .

At last Dr. Shaha again emerged. 'Will you find someone to stay with him, please?' he asked. 'There are only three nurses and many patients.'

It took me a moment to grasp the fact that a patient must bring to hospital not only a disease but also an attendant. It explained the presence of the familiars. I was foxed.

'But all his family are sick. We have no-one!' We both recognised an impasse; there was little we could do. In the midst of bedlam, Mr. Hamid, it seemed, must suffer alone.

Dr. Shaha produced a little paper packet. 'Give one of these pills to each of the family. It will stop vomiting.' I reminded him of the sample. The doctor shrugged. 'He has again loose motion. It does not matter. You may go, please.' I thanked him and started up the engine.

At that moment all hell broke loose in the ward. A thin ragged woman rushed out, her face puckered with grief, from her lips a pitiful ululation. She made off blindly into the darkness. Someone, no doubt, had given up the unequal struggle.

The night was not without its splendour. Back at the College, I delivered the pills. The Adjutant, the housemaster and a handful of others were sitting outside the stricken house. They would stay there all night, mounting guard over the sick. It would not have occurred to them to do anything else. The Bengali enjoys only one form of social security and not a bad one at that – the sympathy and care of his relatives and neighbours when he needs them most.

The story has a happy ending; Mr. Hamid and his family did not have cholera, only food poisoning, which in fact was a euphemism for overeating during the Idh festival.

*   *   *

The tremendous density of population in East Bengal affected us in several ways, not least in the matter of privacy in the area of our own home. The word privacy has in any case little or no meaning to the Bengali; in the earliest days, if I stopped to speak to a boy in passing, a crowd would at once collect to listen in to the fun. Since it was impossible to fence off our compound strongly enough to keep out the passers-by, we were constantly exposed to inquisitive eyes. This was particularly embarrassing when we first arrived, and never more so than on the occasion of the Idh festival two weeks after we had settled in (There are two Idh festivals in the year. This one was the bigger, the nearest Muslim equivalent to Christmas). From miles around, the villagers – mostly women and children, all dressed in their best finery – gathered around the house to gawp at the domestic comings and goings of the strange white foreigners. One would have minded less had they kept their distance – let us suggest fifty yards or so. But when they pressed their noses against the fly-netting of the verandah, chatting, pointing and giggling, we understood, and sympathised with, the feelings of so many monkeys in a zoo. One dashed out shouting and waving, but it was of little avail. In a few minutes they were back; we took refuge in flight to the rooms upstairs.

It was during the second Idh festival, just after the long school holidays had begun, that I happened to look out across the playing fields about five in the afternoon to see, to my astonishment, a full-scale football match in progress with an attendant crowd of spectators. For such an assemblage no permission had been sought or given. This was the locals' way of asserting their rights over desirable territory not at the moment in use by others. I contemplated a display of *force majeure*, of rantings and shoutings and protests, but thought better of it. Some face would be lost; one would too easily have been turned into a figure of fun. Instead I elected to carry out pre-arranged plans – we went up to play tennis. The football crowd at once abandoned interest in their game, and flocked across to line the precincts of the court. The spectacle of four foreigners – the ladies trim and smart in their tennis outfits – playing an incomprehensible game was far more rewarding than a workaday football match.

If the Bengali pays scant attention to the privacy of others, he is a dab hand at shutting himself off from the affairs of this world – he has a unique capacity for sleep. Being more amply cushioned against noise than the average westerner, he puts this advantage to good use. He will nod off literally anywhere – side-saddle on the crossbar of a bicycle (a favoured form of transport); prone on the green verge in the centre of a busy dual carriageway; seated at the office desk (a mid-morning call found the Income Tax officer wrapped in guileless sleep, I tiptoed out); lying under the broken down vehicle; upright against the trunk of the mango tree. Sitting, squatting, standing, lying – any time, any place is right for nature's sweet restorer, balmy sleep.

Part Four

Second Term and After

Second Term and After

Being on holiday in Lahore, we missed the great cyclone that hit Bengal on 13 May, 1965. Two days later, we landed at Dacca. My diary:

'We are on the look-out for evidence of the cyclone. In Dacca many trees down, hoardings grounded, rooftops gone. Obviously the storm struck piecemeal – out in the country damage is less apparent. The college is virtually untouched. From the story of the night given by Deenat and Cyprian – much waving of arms, eyes popping – we are surprised a building is left standing.'

Thoughts of catastrophe reminded me, as we prepared for the new term, that we still had no telephones.

As early as last August, I had sought out the Director of Communications, East Pakistan. I wanted the Top Man, no less (Another Maurice Brown tip: 'Grab the Number One by the short and curlies, and don't let go!') At last I ran him to earth in his Dacca office. For one in so important a post, he cut an unlikely figure. He would have caught the eye of any casting director on the look out for someone to play the Venerable Bede. White hair, long white beard, he wore a long white robe and an air of benignity tinged with dottiness; he looked 108. We got on famously.

'We shall want telephones at my college. Can you help me, please?'

'You wait. I call my Engineer.' Twenty minutes later, the Engineer appeared, we all drew little pictures. A Decision became imminent. Loud spoke the oracle: 'You get telephones November. Maybe sooner, but November sure.' I thanked the Director elaborately; with the usual fandango, we parted company. Unfortunately I failed to ascertain to which November he was referring.

155

We began term without telephone, likewise without money; we had in fact run into a bank overdraft of ten thousand rupees to enable us to meet the wages bill for May. (Wages were paid in the end four days late. One began to see how it was that teachers in Government schools on occasions have to go as long as three months without receiving the salaries due to them.) Meantime our creditors, about 150,000 rupees worth of them, had given up the unequal struggle, and had fallen back on the only weapon left – they back-pedalled on supplies. The sorriest aspect of the whole sorry business – the limitless procrastination and ineptitude of officialdom – was that the chief sufferers were the pupils themselves.

We were, for instance, as yet unable to provide laboratory facilities. Many months ago, in early September to be exact, a small but high-powered meeting was held at the College over which the General himself presided. A senior engineer from Constructions and Buildings had been present; it was agreed and correctly minuted that his department would provide all the furnishings for both the physics and chemistry labs.

When in November I enquired about progress, I was blandly informed that there was nothing doing; without batting an eyelid, C. & B. simply backed out of the commitment, and there was nothing which anyone, however illustrious, could do about it to bring them to heel. Into the commercial market we had to plunge, a process which for so substantial an order took time. While the furniture was being made, our scientists taught in classrooms, concentrating on theoretical work, a somewhat un-satisfactory makeshift. It was our intention to have both labs in full working order for the start of the second term, but two things happened to prevent this. Firstly the contractor ran out of money, in which situation we were unable, for reasons already stated, to help him; secondly, the great cyclone of May 12th blew away his factory. Thus an act of God and the inadequacies of man conspired to deny us our just deserts.

The term was not a day old before I got the old smell of battle in my nostrils; once again Mr. Rahman and I were destined for the breach. This was a situation with which we were both familiar; we had already crossed swords on several occasions, (the most stupefying being the recent 'Forceful Confinement' of Miss Shely and Miss Lilly), with the Bursar as referee and time-keeper, the office staff at the ringside. Mr. Rahman was our head clerk – as such, he considered himself to be a person of consid-erable consequence. When we passed him over for the post of office superintendent – in fact he was never considered for it – he vented his spleen in characteristic fashion by doing his utmost to make life unpleas-ant for the rest of the office staff. He fought with the Bursar, with the

Accountant and with the Office Superintendent. Things got to such a pitch that he would either have to be sacked or transferred. He was not without ability; this, together with the fact that I scented faults on both sides of this hectic bickering, decided me to make him storekeeper and canteen manager with pointed suggestions that he refrain from squabbling in future.

Mr. Rahman, now established in a little kingdom of his own, soon gave proof of his calibre; he was out to extract every ounce of pomp and circumstance in his new responsibilities.

'Sir, I want assistant in canteen, it is much work. I want too one peon to help me.' To command the services of a peon, be it remembered, was a status symbol: Mr. Rahman was staking out his claim.

'Mr. Rahman,' I replied, 'your canteen is open for half-an-hour a day and your daily turn-over is about twenty five rupees. How can you possibly need two assistants?'

'But sir, it takes two, three hours after canteen is closed. I have my ledgers . . .' and so on with much mop and mow.

He lost no time in carrying this self-esteem a stage further which brings me to the battle so early in the second term. The stores over which he presided were in these early days humble – a few brooms, tins of disinfectant, stationery and so on. The Bursar and I had evolved a simple system of issues, and I was therefore not a little surprised to find on my desk a letter typed out in decemplicate for my signature, unmistakably the handiwork of Mr. Rahman:

CIRCULAR
(Serial No.1)

No. MOO/ST/1   Dated 1.6.65
From: Principal   To: All Lecturers, Adjutant,
Momenshahi Cadet College.   and Section-In-Charge of the
                                      Administration of Momenshahi
                                      Cadet College.

Re: Procedure of getting, supply of Stores from General stores.

This is advanced stage of the College and as such it is high time now to introduce perfect systems throughout all the functions of this administration. Towards taking measure in promulgating fundamental system for getting supply of stores from general store, the following procedure is adopted which should be adhered to strictly with immediate effect.

The present temporary system of issuing manuscript memos and receipt to the Store-in-charge for getting supply of stores, should be stopped forthwith. From now on, all kinds of stores are subject to be issued against placement of the prescribed printed, requisition slips only which is called 'Store Issue Requisition Slip'. These requisition slips would be supplied all along by the Store in charge without loss of time, in the form of books, each containing a hundred copies in triplicate which should be preserved by the respective sections in safe custodies for the necessary issues. These requisition slips should be correctly and legibly filled in by the requisitioning party in triplicate by setting carbons with his clear signature underneath. The requisitioning party is required to write down the necessaries on the top and to fill in the columns 1 (Item No) 2 (Description) and 3 (Quantity required) only, to obtain the signature of the Assistant Officer in the place specified for him and to place the same along with the book before the store-in-charge for supply of stores, signature of the Assistant Officer (Bursar) on the requisition slip is invariably necessary, in default of which stores will not be issued. The store-in-charge, on receipt of the requisition duly signed by the Assistant Office, will verify his stock with the required quantity and issue the available Stores after making necessary entries against columns 4 (Unit) 5 (Quantity) and 6 (Remarks and put his signature below in the place fixed for him.). Before parting the stores and requisition book, the store I/C, will take off the Accounts copy leaving behind the original copy to be retained with the book. He (Store I/C) with then send the Accounts copy through peon book (sic) to the accounts section for the necessary, account and audit and file up the stores copy in the proper file of store for record.

For the paper economy, requisition should be issued for a bulk supply of the daily consumable stores so as to cover the consumption for at least a fortnight. Since store is money all are warned against extravagant use of Stores for the sake of the national economy drive.

This is for information of all the staff and act accordingly.

Principal
Momenshahi Cadet College.

The letter was not sent; the well-meaning Mr. Rahman retired to lick his wounds and to await the next opportunity of asserting his ego, of proving himself the epitome of the dear old Baboo.

(Chamber's Twentieth Century Dictionary has this to say – '*Baboo*: an Indian with a superficial English education, using Baboo English, which is more copious than correct, with long and learned words most ingeniously misapplied.' This summary, one would think, could hardly be bettered.)

One might add in conclusion that Mr. Rahman, before he joined us, had been in government service.

*   *   *

From time to time politicians, anxious to win popular acclaim by appealing to national sentiment, would campaign for a reduction in the use of the English language and for the universal adoption of the vernacular tongue. In so doing they were flying in the face of the practical needs of the moment. The abandonment of English would not have been such a futile move had Pakistan been a linguistic entity, but that she most certainly was not. As I have already pointed out, the language of East Pakistan was Bengali, of West Pakistan Urdu and others, notably Pushtu and Sindhi. There are some similarities between Bengali and Urdu, but not enough to make a speaker of one readily comprehensible to a speaker of the other. Since there was a great deal of interchange between the two wings, a lingua franca was essential, and this lingua franca happened to be English.

In Pakistan, the schools taught either in the vernacular or in English. The latter schools were sited mostly in the cities, and enjoyed a fairly high measure of esteem. At them the politicians liked occasionally to have a tilt; English medium schools, they proclaimed, offended national aspirations; they were the stale fug left over from the bad old days of imperialism. The sobering fact remained, however, that the very politicians who played this particular line would many of them be doing their utmost to get their sons admitted to these schools, for not only was English the lingua franca, it was also a prestige symbol. If a young man wanted to get on, if he wanted to be one up on the Jones' (in Bengal one-upmanship is played with resource and subtlety), he had to have some command of the English language.

The extent to which it was the lingua franca was considerable. All government letters were written in English. In the capital city the road signs, the advertisement hoardings, the trade signs were in English and

Bengali, often in English only. However much the political firebrand may have disliked it, the importance of the language to the whole country was immense. The Bengali tongue, moreover, though in many respects a rich one, lacked the vocabular breadth to meet the demands of the day, especially in the fields of science and technology. So a slightly uneasy compromise was adopted, but it was, from the practical viewpoint, the only solution.

Some of the wash from this very big problem trickled into our little backwater. The new Adjutant, who joined us in June, came from West Pakistan; his native tongue was Urdu which meant that he could talk to the cadets, with whom he must of necessity have a good deal of contact, only in English; he was at a distinct disadvantage when it came to establishing the sort of rapport which his predecessor, a Bengali, had effortlessly achieved. There were our five havildars who had no English at all; two had precious little Urdu. Since these men were in the Adjutant's direct charge and since it was to them that he had to pass orders about a number of things affecting our daily life, the possibilities of misunderstanding were legion. The Adjutant was expected, too, to have charge of the work of the sweepers, a class whose linguistic range was decidedly limited. Thus a little grit was inserted into our somewhat shaky administrative machinery just at a time – the early part of the difficult wet weather term – when a generous spot of oil was most needed.

The Adjutant's position was always a difficult one for a number of reasons: his relationship with the teaching staff was tricky, for as an Army Captain his pay was far higher than theirs; he, a regular officer with a career to make, had to serve two masters, the Principal (at Momenshahi a foreigner and a civilian into the bargain) and his military boss in the cantonment; he was subject to the vagaries of army posting, neither of us knew how long he would be around; if he was a West Pakistani, he was a long way from his own environment.

Capt. Wasiq Khan, our June arrival, magnificently overcame all these disadvantages. Well built and of striking features, he established a splendid rapport with the boys, many of whom saw in the handsome captain the apotheosis of their own military aspirations. He was both loyal and shrewd; he kept a finger on the pulse, his judgement was always worth attention. I was lucky to have him as an adviser for most of my time at the College.

Another arrival was Robin Webster, out for a year on the Voluntary Service Overseas scheme. Resourceful and intelligent, he was a tower of strength, as popular with colleagues and pupils as with management.

*   *   *

To give an impression of the day-to-day life of the College, here are some extracts from my diary of the first few days of the new term:

June 6th

I have never been enamoured of staff meetings, seeing them as necessary chores to be indulged in as infrequently as possible. At home one had become used to their peculiar ethos – a good deal of healthy give-and-take, some shared laughter, the 'characters' on the staff playing their parts with gusto, the termly resurrection of pet grievances (I recall the issue of blotting-paper and the delightful character of the man who unfailingly raised it), the Headmaster feeling his way with caution and tact. One was conscious too of being seldom more than *primus inter pares*; here it was difficult to adjust oneself to the aura of majesty which hung, so undeservedly, about one's person. If the king can do no wrong, nor, in Bengal, can a Principal, at least not to his face. At staff meetings one knew how Dr. Arnold must have felt when presiding over a concourse of sixth-formers. It was not easy to get the lecturers to speak out, and, when they did, to keep them to the point at issue. This reluctance to give tongue may have had its advantages, but one wished at times that someone would express a definite view about something.

As I look at the agenda of our ritual beginning-of-term meeting –
1. Welcome.
2. Time table alterations.
3. Beginning of term routine.
4. Stationery issues.
5. Arrangements for Friday prayers.
6. Summer term routine. ⸴
7. Dress-staff.
8. Duty masters, duties of.
9. Furniture – staff room.
10. Marks, new system of monthly orders.
11. Transport – staff.
12. Any other business.

I know that, save for item 5, such could do duty on a universal scale. The fact that we swallow this little mouthful in forty-five minutes is testimony not to the incisiveness of the chairman but to the reticence of delegates.

June 7th

Whit Monday. Up at five, and out into a morning of greyness and cloud to watch the boys at drill. The humidity is appalling; by seven o'clock my shirt is wet with sweat after no more exertion than walking around classrooms to see that everything gets under way. We are trying out this early start as a means of combatting the heat. Teach a period of English – what an infernal language it must be for the foreigner to learn! I am in poor form, and come out of the period feeling that not much has got across. Drop my Parker on the stone floor, bang on the point of the nib. This is *not* being a good morning.

Interview a funny little man like an under-nourished weasel; he wants to be a laboratory attendant. He is teaching Maths at a Primary school on a salary of sixty rupees a month which is rather less than a sweeper is paid here.

'Bursar, how can this country cope if it pays its teachers like this?'

'It is the way in the under-developed countries,' he replies. 'They do not think that teachers are important.'

We engage the little fellow at one hundred a month, and he scampers off with his tail up. Teach again late morning. The boys seem lethargic; obviously the weather affects them as much as it does me. One has already noticed that there is a good deal less zip about them than last term.

Talk to the Islamiat expert re Friday prayers which we are now taking on a communal basis. We need a prayer-book – no-one on the premises has one, it seems – a pulpit and cloth to cover the floor, the last rather important as the worshippers prostrate themselves from time to time. Upbraid a clerk for expectorating too loudly outside my office. (In our neck of the woods, spitting was no trivial affair. It started deep down, and crescendoed through a whole range of guttural variations to the final triumphant emission).

Shall we start baking our own bread? 'It will save money,' says the mess manager, 'if only we can find a baker.' He follows me out into the sunlight. 'Sir, I'm very short of money. Perhaps you can help me?'

'I'll think it over, Mr. Barbhuyhan.'

Off and on during the morning I talk with the Bursar; of money – yes, we'll give Mr. B. a rise, he's earned it; of the lecturer who refuses to pay his electricity bill; of barbers; of stores issues; of the iniquities of C & B. Time passes quickly, I'm soon in boys' lunch, watching piles of rice disappear with frightening speed.

Football on grass for the first time, football with the players wearing boots instead of canvas shoes or barefoot; with more length in the kick the game is improved.

On the way into Dacca for a social evening we are caught in the baby brother of a cyclone. Rain reduces visibility to two feet, the astonishing wind makes the car buck like a randy stallion. There is nothing for it but to heave to and sweat it out in our little metal prison. We are as helpless as a bankrupt in a Stock market. Even by tropical standards the lightning is impressive. It is all over in ten minutes, and we motor on along roads two inches deep in water. By and large, a memorable Whit Monday.

June 8th

As usual I spend a good deal of the morning pacing up and down outside the classrooms, occasionally diving inside to catch samples of the wisdom being imparted. If discipline of any sort is to be maintained this vigilance is essential.

Can I put up with my secretary much longer? A young man, he thinks his English is above average. I draft a short letter to the Principal of Aichison College, Lahore; it comes back with three mistakes. 'Do it again,' I mutter with a tired sigh. This time there are only two mistakes, one of which makes nonsense of a complete sentence. 'Do it again,' I shout, curbing temper with an effort. Secretaries with shorthand – this man has none – and a good knowledge of English are very hard to find. The best lie fallow – English housewives with secretarial training and nothing whatever to do. Many of them would be glad of a job, but government puts every obstacle in the path of their employment, while providing miserably inadequate facilities for training their own people.

I spend a few minutes on the roof of the College building taking photographs with my new camera (Zeiss Eikon Contina III) bought from a friend at a bargain price.

In the nearly completed library three coolies have set up house complete with cooking pots, clothes lines, rolls of bedding. I remove them. We are, as so often, in difficulties with transport.

The jeep waggoneer was returned for an overhaul to the garage whence it was bought. On calling for it three weeks later, we find it has not been touched. The manager shrugs his shoulders; protest is futile. Happily, for the other vehicles we get good service from a firm whose managers keep things moving.

I protest to the Office Superintendent about the infernal din which goes on perpetually in the administrative block. The ceaseless chatter combined with the roar of lavatory cisterns – for some reason they installed no fewer than five in this small building, showing thereby an affection for lavatories that is strange in view of the speed with which they allow them to deteriorate – makes concentration difficult.

I decide to form a committee with the pompous title of College Council to meet every three weeks for discussion and airing of grievances. This may yet prove to be a Big Mistake.

The librarian arrives, a pleasant little man and seemingly able. He loses no time in complaining that he has been given a C rather than B Quarter. (We have four grades – A for senior lecturers, B for junior lecturers, C for admin. staff and D for 'menials' as they are distressingly known, a feudal but on the whole realistic arrangement in a country where class distinctions are subtly defined and universally accepted). 'You see, sir, I have large family,' he pleads. 'And so say all of us,' I feel like countering, but refrain, falling back instead on Regulations which effectually silences his complaint. Watch a pair of blue jays in the garden raucous in their courtship; watch too the boys at play until a monsoon storm sends everyone pell-mell for shelter.

'I told them to build your College nearer Dacca,' says Maurice Brown up with his wife for an overnight visit. 'There's an ideal site for it twenty miles out, an old palace that used to belong to a rajah. Beautiful grounds, plenty of water and a building which could have been adapted for a lak or two. Masses of room for development. Main line less than half a mile away, none of these marketing problems for you – absolutely perfect.'

'Why didn't they take it?'

'Oh, the family that used to own it were Hindus . . .'

Maurice tells an intriguing story connected with this palace. Some thirty five years ago the Rajah died while on holiday in Darjeeling and was carried off on a litter to the Hindu burning ghat. A sudden violent storm dispersed the mourners who returned after an hour or so to complete the funeral rites. Twenty-five years later the corpse turned up as large as life. 'I am the Rajah of Jaiwalpur,' he announced.

'You can't be,' they said. 'He is long dead.'

His story was unlikely but faintly possible. He had, he said, been awoken by rain, and had made off into the hills knowing neither who he was nor what he was about. For a long time he had lived the life of a hermit until one day a bang on the head restored memory. As to who the corpse was they burnt on that afternoon so long ago he had no idea, except that it wasn't he! His wife was emphatic – this was no rajah but an impostor. The case went to court, the 'rajah' won; the wife appealed, the 'rajah' lost. A still higher court ruled in his favour, and rajah he remained until his death a few years later. To this day he is still a figure of lively controversy, the people on his estate convinced he was the man, others equally convinced he was an impostor.

June 9th

There's a good deal of builders' mess in the courtyards – or what will one day be courtyards – behind the College building. I watch a gang of eight coolies at work. With infinite care each picks up twelve bricks from a pile, puts them in a basket, lifts it to his head, walks nine paces and throws the bricks to the ground in a new pile. The object of the exercise is not at once apparent. I have more sharp words with my secretary who keeps charging out of his little office next to mine in order to blow the contents of an overloaded nose into the flower bed. While thankful that at least he performs this function out of doors, I nonetheless find it distracting. The Adjutant presents us with a big hunk of newly killed lamb. Butchery here is cosier, more domestic than anything one has met before – more painful, one fears, to the animal. Driver Nazir for instance has just bought a little white bullock and will slaughter it to-morrow. It cost him one hundred and ten rupees. To buy one's dinner on the hoof is quite common practice.

June 10th

Over twenty boys absent on early P.T. this morning. With the Adjutant I storm around the dormitories on the look-out for malingerers. 'Have muscle pain, sir,' says one pointing vaguely at his tibia. 'Have muscle pain, sir,' says another, pointing vaguely at his ankle. And so on. These boys are not, by their lights, malingerers; they genuinely have got some pain, a twinge here and there, caused mostly at football. But the sad fact is that the old familiar weaknesses are coming out; they collapse at once, not because they do not want exercise but because they want to do justice to their aches.

My post to-day is varied and largely futile; a request from G.H.Q. for .22 ammunition requirements for 1967-68; a 'prayer' for raising the rate of mutton from rupees 3.25 to rupees 3.75 a seer – 'with due respect I beg to state that because of the high price of goats it has become very difficult to supply mutton at this low price'; a request to submit the names of three teachers 'in order of preference' for the possible attachment of one of them to Fettes College in September, although I know that a man has already been selected from West Pakistan; a letter from a parent beginning 'I on behalf of the guardians of some of your cadets take this opportunity to congratulate you for the keen and fatherly interest you take in our children who speak very highly of your affectionate dealings with them. Nevertheless I as a sincere wellwisher of your learned person, deem it morally obligatory on me to invite your vigilant attention to some of the very important aspects of the Cadet College designed to build up an ideal progeny for our nation' – and going on with a plea for compulsory prayer sessions five times a day; a note from the postmaster of the College Post Office asking me to intercede on his behalf to the P.M.G. for his salary to be raised from twenty two rupees a month to fifty – 'my family consists of nine members and in this hard days it is quite impossible for me to maintain the family with this humble pay as I am the only earning member of my family'.

I write a long letter to the Chief Engineer beefing about the multiple delays in finishing off so many of the facilities we should have had months ago. The President is expected here in the fall and this fact is used as a spur to action.

A man walks up the drive in a blue shirt and dark red longhi, umbrella aloft to ward off the sun; his wife, in a cerise sari, trots behind him without benefit of umbrella. The pair make a joyous splash of colour against the green background, against the rust red earth about their feet.

For lunch two of East Bengal's best products – fat, succulent shrimps dipped in batter and served with a tart white sauce, and green mangoes.

A woman comes into our compound carrying a small baby. 'Who is she?' we ask.

'She is the mother of Daniel,' replies Deenat.

'What does she want?'

'She lose her house in storm. She want money.'

Daniel, our Christian sweeper, earns seventy a month of which he gives his mother forty. Through this incident we learn a little of the domestic economy of life below stairs. Each of our three contributes twenty a month into the food kitty – we provide bread, tea, milk and sugar – and Cyprian the cook runs the mess on this bounty. Judging by the rings on young Deenat's fingers he is not doing so badly, the two cost him a hundred rupees. 'What are you doing with all your money these days, Deenat?' I ask him.

'I buy tin shed in my village.'

'How much will that cost you?'

'About four hundred rupees. It is for when I marry.'

So our Deenat is in the property market.

June 11th

Every morning I take post inside the narrow door through which the boys have to pass to enter the College building. This has several objects – to exchange the time of day with each boy, to check on dress, to bolster up my poor memory for names, to discourage the tardy. Of the last, after an explosion, there are none. I then resume my 'bobby-on-the-beat' role, pacing up and down the corridors until the boom of the 7 a.m. gong brings the lecturers out of the staffroom about their tasks. Thus the day's business is, as it were, launched. I go back to my office to parry the slings and arrows of the daily round.

The question of how often one should be seen around 'on the beat' is one which bothers headmasters everywhere: overdo it and you're interfering; spend too long in the office and you're out of touch. Much depends on the type of school. Here, for better or for worse, I get out into the action whenever possible, prompted by a feeling, possibly erroneous, that one's presence assists smooth running.

I watch a tiny lizard which decorates the office wall, welcome both for its delicate appearance and for its appetite for insects. These creatures are abnormally timid; at the human touch, no matter how gentle, they are seized with paralysis and die. The Librarian comes in with a list of newspapers and magazines to be purchased for the library, one hundred and twenty nine in all, including such titles as the *British Medical Journal, The Dock and Harbour Authority* (articles on port engineering subjects; and port operation and administration) and *Heredity: an International Journal of Genetics.* Another list, this time of reference books, suggests twenty-four titles including *The Oxford English Dictionary* (12 Vols.) and the *Encyclopedia Brittanica* (24 Vols.) 'Sir, I shall want an assistant,' he says. Gently and firmly, this eager character must be scaled down to size.

In the hot midday sun we see in the garden a most unusual spectacle. Twenty five yards from the verandah is a shallow pile of white builders' sand. Suddenly there touches down in the middle of it a big blue jay who stretches himself flat on his belly, glorious wings outstretched, a dust bather naked and unashamed. He lies so still one might think him dead. The blue of royal and turquoise blue against the pale background is resplendent; I lament my lack of a telephoto lens.

June 12th

Oversleep, and have to scramble to be on time to teach the first two periods. A bad start to a morning which develops along similar lines. It is cripplingly hot – the rain has temporarily retracted – which makes the day's big problem the more acute. The dhobi is giving trouble just at the time when his efficient services are most urgently needed – at the moment a shirt is good for nothing but a morning's wear. Spend a good deal of time listening to complaints of, and trying to do something about, his multiple shortcomings.

Owing to the curious system of placing the water tanks on the roof, the water runs so hot from the cold tap that we cannot bear our hands in it. We fall back on the fat clay chatti-jars, village-made at less than a rupee apiece, pouring the cool contents over our heads in a crude but effective imitation of a shower.

We do some early evening shopping in Mirzapur market, taking with us a bucket of water for this is the Season of the Bad Egg. If the clutch sinks, we buy. We direct operations from the car while Deenat bargains at the rickety stalls. We are quickly surrounded by a gaping throng of all ages. As a shopping expedition it has the merit of novelty.

I am vexed by the situation in the photographic world. Urgently needing black and white 35mm. film I scour every shop in Dacca – none to be had, only colour. I buy two colour films and find that these cannot, owing to lack of materials and know-how, be printed locally but must be sent to London, which means a long delay before we can hope to see the finished product. Hardly an important issue, merely another irritation in the flow which never dries up.

June 13th

Inspecting boys' clothes is not most people's idea of the best way to spend a Sunday morning, nor mine. But it has to be done. As I have intimated elsewhere, the boys were clothed free of charge from head to foot with a generous margin of spares. In addition to blue shirts and khaki slacks – the daily wear – a boy had white slacks and white shirts, pyjamas (or sleeping suits as they are called here), underclothing, black shoes, socks, games clothes, handkerchiefs, sheets, towels, pillow-cases, mosquito nets – it all added up to a formidable and costly list. We were beset from the start by twin difficulties: the very poor quality of material available – there was no question of buying ready-made, retailers carry tiny stocks while clothing wholesalers appear not to exist – and the inadequate workmanship of tailors. To these could be added a third, the rough and ready ways of the dhobi who by methods literally slaphazard will quickly reduce a garment to rags. Dyes were not fast, the shirts soon assumed all the shades in the light blue range; trousers were so far from being shrinkproof as to creep up the shins of the wearer at a pace almost visible.

On this Sunday morning when the boys lay out their clothes on the bed after the manner of an army kit inspection, I am horrified by the effect of six months wear – gym shoes with gaunt hollows in the soles, socks more hole than sock, trousers frayed and exhausted. Nothing is laid down as to when a boy is entitled to fresh issues, thus leaving us unshackled by regulations. Several boys complain that their shoes pinch. The Adjutant remonstrates with them. 'But you did not say so when they were issued to you!' 'Don't forget, Captain, that boys grow,' I reply, at which he grins ruefully. It is unlikely that the official mind would ever have grasped this fact. A second salutary factor is that we now have our own tailors where previously we had to rely on a contractor, and we can replace at leisure. But it is useless to pretend that this will be anything but a headache as long as it is impossible to buy cloth of anything but poor quality.

We sit on the darkened verandah before dinner watching a wonderful display of sheet lightning in the East. The white flashes illuminate tall bamboo trees, graceful black silhouettes against the thick nimbused background. It is cooler and there is a feeling of rain in the air.

One of the havildars is in hospital for a stomach operation. I ask a senior boy to write him a letter of good wishes from the boys of the College.

'How are you?' he writes. 'We were stunned with shock when we heard of you. We have been without you for about ten days. But none of those nights during these days could we sleep peacefully. When we go on parade we see No. 2 Platoon boys standing with No. 1 Platoon boys with blue faces. How we wish you were with us!'

I suspect that this fulsomeness will be apparent in the accounts some of the boys have written for me of their experiences on the night of the cyclone. In fact it is soon obvious that the storm itself was of such magnitude as to dwarf the descriptive powers of even the most agitated pen. I find Qamrum Noor's story of the calamity simple and graphic:

'Shut the windows?' came a cry behind me but before I could look a gust of wind with rain splashed right into my face. With desperate strength I tried to close the shutters but in vain. Rain began to beat hard and started pouring into our house like an ants' home being drenched with a bucket of water. For the last time I tried to close the window. But the shutter is nowhere so I concluded that it must have been blown off. With the help of others I put a piece of old cloth in place of the shutter and we waited to see the result.

While we are waiting the result let me introduce you to me. I am Qamrum Noor. On this stormy day which I had seen from head to tail, I was in my room most of the time. Before the storm started there was a lull in the weather. No-one expected a cyclone on that night; to tell the truth how little did they realise this night was going to be the most ruthless night ever experienced.

The cloth which we put for protection proved useful. I was tired and worn out so I took some rest. As I lay weathering the merciless storm at its full height the floor gradually was immersing in water. Suddenly I heard a crack near the kitchen. I ran to find broken pieces of stone lying all around and I looked up to find that the roof had given way. Now the storm rose to its full height placing us in a very critical situation. Suddenly the light went off leaving us in gloom. I groped my way to my Father's room where my parents were planning something. They decided to take shelter in the car which was parked in the porch. As my father entered the car a large tree crashed on the car crushing my poor brother to death. I prayed and wept for about two hours, and my prayer was answered. The storm stopped and my brother did not die. Morning came calmly with all the ruins of nature's weapon lying on the ground. By now I hope you can well imagine how ruthless was the night of terror.

June 14th

Can I capture in words the tumult of ten thousand frogs? Last night's storm brought out the choruses in swollen diapason. I use the plural deliberately for the frogs sing in choruses as disciplined as the Bach or Huddersfield. The steady refrain is honked out allegro by powerful tenor and bass parts; off and on there enters from the wings an alto descant – alas, no frog has yet sung treble – to give harmonic poise to the vibrant song. The beat is there, as insistent as that of any pop group. To describe the noise as thunderous would be misleading, for the din is, off and on, drowned by the claps which resound stentoriously across the sky. Over the great swish of rain in the trees, the ranarian choirs are master.

'Is it raining still?' we cry above the shouts of frog and thunder. A question nags me as I am kept wakeful by the storm. Is this a chorus of praise and thanksgiving for a pluvial benediction, or a lamentation at being caught out in the open without umbrella? I wish I knew the answer, for the frogs, which of an evening visit our bathrooms via the waste pipes – welcome guests whose

extinction at the express desire of the servants we sternly disallow
– are equal to a situation that reduces most livestock to a state of
numbed despair. As the natural elements go momentarily berserk,
the frogs give tongue in clamant defiance, challenging, as it were,
the weather to do its damnedest. It is a splendid example of
refusal to be dwarfed by circumstances. No wonder Aristophanes
wrote a play and called it *Frogs*. There is a lot of character out
there in the warm wet night.

Driver Nazir greets me as I leave the house, he has been polishing the car in preparation for its quarter-mile journey to the office.
To-day he is wearing his medals, and looks sprucer than usual.
This puzzles me, for we have, to the best of my belief, no V.I.P.
visitors, the common pretext for a display of metalwork. I ask no
questions and wait on events which quickly catch up with me.

'The drivers have a complaint,' says the Adjutant.

'What's it all about?'

'Driver Asgah says he was insulted by the Librarian when he
refused to give him a lift to Mirzapur. He used abusive language.'

'All right, I'll see them,' I reply, trying to keep the weariness
out of my voice. (Why must all these grown people behave like
children?)

There is a stentorian bellow from the door which nearly lifts me
out of my seat.

'Driver Asgah, attenshun! Quick march – left, right – left, right
– Driver Asgah, halt! Salute!' Bless my soul, Driver Nazir, gen-
tlest of creatures, has suddenly donned the mantle reserved for the
sergeant-major. The meaning of the medals is instantly clear; for
him this is a golden morning, a purple patch in his humdrum
existence.

Later I interview an Imam, we need someone to conduct our
Friday Jumma prayer. Above a beard dyed red and a pair of horn-
rimmed glasses, he sports a coloured pillarbox hat which would
earn respect on Blackpool's golden mile. He gives his age as
forty, yet contrives to look seventy. This must be a part-time
appointment, one hour a week, once a week; main interest centres
on the rate for the job. We ask his terms. 'A hundred and twenty
five rupees.' he says. The Bursar and I exchange meaningful
glances, and frown with contemptuous disbelief. He comes down
to a hundred, then eighty. We offer fifty, he goes away to think it
over. Within the hour he is back, his mind made up. Fifty it is.

June 15th

I go to a lecture in Dacca on Population Growth given by Lawrence Green, an American working on family planning for the Ford Foundation. He forecasts that East Pakistan's population will double by 1985, and that no form of government nor foreign aid could feed such a population.

My interest in this family planning question has been heightened by two items in a recent *Pakistan Times.*

Here is a notice set in double column –
The First Ever
Family Planning Exhibition.
Inauguration by
Mr. Abdul Monem Khan
Governor, East Pakistan,
at Pakistan Council, Lahore,
on Tuesday, March 10th at 5.30 p.m.

Taking up a whole centre page of this very same edition was an article headed 'The Quoran on Sex', which roundly condemned family planning, calling it a whim of the Western World to restrict the growth of 'the coloured races'.

After the lecture, I collar Lawrence Green in the bar of the Shahbagh Hotel.

'To what extent is religion a stumbling-block to family planning?'

'Nothing like as bad as you might think,' he replies. 'It doesn't seem to occur to the villagers that there could be religious objections.'

'Don't the mullahs get at them?'

'By and large, no. If the villagers show interest, they don't interfere.'

He dismisses the *Pakistan Times* article as fanatical propaganda which will cut little ice.

'Believe me, the Government really is behind us on this one. Increasingly money is being allotted for education in family planning.'

'In the Calcutta newspapers, Mr. Green, you see panels urging men to get themselves sterilised. I haven't seen anything of that sort here.'

'Correct. Yet sterilisation has been strongly advocated by this Government, but facilities are poor. They've had little success with men, which is a pity, because it's a simple operation, whereas it's a rather bigger thing for women.'

'Any adverse effects?'

'None. It makes no difference at all to sexual performance.'

The sale of inexpensive contraceptives has, I gather, been disappointingly low.

I begin to wonder whether what the cynics say is right: until electric light reaches the peasantry, the early 'lights out', now the habit in millions of basha huts, will keep the population rate going the wrong way – steadily upwards.

June 16th

All around us, as the summer rains belt down and the waters rise, we watch the garnering of a nation's wealth. Far and away the biggest foreign exchange earner for Pakistan is jute; due to climate and soil, the best quality jute in the world is grown on our very doorstep, produced, not on big modern farms, but by millions of families farming two or three acres, each with implements which would have been familiar to Moses and the Prophets.

The farmer lives in a mud hut roofed with rough thatch or, if he is well-to-do, corrugated iron. He has positively no mod cons, and will perform his natural functions into the surrounding waters either in the open or in a communal shed. Much of his small acreage will be sown with rice: on this he will feed himself and his family. But the farmer will give as much space as he can to jute – his one cash crop.

Jute grows high and handsome. There is no flower, but each plant is topped off with a cluster of dark green leaves. The chunks of growing jute transform the appearance of the countryside, especially in the later stages when, six to eight feet high, the slender plants sway in the breeze above the water-logged earth, giving welcome variety to the landscape.

When little Abdul cuts his jute he leaves a few inches of stump in the ground; he then puts his crop through the process of retting, a simple and crude – some would say far too crude – operation. He bundles it together and shoves it under water in a nearby pond, where, weighted down by tree branches, it will soak for ten days or so. This retting process is important, for on it depends to some extent the quality of the final product. Unfortunately little Abdul often lacks a supply of clean and flowing water necessary for good retting. The process complete, he removes the sodden remains of the leaves, and then strips the cane of its outer bark. This is the precious fibre, the main object of the whole exercise. The stringy pieces little Abdul now dries in bundles – no easy matter in rain-soaked Bengal. Bridge parapets are favoured spots, and, from July to September, the fat bunches of dirty white fibre, guarded by women and children, decorate the sides of the long road bridges; the smell is pungent.

After drying and a little rudimentary cleaning, little Abdul now sells his crop to a middle man for the best sum he can get; when prices are low, he may store it against better times. If the quality of the product is good and the market firm, he will collect about three hundred rupees from a one-acre field. The jute canes will be stooked, dried out and used for thatch or fuel.

Little Abdul is at the base of a vast and complex structure with millions of rupees, pounds and dollars at stake each year. Middlemen abound – it is a position much coveted in the East. After them, export agents, shippers, insurers, financiers, advisers, millowners, salesmen – all have a part to play in satisfying world demand. That fortunes have been, and still are, made in jute is not so apparent to us in our jungle fastness, as we watch little Abdul and his like going about their business. As the *Pakistan Observer* puts it – 'We earn crores of rupees in foreign exchange by exporting jute. Thousands of traders, marketeers, exporters and millowners are becoming richer every year by means of jute. But who cares about the growers who are the primary source of this wealth?'

June 17th

A visit to-day from a small group of Americans, out here on some fact-finding mission. They are more than welcome, because I find the candour and enthusiasm of Americans so invigorating. These do not disappoint; the air fairly crackles with mid-western cries of wonder. When I tell them how Uncle came into our midst, they insist on an introduction – 'Gee, we godda meet this guy.'

Uncle is at the top of his form.

'I am son of Pakistan,' he says, 'I love my country, I love my College.'

This remark is received with ecstasy; I get the impression that our visitors want nothing so much as to cart Uncle back with them to the States there and then. Eventually I part them, with reluctance on all sides.

After an excellent lunch – Cyprian rises to the occasion as always – they leave to shouts of mutual esteem. My wife and I agree that we could do with more visitors like these.

*   *   *

Less than three weeks after start of term, we ran head-on into trouble over food. I was busying myself one evening with the pre-dinner aperitif when the Adjutant bustled in looking grave. When wearing that expression he was inevitably the bearer of ill tidings – an attempted murder at worst, a broken down vehicle at best. 'Sir, the boys are refusing to eat dinner. They say the food is bad.' I hurried up to the dining-hall wondering just what I would find there. Grumbles from boys about school food had been at one time a part and parcel of my daily life; a hunger strike was a new experience.

As I walked into the hall, everyone stood up; clearly I was expected. The mess manager, waiters, a little gaggle of cooks and the lecturer on duty were looking forlorn and obviously at a loss. The atmosphere was quiet and very orderly; it was resistance of the most passive kind. I made a short speech promising that complaints would be investigated, and leaving to the individual the choice as to whether he ate the meal or went hungry. Most of them then got down to the business of eating. Later that same evening we held a meeting, some senior staff and boys, where we listened to grumbles, many of them entirely justified.

We were the victims in the main of the summer food situation in East Bengal – the difficulty of getting vegetables, fish and any variety of meat or fruit. This basic lack was made in our case the more acute by marketing problems, a matter which the authorities had not investigated with sufficient thoroughness before choosing a site so remote. Local sources of supply were desperately meagre, and quite insufficient to cope with the appetites of a very large family indeed. The menu had become monotonous even to palates unused to great variety. Curried mutton (which is in fact goat) followed curried beef day after day, and that was about the extent of the matter. Sometimes we served chicken but they were very

different birds from the succulent roasts that one can still find occasionally on the English dinner table. No, these were poor skinny things lacking flesh and flavour.

The meeting did a lot to ease tensions, certainly the consumers were
brought to a fuller understanding of the difficulties we were up against. At
times, I might have been back in my Yorkshire school chairing an identi-
cal meeting, so familiar were some of the complaints: slipshod washing-
up – cold toast – 'can't we have milk and sugar served separately with
porridge?' – meat too tough – I had heard it all before. So, too, the utter
impracticality of some suggestions: the sudden comprehension that food
costs money and that supply of the latter is not unlimited; the attitude –
half defensive, a shade resentful – of the caterer; the difficulty of getting a
group of people to achieve unanimity when it is a question of the palate;
all these were echoed back over seven thousand miles to the Pennine
Hills. I ended the meeting on a mildly aggressive note. 'This form of
protest,' I said, 'must not happen again. In a country where millions of
people are poor and have barely enough to live on, waste of food is a sin.'
I think they got the message.

There was one corner of the College area upon which we frequently cast
envious eyes. We called it the C & B compound; it comprised three big
sheds, a storage bungalow of five rooms, and three bungalows for housing
purposes. One of these was by local standards commodious, even stylish,
being separated from the rest by a low but meaningful wall. This was
reserved for top C & B executives who might, but in fact never once did,
feel the urge to spend a night on the site. All these buildings were
equipped with running water, electricity and fans – a solid testimony to
the ability of government departments to squander public money. Broadly
speaking the idea was that the College would take them over as the
requirements of the builders slackened, but this was a situation which our
friends in C & B were loath to recognise. They surrendered two storage
sheds without much of a struggle, for the very good reason that they
contributed not an iota to the personal comforts of the executive staff.
Over the bungalows a squabble simmered spasmodically for months;
meanwhile the buildings themselves became more dilapidated as the effects of weather took their toll.

At last, late in June, the Bursar and I stood under umbrellas up to our
ankles in mud in the middle of the compound, officially 'taking over' one
of these desirable residences.

'What are we going to do with it now we've got it?' I asked.
'It will do for two families,' said the Bursar.
I had by now almost become hardened to local housing conditions, and agreed, though not without qualms. Each family would have two rooms, fifteen by twelve, with a tiny kitchen and lavatory attached. Since a family would be inflated by hordes of children and, like as not, an elderly dependant or two for good measure, I could not escape a feeling of guilt that I might be fostering a certain measure of overcrowding. But no, this would do, and would moreover be perfectly acceptable to clerical grades. So two clerks each with multiple progeny moved in. The really surprising thing was that from such congested dwellings the two estimable fellows would turn out every morning crisp and laundered as if they had spent the night in a four-star hotel.

*   *   *

A legitimate way of making money in the subcontinent was to buy a decrepit building, patch it up, instal screen and projector, and show films. It mattered not a whit what the films were; the Bengali was an inveterate cinema goer, and every performance of every film was packed. On seating, cleaning and maintenance one would spend the bare minimum, as none of the audience would be worried by the discomfort. A small capital outlay, guaranteed full houses, the cheapest of films and the lowest possible day to day running costs – it all added up to thoroughly sound business.

Thanks to the assistance of the British Information Services and the United States equivalent, we were able to show films at the College right from the start. Everything was provided for us – films, operators, screen and projector – without any charge. We were confined to documentaries, but the range was so wide that this was little disadvantage. On the cool rainless evenings we held the shows in the open air; it was pleasant to sit there in the car after the manner of a drive-in cinema. Of all the films shown during the term the one that the boys enjoyed most was a ten minute reel in colour of the Trooping the Colour ceremony on Horse Guards Parade.

For live entertainment we were invited, my family and I, to a girls' school nearby on occasions when they abandoned themselves to the drama. Two performances stand out in my mind though for different reasons. The first was a polished and colourful production of *Ali Baba and the Forty Thieves*, given in Bengali with song and dance into the bargain. This took place on a winter's evening, and, though rather long drawn-out, provided pleasant entertainment. When the play was over we were treated to a precision exercise which would have done credit to the Brigade of Guards. Great strapping girls clad in a sort of gym outfit went through a series of manoeuvres on stage both impressive and a little scaring. One would think twice before making unsolicited advances to any of these young Amazons – one would be flat on one's back before you could say Errol Flynn. It all seemed a long way from the purdah room and from the role traditionally assigned to women in the Islamic society.

Nine thirty on a Sunday morning is not a time one usually associates with visits to the theatre, but *Beauty and the Beast* – the second of these memorable performances – was given at this peculiar hour in order to defeat, unsuccessfully as it turned out, the cruel heat of mid-summer. Things got off to a poor start – we simply sat there in the crowded little hall while for half-an-hour nothing whatever happened. A good lady then stood forth full of apology – the players had been overcome by the weather. That the audience was reduced to the same state was pitifully obvious from the turgid reaction to the drama when finally it got under way. It lasted one hour, but as three-quarters of this time was spent on scenery and costume changes, there was little to divert attention from the soaring temperature. I remember sitting there incapable of thought or movement, feeling the sweat trickling down the inside of my shirt, and wondering why precisely I had allowed myself to be subjected to such an ordeal. Beside me my wife and daughters dripped in unison. When mercifully the final curtain fell, a few spongy hand-claps testified to the fact that native and foreigner had suffered alike.

*   *   *

The first College football match produced, as one might have expected, a number of shocks. We had accepted a challenge from the local Boys' Club, the game to be contested on our ground. Deliberately I played the occasion up. This as it turned out was a mistake; it was an occasion which should have been played down.

The ground was dressed overall; flags were two a penny, the sun shone on close cut grass; the College team, decked out in white, posed in front of cameras. An atmosphere had been created. Opposite the centre-line, an upholstered couch, salvaged from goodness-knows-where, was topped by a white sheet stretched between poles to provide a tiny oasis of shade. On to this couch sank our beloved Principal, still unused to such treatment and wondering just what he had done to deserve it.

It was five minutes to kick-off. 'Where's the other team?' I asked the senior cadet who at my invitation had perched himself gingerly on one end of the regal couch.

'They come from there, sir, from the bazaar,' he said, pointing across the compound.

Sure enough, in the middle distance a vast crowd was approaching; here and there one could discern a figure clad for football.

'They look rather big,' I said.

They were big; for a Boys' Club they made a startling ensemble. I put their average age at twenty four. Solemnly they trooped past me, I shook eleven hot hands. The teams lined up in the middle of the field to be harangued by the havildar-major in the manner of boxers before a fight; as a referee he considered it beneath his dignity ever to break into a trot, which meant that he was usually a long way from the centre of operations. But at least he was prepared to blow his whistle authoritatively, and this was all that really mattered. 'Atten-shun!' he roared, his monologue done. He strutted over to click his heels in front of the regal couch. 'Let battle commence, havildar-major!' I cried, still living it up as the grand seigneur. The metaphor was singularly apt. The whistle went and we were off.

It was soon plain that we were in for a roughish ride. The club boys were a jungly crew, barefooted and dressed anything but stylishly, but they could play football. They kicked the ball huge distances and ran very fast in pursuit of it. The cadets, pathetically nervous, were shaken by the speed and vigour of the opposition. Fortunately for them, the visitors completely lost their heads whenever they got near goal; the prospect of shooting the ball into the net was too much for them. They either muffed their kicks completely, or more often tried to walk the ball into the goal.

Our visitors did not suffer from lack of support. Their camp followers, a colourful throng, numbered about five hundred and sounded like five thousand. On a football special, they would have added to the cares of B.R. officials. But yell as hard as they might, nothing would persuade their forwards to shoot a goal. Half way through the first half and absurdly against the run of the play, the College scored. A speculative shot from the outside right – it was intended, I think, as a centre – so astonished the goalkeeper, who was not used to action so direct, that he let it bounce off his naked torso into the goal. I then had my first big shock of the day. All bedlam broke loose; the spectators surged on to the field, screaming their heads off and capering like hell's angels. They came not from the ranks of the visitors' supporters but from our pupils. I began to compose a sermon on self-control.

The game became rougher, both sides contributing some sharply illegal practices. The College conceded a penalty; it seemed that justice might at last be done. Not a bit of it – the marksman tapped his shot gently along the ground straight into the goalkeeper's hands; he was so surprised that he nearly let it through.

Came half-time, and I exhorted the team to start playing football. They looked aggrieved; after all, they were winning, weren't they? What more could I expect?

As the second half progressed, so the superiority of our opponents grew more marked; the College goalmouth became a scene of recurrent chaos, of flying bodies, legs, heads, as players plunged and kicked their way into and out of trouble. The defence tackled and tackled again; still the attackers failed to realise that a few hefty shots would do the trick. They tried it once, from three yards out, and the young goalkeeper produced a virtuoso save. Sporadically one or two of the College forwards made sallies into the other half of the field, but they looked no more likely to bring their efforts to a successful conclusion than a pickpocket in a nudist colony. Just as it began to look as if two miracles could happen, one that the College might win, and two the game end without an incident, an ugly tackle brought our outside right to the ground, where he lay writhing in some distress. What followed almost defies description.

Had the unlucky youth been riddled with gunshot, the reactions of the crowd could hardly have been more explosive. Spectators of all ages swarmed on to the field; it could surely be only a matter of moments before the knives would be out and butchery begun. The injured player was carried to a spot near the regal couch where he became the centre of a milling mob crowding hot and thick about him, thus making doubly difficult the attempts of the medical men to restore him to health. Two of the lecturers considered that the surest way to restore order was to rush about screaming and hitting out with abandon, their blows for the most part striking the empty air. Shouts of rage vied with moans of sympathy for the afflicted youth; it was the 'rash fierce blaze of riot' and no mistake. I sat stock still on the regal couch, as quiet as the eye of a cyclone, wondering how on earth to bring the situation under some sort of control. All seignioral feelings had long since disappeared.

I grabbed the referee. 'Blow your whistle, man, and get on with the game!' I yelled. Being a soldier and this being the first coherent notion that had entered his head for the past five minutes, he was quick to obey. He blew hard, though not hard enough to penetrate the mind of Uncle, our centre-half, whom I intercepted as he wandered off the field, tears in his eyes, towards his fallen comrade. 'Get back on the field, boy. The game's restarting!' He gave me an uncomprehending stare and trotted back to the scene of battle in a bemused state. The game – if it could still merit the epithet – was resumed, while the outside right was carted off to hospital. Ten minutes later it was over, and the College had gained the luckiest victory ever won on a football field.

A few days later, Jim Chaffey, himself a fine footballer, collected from Dacca a team which we dubbed, not without justification, an International XI – an Englishman, a Welshman, a Pakistani, an Anglo-Indian, a Finn and three Dutchmen. To this medley we added three cadets to make up the complement. The match caught the imagination of the surrounding countryside; although it was only officially declared 'on' a few hours before kick-off, the populace turned out in shoals from miles around. One got a new respect for the jungle telegraph. At a conservative estimate there were no less than a thousand standing three and four deep round three sides of the field.

The international team's approach to the game was whole-hearted rather than skilful. Roger Davies, a seventy-three inch graduate from the depths of a Welsh Rugby scrum, plunged about like a baited bull, often, to the huge delight of the crowd, shaking the earth with spectacular tumbles; the Finn, a vast doctor with herculean shoulders, had as much skill in his feet as a hippopotamus; the Pakistani, Mr. Nabbi, had once been a good player, but the years had thickened his figure and reduced his speed to that of a steam-roller. No, the soccer virtuosity came from one player, energy and determination from the whole team. The game was as interesting and pleasant as the previous one had been dull and ill-tempered. The College won by two goals to nothing, but as the second goal came over very near the end there was plenty of excitement. The result gave everyone great satisfaction, for we were anxious for the College to win, and for the visitors not to lose by a discreditable margin.

*   *   *

If you subscribe to the view that a parish church, to do its job properly, ought to be situated in among the people, then St. Thomas' Anglican Church, Dacca, would be at the top of your league. Or would it?

St. Thomas' was a substantial Victorian-style building with a parsonage adjacent, set in a tiny compound, completely engulfed by the clamorous, occasionally riotous, always hectic life which was the old city of Dacca. It could be seen both as a bold witness to Christianity stuck there in the middle of so many 'unbelievers', and as a silent testimony to the tolerance of Muslims, who not only put up with this little foreign bastion in their midst, but also managed not to knock it down or set it on fire in times of riot.

In a sense, though, St. Thomas' Church was in the wrong place. Only the merest handful of British lived in the old city; one had to be a very zealous church-goer indeed to undertake that journey through narrow, congested streets on a hot spring or summer morning. The church existed, of course, both for the expatriate and the Bengali Anglican. Yet, just as the Church of England on its home ground has never quite succeeded in coming to terms with the less well endowed section of the population, so in Dacca it was Mr. Ahmed, chief clerk in a business house, rather than little Abdul, the rickshaw wallah, who typified the small number of Bengali Anglicans in the parish. (The same was not quite true of the countryside where, in the widely scattered Christian communities, people of the most humble origin would stand up to be counted). Since Mr. Ahmed and his like were tending to move out of the old city into New Dacca and its suburbs, St. Thomas' Church lived with a congregation problem. I can remember a beautiful Christmas Carol Service there. The church was barely half full; that was considered, in the words of one of the churchwardens, 'about par for the course.'

Ministering to the spiritual welfare of East Pakistan's Anglicans was a very remarkable man indeed – the Rt. Revd. James Blair, Bishop of Dacca. No-one would have raised an eyebrow had the Bishop chosen to live in the comparative calm of New Dacca, among, after all, the bulk of his flock. That was not James Blair's way; a bachelor – he had taken the vows of the Brotherhood of the Epiphany – he had a tiny bedroom and office in the parsonage, right down there in the old city, the rest of the accommodation being given over to the vicar of the parish of Dacca.

James Blair would call on us at the College, not as a prince of the church visiting a school, but as a pastor visiting the only three Anglicans for miles around. He would either be at the wheel of a rather rickety van, or, the vehicle temporarily out of action, on his feet, having walked twenty miles or more – sandals, white cotton cassock, bare-headed, staff in hand, a small rucksack on his back. He covered vast distances in all kinds of weather, in all kinds of 'troubles', as a pastoral prelate ministering to his see. Periodically he would publish a news sheet which would be an account, often hilarious, of his latest adventures among the jungles and swamps he traversed with such effortless ease. He was rising sixty and looked a very fit forty. Like other notable wayfarers before him, he must have been possessed of a cast-iron digestive system, for he was capable of taking on food and water of a kind which would have sent most Europeans scuttling to the dysentery wards.

The second half of the 20th century has not been kind to the notion of missionary work. The right of any one religion to proselytise is now a debatable point which would simply not have occurred to our forebears. By opening the doors of modern civilisation to primitive people, we are, it is said, not only destroying cultures of singular simplicity and naturalness, but also offering in the wake of the Gospel the decadence, diseases and malpractices of westernised society. These views are widely held. They have not, however, deterred men of great courage from going about their work in a totally selfless manner, firm in the belief that what they are doing is for the good of their fellow men. Such a one was James Blair; it was a privilege to know him.

*   *   *

Every Sunday morning I had an inspection unashamedly military in character; the boys stood to their beds', there was a good deal of shouting – 'room, attenshun!' – and so on. The boys themselves seemed not to mind this; indeed they encouraged it by adding on their own initiative little side effects that heightened the martial atmosphere, as when a sprightly child, fifty four inches of incarnate mischief, planted beside his foot an explosive cap, so that the action of coming to attention triggered off an almighty bang.

The dormitories were small, none holding more than eight, with good cross-ventilation and enough fans to set up the electrical contractor for a lifetime. A boy enjoyed a very reasonable degree of comfort, having beside his bed a chair, table and wardrobe – the last we designed ourselves after much trial and error to give him room for all his belongings under lock and key. Whether it was a mark of appreciation of their surroundings or whether it was part of their make-up, I do not know, but the boys went to immense trouble to deck out their rooms with finery on days, for instance, when parents were about. The trappings were gaudy –'Welcome to Room 7' would be plastered across a doorway in the rather insipid pastel shades which they loved to reproduce – but occasionally, the more so when they used greenery plucked from jungle shrubs, pleasant to the eye. Both houses – or hostels as they were regrettably called – had a recreation room with various facilities for making life more agreeable and leisure more profitable. Of bathrooms and lavatories there was no lack, one shower and one lavatory basin to every six boys. It was impossible to escape the conclusion that they were better off in terms of space and comfort than many boys of their age in some of the more old-fashioned boarding schools in Britain.

On this Sunday inspection, then, I trooped around attended by a little band, looking all the time for evidence of dirt and decay in corners and crevices, peering at boys – to do this one often had to stoop low, so small were many of them; some half dozen were tall enough to be almost at eye level – for evidence of cleanliness and tidy dress. In a country where the inhabitants, though personally clean (frequent ablution is obligatory to the Muslim), are inclined not to worry too much about the dirtiness of their surroundings, this sort of inspection was rather necessary. In fairness it should be added that, once it was established that a certain standard of cleanliness was expected, more than half the battle was won, while the quasi-military atmosphere provided its own momentum. To do this in-spection on a Sunday would have been unseemly in a Christian country; here it was entirely in order, for the day has no religious significance for the Muslim, while it had the added advantage, not unintentionally seized, of giving the boys in their cleansing and polishing something with which to occupy themselves in the early hours of an otherwise carefree day.

*   *   *

Quickly and almost uneventfully – if one dare use such an epithet in such a setting – the monsoon term slipped past. There were innumerable squab-bles between man and man, mostly among the administrative staff, ob-sessed every one of them with the struggle to maintain position and not to lose face. There was the time when the Adjutant threw a file at the Office Superintendent. This drew from the latter an outraged letter of protest concluding: 'At this he grew angry and threw the file towards me with the remarks, '"I am first-class Gazetted Officer and I am competent enough to deal with the cases of my N.C.Os and I will not be guided by the pitty (sic) clerks."'

In the midst of the heat, the rain and the humidity, there was a good deal of fun to be had. It was generally possible to squeeze a laugh out of most situations even if the laugh was delayed until later. There was the occa-sion on an early morning parade when a cadet platoon commander got as far as 'Stand at ———' and then blacked out on the executive word. There was the day, a Sunday of course, when the water pump packed up, leaving us, in a temperature of over ninety degrees, without drinking, washing or sanitary water. There was the night the madman came; he crept into a dormitory at dead of night, and quietly, for he was a placid lunatic, lay down on the floor beside a boy's bed and went to sleep. 'He was stark naked!' exclaimed the horrified housemaster, dotting the Is and crossing the Ts of what might have been an unpleasant incident. There was the case of the Hairless Horrors . . .

Most school authorities are faced with problems centering upon their pupils' hair styles, male and female. Mine was a strange one, if not unique. I was astonished on one early morning P.T. to see some half dozen boys with their heads completely shaven, as bald as stones and as distinctive as Buddhist monks. There was a good deal of tittering as the reactions of our beloved Principal to this phenomenon were observed by the multitude. I was completely foxed. Was this some sort of a joke, or was it a form of protest peculiar to the mysterious East? It so happened that the day before I had given short shift to a little deputation which had voiced its disapproval of a certain lecturer's marking system. Was it a coincidence that most of that deputation now stood in front of me in hairless indignation? I took counsel with a housemaster.

'I have enquired of the students, sir,' he replied, 'they have some slight trouble of a medical kind . . .'

And, on further enquiry, medical indeed it was. We published an order forbidding such tonsorial practices without sanction from on high, while pouring gentle scorn on the baldheads, dubbing them 'hairless horrors'. It was all very good humoured and appealed enormously to the Bengali boys' keen sense of fun. There were no more naked scalps.

We tackled, and not before it was due, the problem of the public's insatiable curiosity in our daily doings. Our football matches, it may be recalled, attracted large crowds. When, on the Saturday following the second of these matches, a like multitude turned out to watch a common or garden practice game, I decided we had had enough. We engaged six additional chowkidhars, put them into khaki drill and issued them with staves and an instruction that they were to remain on duty from sunrise to sunset. In the anticipation of trouble, I solicited the help of a parent who was high up in the police hierarchy; he sent us a small posse on a fortnight's attachment. In fact they stayed over a month, not because of trouble (of that there was none whatever) but because the assignment was a particularly cushy one, involving, I was assured, a good deal of profitable extortion. No sooner had we rid the premises of the human hordes than a new nuisance became evident – dogs.

To those Anglo-Saxons who know not the East, a dog is a pleasant domestic companion recognised by the State through virtue of a licence.

In the subcontinent there are domestic dogs, but they are in a very, very, small minority. The canine population is concentrated in the main into packs of skeletal mongrels which hunt in clamorous hordes, feeding off scraps and taking shelter wherever they can find it. They make an infernal din and a lot of mess. In the College they showed understandable partiality for the big covered verandahs of the main building, which they fouled profusely while assailing our ears with their fights and amorous adventures. The only answer was a shot gun, and to this we had recourse from time to time. Lest any dog-lovers – and we number ourselves among them – should be shocked by such apparent callousness, they should rest assured that the pitiful condition of many of these animals, covered with sores and unimaginably thin, warranted only one solution.

One afternoon early in August we stood on the tarmac of Dacca Airport watching with sad hearts the Indian Airways Dakota take off for Calcutta carrying the twins on the first leg of their journey back to England. They had been with us for ten months, studying through a correspondence course – with help here and there from Father – for 'O' levels which they sat at the British High Commission in June. They were then just short of sixteen, and it was time they went home to continue their schooling on more conventional lines.

We walked in close companionship with the frailties of human nature. We commissioned the two College carpenters to make a house for Gertie and Gilbert. This they did with speed and enthusiasm, proudly producing a structure quite excellent save for the fact that the door was too small by half for a goose to enter. With the approach of a twenty-eight day break, I was inundated with requests for huge slabs of leave, every conceivable reason being put forward – a wife's pregnancy, the building of a new house, the applicant's blood-pressure, a brother's law-suit, a grandfather's slow decline. One morning the din coming from the College main office was so clamant that I could stand it no longer. I stalked in – the office superintendent, the accountant, the senior clerk, the junior clerk, two peons, the ration storeman, a pump operator and the plumber were all talking at once.

'Shut up!' I roared, 'Let's have a little less noise and a little more work in here.' A shame-faced silence. It was just like dealing with the Lower Fourth really.

As I once again stood outside the office grinning fatuously and waving at the busloads of boys moving away for the holidays, I noticed a small van approaching up the drive. Out of it tumbled seven men. They had come to instal two telephone instruments, almost a year to the day since I

made my first approach to the All Highest of East Pakistan Telephonic
Communications. One began to believe in miracles.

*   *   *

When we had contracted to do a stint of work in Bengal, we had taken
certain adverse factors into the reckoning – a reputedly vile climate,
family separations, isolation, frustration and a few others. These we had
weighed in the balance and found acceptable. The one thing for which we
had not bargained was a war.

At the end of the raj, Kashmir, having a strong Muslim population, was
split into two – Azad Kashmir, belonging to Pakistan, and Indian Kashmir. Since that day the two countries had never ceased to trumpet the
rights and wrongs of the case. Pakistan was convinced that Indian Kashmir was full of oppressed Muslims groaning under Indian tyranny; India
was convinced that no such situation existed. A grotesque see-saw of
argument and counter-argument blasted the air. Meanwhile, the bulk of
the Kashmiris – not the most martial race on earth – didn't give a damn,
being far too intent on flogging carpets and renting houseboats to tourists
in what is arguably the loveliest country in the world.

Things really began to hot up on 5 August 1965, on which day armed
groups of Pakistan soldiery infiltrated into Indian Kashmir to support
what they claimed was an anti-Indian uprising among the populace. India
vigorously denied that such a revolt had taken place. In a broadcast on 13
August, Prime Minister Shastri warned Pakistan that 'force will be met
with force,' to which President Ayub Khan countered with 'the threat of
war in Kashmir is being forced on us by India'. On 6 September, Indian
troops, without a declaration of war, launched an offensive across the
Punjab into West Pakistan.

It was on the following day that we came face to face for the first time with
the hard facts. Armed with shopping list and a batch of letters for the post,
we set off to Dacca with little sense of apprehension. Passing through the
cantonments we sensed an atmosphere more purposeful and sinister than we
had come across before: a troop train in a siding, camouflaged vehicles being
loaded onto flats, soldiers tin-hatted and crowned with sprouts of greenery.
But the airport gave the first real cause for what sailors call tooth-sucking. It
was decidedly quiet, the usual hordes missing; the Air Force had taken over
and P.I.A. was grounded. It did not take long for the significance of this to
sink in; it meant that we were cut off from West Pakistan, and therefore from
U.K. Our little pile of letters looked singularly forlorn.

The city itself was calm, in spite of the bannered headlines, quoting the President's latest broadcast – 'We Are At War'. Calm is not quite the right word for Dacca, because a million Bengalis, concentrated within a few square miles, are incapable of creating such an atmosphere at any time. Rather would it be truer to suggest 'business as usual'. Rumour was having a field day: an Indian bomber had been shot down over the golf-course (possible); Pakistani paratroopers were on their way to Delhi (highly improbable); the Royal Navy was steaming for Chittagong (too good to be true); a top U.N. man had dubbed India 'the aggressor' (wishful thinking); Prime Minister Shastri had been lynched by his own mobsters (you could laugh that one off).

When we returned to the College that evening, I was met by the Adjutant, booted and spurred. Accoutred for the field, he, an officer of the Army Education Corps, was preparing to sell his life dearly, 'We must all report, sir. We have had orders on the wireless.'

I said a not unemotional farewell to our gallant captain and the havildars. If not with sobs, at least with lumps in the throat, we waved them away to the wars. Next day, they were back.

Our captain's ear had been enlarged by an outsize flea; he had, in his martial ardour, quite misinterpreted the radio announcement. Authority – in the person of Col. Rahman – was displeased, and delivered a fizzing rocket verbally and in writing, to which the captain replied with some dignity:

'I am proud,' he wrote, 'of being an Officer in the Pakistan Army, and I considered it my duty to move without loss of a second. I have been maintained and trained by the Army all these years to be of service to my profession and to the Nation. I take it as an honour that my country has selected me to join the ranks of her defenders. I did not like to be deprived of the supreme honour of staking and sacrificing my life in the path of duty and service to the Nation when the very existence of my country is at stake and the enemy is knocking at the door of the Nation.'

Fighting talk – our sympathies were very much with our gallant captain.

East Pakistan was dependent for most of its essentials on imports. With the port of Chittagong more constipated than usual and the air routes closed, it was clear that we would soon be running short of a good many essential things. It was no surprise when, very early on, petrol rationing – two gallons a week – was introduced, and no surprise at all that ration cards were not available – a truly Asian impasse. For us the situation looked bad – two gallons a week was a nasty comedown from the fifty-odd we used normally. In common with every other vehicle owner in the land we stocked up to the limit of tanks and available cans. Prices of food, tobacco and kerosene shot up.

News bulletins were notably unhelpful: these came either from Radio Pakistan which told of 'our gallant soldiers who are inflicting heavy casualties', and 'our gallant airmen who have shot down fifty Indian planes'; or from Radio Calcutta which told of 'our gallant soldiers who are inflicting heavy casualties', and 'our gallant airmen who have shot down fifty Pakistani planes.' Newspaper reports were even more fanciful: 'Dacca Bombed' in huge headlines – one small bomb was believed to have been dropped on an empty store shed ten miles from the city – this was, of course, the familiar mumbo jumbo of war propaganda. From all such extravagant eye-wash, we tried to ferret out some truth. We gave thought to black-out and the advisability of a slit trench in the garden.

One watched admiringly the stiff upper lip in action. We kept in touch with the British High Commission as closely as limited petrol would permit. What we gleaned there was impressive – British phlegm at work again. 'We are advising,' said the First Secretary, 'all non-essential personnel to concentrate centrally – that means women and children, of course. Men should stay on post; there is no question yet of any evacuation.' My wife, stiff upper lip again, refused point-blank to leave the home for Dacca. So, with the car ready and suitcases dusted – not packed – we continued to enjoy life in our peaceful country retreat. To the thousands of peasants who were our neighbours the war appeared to mean nothing, though they may have had to pay more for their frugal purchases, and to suffer inconvenience from shortage of oil for their lamps. They went about their tasks just as their forefathers had done for centuries, apparently impervious to the trend of events in the world around them.

It would be idle to pretend that the days did not tend to drag. The College was on holiday, and so supposedly were we. But a visit to friends in the tea plantations of Sylhet had to be abandoned; there was nothing for it but to sit back and wait upon events.

We were not left in peace for long. On a Friday – it must have been the fifth day of the war – our afternoon siesta was interrupted by the arrival of a motor-car. As soon as I peered down from the balcony and recognised a British Council vehicle, I knew something was up. The driver handed me a note: we were to leave at once for Dacca, all Europeans having been summoned to congregate in the capital. Not without irritation we stuffed suitcases with 'essential' chattels – tricky little decisions had to be made in the course of that operation – bade farewell to the servants with a good deal of 'we'll be back soon' and 'look after the house', and set off, acutely aware of the incongruity of leaving the somnolent countryside for the turmoil of the city. However, orders were orders, and when we learnt that Tim and Mary Kidd had invited us to be their guests in Dacca for as long as needs be, all our irritation evaporated.

There now began for us a curious period of time during which we lived on rumour, B.B.C. World News bulletins, endless talk and speculation. Evacuation was the question which obsessed us – evacuation, that is, of women, children and such non-essentials as the little group of visiting businessmen, stranded and fuming with frustration in the Shabagh Hotel. The Americans set the pace. On a hot Sunday morning we watched the big U.S.A.F. transports rumbling into and out of the airport with their loads of redundant Yanks. It appeared to be – and was – a most efficient operation; in the course of a few hours the whole American overspill was off and away to distant Manila. Meanwhile, no decision had been taken for the rest of the expatriates, who sat back to await developments with the smug satisfaction of those who have watched the launching of the lifeboats before themselves taking to the rafts.

It was, as I have suggested, a curious period of time; certainly we had experienced nothing like it before. The war went on, the pattern of events being hopelessly blurred by communiqués of risible exaggeration. After the first week we knew full well that in Britain the hostilities would by now have been shoved off the front pages of the newspapers; already it would have been relegated to the status of another, rather boring, foreign war. To us the situation was very different: we were foreigners in a country at war, the victim, so that country proclaimed, of an oppression which threatened the survival of the State. Under such circumstances foreigners, though they had to be tolerated, were something of an embarrassment. The Bengalis, moreover, were astonished that we British did not throw in our lot wholeheartedly with Pakistan. The suggestion that India, too, was a member of the Commonwealth fell on unreceptive ears, while it would have been a bold man who ventured to suggest that the Indians might conceivably have been provoked into doing what they did. To the Bengalis, Pakistan was the victim of a treacherous act of aggression, and that was that. Nor was the idea of a quick peace agreeable. Dacca, its inhabitants quite ignorant of what war means, struck an attitude of uncharacteristic aggression. 'Crush India' was the slogan painted on walls, or stuck on car rear windows in neatly printed capitals. East Bengal was breathing fire and slaughter, anxious to have a go.

We lived from day to day. Our anxieties·were focused on two points: the sense of being cut off, and the threat of street riots. As for the latter, it only needed a news editor or politician in London to make a public pronouncement expressing disapproval of Pakistan for the mobs to take to the streets, hellbent on trouble. The Bengali is at heart a gentle, peace-loving creature; put him in a mob and feed him with xenophobic slogans, and he is transformed into one of the most dangerous creatures on earth.

I had little or nothing to do. Owing to the emergency, passage through the cantonment was closed; no amount of pleading with the soldiery could get me a pass. I was thus neatly cut off from both home and work. The plea that, if I was considered a fit person to have charge of Pakistan's younger sons, I might be entrusted to pass through the cantonments without lapsing into espionage – this plea got me precisely nowhere. I was a foreigner, and that was that. Cut off from the place that was both home and *raison d'être*, we relaxed in frustration made lighter by the generous hospitality of our friends.

As the war moved into its second week, a threat to world peace loomed out of the North in the shape of possible Chinese intervention. Having crossed swords with India two years earlier, China saw in this new conflict a heaven-sent opportunity to stir up trouble. She declared herself for Pakistan, and appeared to be rolling up her sleeves to do battle against India. Thus what had been a local struggle suddenly took on an entirely new aspect; it looked very much as if the whole thing might blow up into a major war. It was this threat that finally decided the British Government to act; on 20 September the news came through – evacuation to-morrow. That night the B.B.C. news could hardly have been worse – a Chinese ultimatum, serious riots in Karachi against American institutions. Those of us who had been sceptical about evacuation appeared, for the moment, to have got our sums wrong.

An evacuation is a painful and trying experience, although in this Dacca exodus there were factors which made things easier. Matters were very well organised, both by the staff of the High Commission and by the Committee of the U.K. Association for Pakistan – a rather pompous title for an organisation which, in more relaxed times, organised jolly-boy gatherings, while being always on the alert to cope with just such an emergency as the one we now faced. The whole of Dacca was divided into zones, each having one or two Committee members to act as wardens. Thus we took our orders, always verbal, from our warden, whom we knew and who knew us. With dexterity, and, having regard to the nature of the occasion, with a minimum of fuss, the proceedings got under way. Scarcely had the roar of the R.A.F. Brittanias – three flown out from

Lyneham in Wiltshire – faded from our ears, when news came through that a cease-fire would become effective at 3.30 a.m. on 23 September. We then got involved in a ludicrous cat-and-mouse game with, of all people, H.M. Government. As the days slipped by, there seemed no reason to us men why our families should not rejoin us. The cease-fire was holding, tempers fast cooling. I was even permitted to drive through the cantonments to the College.

The British Foreign Office did not see things in that light at all; having effected an evacuation, they were clearly anxious to make it stick. They were adamant that 'official' wives must toe the line, while admitting that wives of the business community were free to please themselves and return when they felt so inclined.

There were heated argument about these 'official' wives; what was an 'official' wife? No-one doubted that the wives of diplomats fitted this curious description, and the same could be said, perhaps with a little less conviction, of the wives of British Council officers. But what of us creatures on the periphery, the likes of Maurice Brown and myself? We mustered arguments that we most certainly did not consider our wives to be in any way 'official'.

Maurice brought all his formidable guns into the fray. He ferreted out useful information that our nearest and dearest were in Singapore. 'Have just heard from Maurice where you are – there have been all kinds of rumours', I wrote to my wife on 29 September. 'Officially wives are not yet permitted to return, but I wouldn't let that worry you too much if you can see your way clear. Maurice has cabled ideas to Beryl, but I'm sure that between you you're leaving no stone unturned at your end.'

Perfectly true, they were not. 1,700-odd miles away in Singapore, our wives, or some of them, were also fighting a battle. The two Cadet College ladies were accommodated in a modest but comfortable hotel under the care of the British Council man-on-the-spot, Tim Scott. Other damsels in distress, the wives of the businessmen, were housed rather more expensively at the Hilton. The British High Commission in Singapore, none too pleased at this influx, was quite adamant that all wives and families must be flown on to U.K. as soon as transport was available. Mesdames Brown and Pitt refused to have any truck with such notions, and vociferously demanded that they be returned to homes and husbands without further ado. With this viewpoint Tim Scott, to whom they both owed much for his unceasing care and good humour, was inclined to be sympathetic.

At last, after three weeks spent, not without enjoyment, in what was once the bastion of our Far Eastern strategy, they managed, unbeknown to the High Commission, to book themselves on to a B.O.A.C. flight to Rangoon, whence a Burma Air Lines Viscount would lift them to Chittagong. There they would part company, my wife doing the last short leg to Dacca by P.I.A. Dakota.

These dauntless ladies were rewarded by uneventful flights, if at times a little rough: of Burma Air Lines, Anwar Hossain, B.O.A.C. Manager in Dacca, once said that it was the only airline in the world known to have produced a cockroach out of the folds of a passenger seat. The journey was a triumph of pertinacity, and, it must be added, loyalty.

While all this was happening in Singapore, the arguments were hotting up in Bengal. On 11 October, a despatch rider shattered the peace of my front garden at the College, and handed me a very official envelope. The letter, headed British High Commission, Dacca, read –

11th October '65

Dear Michael,

I have now had a telegram from Singapore indicating that Helen together with Beryl Brown, called on our representative in Singapore recently about their return. Despite strong advice to the contrary, they apparently insisted that they were leaving as soon as possible by air for Dacca.

I must honestly tell you that if Helen returns at this time, especially accompanied by your daughter, this will seriously embarrass the High Commissioner . . .

All other 'official' wives, without exception, have now followed the advice given them and have returned, or are on their way to, Britain.

It can of course be argued that Helen does not fall into this category. But I have no doubt that she would be regarded by the community as being an 'official' wife. Her return therefore would be seen in direct disregard of the High Commissioner's strong recommendation.

I hope I may now ask you to cable her at once advising against her return to Dacca before the High Commissioner thinks it wise for her to do so.

I should be grateful for an urgent reply so that I may reply to the High Commissioner.

As regards the ordinary commercial wives etc. it already is, and is known to be, a matter for the individual to decide whether or not his wife should return. As regards official wives it is not, and cannot be.'

We stood firm on the grounds that our spouses came not within the 'official' category but were to be numbered among 'the ordinary commercial wives etc.' A reply to this effect produced a request that I would kindly present myself at the High Commission at 11 a.m. on 14 October, when the Deputy High Commissioner himself would be pleased to clarify the Government's view. At 6 o'clock on the evening before, I received this unsigned cable – 'Arriving Dacca 11.30 Oct. 14.'

Presenting myself next morning at the High Commission as requested, I listened to the measured, polite tones explaining H.M. Government's reason why wife and child should not return yet. I sat mumchance while keeping an eye on my watch and an ear cocked for the sound of aircraft which would mean wife and child directly overhead. I thanked the Deputy High Commissioner for his patient explanation, and dashed off just in time to see the Dakota touch down at the airport. The family was bundled into the car and whisked off to Momenshahi, there to lie low for a week or two until the situation had cooled even further. Maurice Brown and I exchanged congratulatory telegrams . . .

*   *   *

It was a great day when, the war over and another term well under way, we were at last in a position to open the library. To the very end the struggle, though episodal, was keenly fought and often bitter. I have hinted earlier that alarm and despondency had reigned over the question of where to put the library. In the original plan it had been sited on the lower floor of a two-storied structure, which projected from the back of the main building like the middle bar of letter E. The hall was above it. Maurice Brown on his archiepiscopal visitation had put the kibosh on this. 'You can't possibly have an assembly hall on the first floor,' he had pronounced, whereupon the two rooms were interchanged and for a while everyone was happy. Then the architect awoke to the fact that a library is heavy, and so, to support the weight of printed word, he had dotted the assembly hall with so many concrete pillars that is resembled faintly the Giants' Causeway, and afforded no view whatever of the stage to anybody sitting further than ten paces from it.

Everyone ceased to be happy, at which moment I arrived on the scene from England, a coin newly minted, and endeavoured to restore a situation which was rapidly going downhill. Finally we settled for a single storey block with the library attached to the hall at right angles to it. Thereupon a couple of mistris began to chop down the pillars they had so recently and so laboriously built up.

Unquestionably the library was a casualty in the cold war which raged in the C & B department. 'Buildings' had played their part reasonably well. The room – a handsome one sixty-five feet by twenty-seven feet with plenty of height and copiously windowed – was completed by the summer of '65. It was even decorated, rashly in view of the fact that 'Electrical' were yet to come on the scene to reap their havoc on ceilings and walls. They took their time over the wiring, and then for no reason vanished altogether from the scene. No amount of coaxing or threats could persuade them back to finish off the job. For months on end the big room lay forlorn and wretched, its tiled floor and newly painted walls stained with the filth left over from the wiring operation. The Engineer (Buildings) summarised my feelings on the whole sorry business – 'Electrical people they no damned good'. He was cross, too, that all his decorations would have to be redone. When at last the electricians got down to work again in earnest, they installed no fewer then twenty five big double strip lighting panels, pendant from the roof on black metal rods, not all of them straight. The effect of these, added to the fans also hanging from the ceiling in profusion, was bizarre in the extreme, like a petrified forest upside down. There was a scene; half the fittings were removed, to the chagrin of the electrical contractor whose profit margin was thereby cut by fifty per cent.

Meanwhile there had been activity on the furniture front. I had taken counsel with Tom Maughan, the British Council Librarian in Dacca, who was always ready to help with expert advice. We measured, plotted, drew little plans. In the end we settled for adjustable shelving set at right angles to the long wall, giving six reading bays each with window, table and chairs. The librarian's area was a wide semi-circular counter giving him plenty of space and a cosy corner from which to operate. The room had two doors.

'Keep one of them permanently locked,' said Tom, 'or you'll lose half your stock. No librarian can watch two doors at once.' This was the voice of experience. We entrusted the making of the furniture to a tubby little Burmese who had, after my experiences with Mr. Alam, rather endeared himself to me by declaring roundly, 'There is no seasoned wood in East Pakistan, and I can't provide it.' He agreed to make for a little under one thousand pounds five double adjustable book-cases, eight tables, fifty chairs, a counter twenty-foot long with fitted cupboards etc., two display racks and a card index cabinet. He failed on his delivery dates but this was hardly his fault. A high wind ripped the roof off his factory, and despatched most of his wares down river on a flood tide. I trembled to think to what advantage Mr. Alam would have turned so singular a catastrophe.

And what of books? Here too there were set-backs. One of the best bookshops in Pakistan, some would say the best, was in Lahore. When visiting there for a conference, I called at the shop, selected about a hundred books (there was not a very wide variety in stock) and extracted a promise that a full list of suitable books would be despatched with my order in less than a fortnight. For weeks nothing whatever happened. My letters went unanswered; neither list nor order arrived. Two months later contact was re-established – a long rambling letter, its meaning largely obscure, from which one gleaned that the books had not yet been despatched because of difficulties with the postal authorities, and the charges – about thirty rupees – which the latter were proposing to levy. With a very big order in prospect – prompt service at this stage would certainly have established the firm as the main supplier for a complete school library – this supposed doyen of the book trade had dallied and dithered over a postal charge of a few rupees. In a tempest of indignation, I cancelled the order and shopped elsewhere.

We were not in fact without books. Both the Asia Foundation – an American organisation with generous impulses – and the British Council made splendid donations, and from these we were able gradually to build up a stock. When at last the library was opened for the use of the boys, we forgot the many ups and downs which had attended its creation; in size, ventilation, lighting, furnishing and appearance, if not yet in books, it was a library of which any school might feel proud.

* * *

'Are you not afraid to live out here so far away?'

This was a question we were frequently asked by our Pakistani friends from the city.

'Afraid of what?'

'Oh, snakes and dacoits and er –', with a sidelong glance at the trees, – 'the wild beasts?'

This parochialism, this townees' mistrust of the countryside, was reflected in the attitude of some of the boys. The geography masters took a few of the seniors on an unspectacular walk round the local countryside, spying out the land as geographers are wont to do, and having a close look at rural economy in the villages. The boys were required to write up an account of their findings. These I read, deriving amusement from the several who wrote of their 'terrors' in the woods, and how 'with fearful hearts' they had run from noises in the undergrowth. There was widespread ignorance of natural history, which was a pity, for Bengal is exceptionally rich in this respect.

It was impossible, for instance, to live at Momenshahi without being aware of birds. The jungle encroached right up to the edge of one side of our garden, and birds in abundance were evident to the eye and ear. Five minutes' walk took us to the point where a river ran out into a great jheel, in winter mostly dried up, in summer quite the opposite. Here we would sit under the shade of a mango tree armed with a pair of powerful binoculars, and, when I could borrow a copy (for it was long out of print), Dr. Salim Ali's *The Birds of India*.

Best of all we enjoyed the kingfishers; less common and so doubly welcome were the white-breasted, on the wing a flash of brilliant turquoise blue. The more common pied variety always put up a splendid exhibition of which we never tired. Immediately a meal is sighted, the bird halts dead in its flight and remains poised, its wings revolving frantically like the rotors of a helicopter. The long dark bill points intently downwards, a masterly study in concentration. When the prey is in position, the bird closes its wings and hurls itself from fifteen to thirty feet with astonishing speed and certain aim. Sometimes we would see, on a small wooden hoop sticking out of the river, as many as six of these delightful creatures, sitting pensive and watchful like councillors in conclave. Pond herons were everywhere, hunched up in the shallows or picking their way with fastidious care through the reeds, necks forward and bills poised in readiness. On the ground their colouring was earthy brown; in flight they flashed white wings, and so transformed themselves into creatures of unexpected beauty.

We enjoyed the lanky cattle egret, slender and graceful in repose or in flight, and the cormorant, elegant on a favoured perch such as the pointed prow of a sunken boat. At evening big flights would cross the jheel, tempting the guns which we did not possess. Also favoured was the crow-pheasant or coucal, both for its chestnut wings and for its deep resonant call, broken, when in a fuss, by harsh croaks and pheasant-like chuckles. By their calls we became familiar with the hawk-cuckoo, silent in winter, but, with the approach of the rains, gladdening the air with the repeated scream – 'brain-fever' – rising in a hectic crescendo; with the koel, another crescendo singer; with, above all, the common Indian nightjar whose call so puzzled us when first we arrived. The sound is like the whip of a thin cane, or, better still, a stone flung across a sheet of ice. This peculiar noise gently smote our ears the whole night through. Which, added to the clamour of frogs, tree-crickets, owls, jackals, geckoes, dogs and wild cat, made us conscious of much nocturnal company close at hand.

More rarely seen and greatly prized were the blue-tailed bee-eaters, the paradise fly-catchers, and, loveliest of all, the orioles. The black-headed variety nested in the jungle close to the house, but was shy of showing off its glorious golden yellow body. My friend Roy Crook, on whose considerable knowledge I leant heavily, was certain that he had seen that bird which Malcolm Macdonald considers finest of all, the golden-headed oriole, in spite of Dr. Ali's categorical assertion that it is not to be found in East Bengal.

From the verandah, over the teacups, we would watch the small fry hunting on the lawn a few yards from where we were sitting: magpie-robins continually jerking and spreading their small pretty tails, white-backed munias, house sparrows as cocksure here as in the back gardens of Bolton or Bournemouth, red-starts, the fearless drongoes, the various members of the bulbul family. About the cotton trees the mynas swarmed, busy and chattering, anxious always to be off and joining the pigeons at a fruit feast in the banyan tree. The gentle drowsy call of the pigeon in the jungle was a frequent reminder of summer walks in the English countryside.

There were always the big battalions, the bomber squadrons of the avian air force – kites, vultures, eagles. Of these the vultures are commonly thought repulsive – a disgusting carnivore, ugly in appearance and ugly in habit. But watch a vulture in flight against a cloudless sky, and you understand anew the poetry of motion. Certainly their instinct for death is uncanny; I can recall few sights so pathetic as the donkey dying by the roadside feebly twitching its backlegs to disturb the Bengal vulture already nibbling at the big feast to come. In Dr. Salim Ali's words:

'Their eyesight is remarkably keen, and large numbers will gather at a carcase from nowhere within an incredibly short time. The speed and thoroughness with which a company will dispose of a bullock or other large animal dumped in the precincts of a village is astonishing. These gruesome obsequies are attended by an incessant jostling and bickering among the birds, and by much harsh, unpleasant screeching and hissing as one bird tries to oust another from a coveted vantage point at the feast or to deprive it of a gobbet of flesh. The combatants spread their wings and prance around ludicrously, tugging and pulling at the morsel from either end. They sometimes gorge themselves to such an extent that they become incapable of flight and are compelled to pass the night on the ground.

Nauseating as these habits may be, the vulture is in fact fulfilling a very useful function. There is on the subcontinent no human force to clear the highways and byways of dead animals (the big cities excepted, and there only on the busier thoroughfares). The vultures gnaw flesh to the very bone, thus disposing of matter which would otherwise befoul the air and spread disease. The white scavenger vulture moreover feeds largely on human excrement, of which he finds abundance in the slums of the cities and in the precincts of villages. The kite assists him in this useful scavenging, foreswearing corpses and nightsoil but avid for garbage. The resplendent eagle disdains such practices, preying only on small birds, fish, rats, mice, frogs and snakes.

All these birds – and many others not mentioned – lightened our days in Bengal with their colourful plumage, soaring flight and incessant song. We were glad of their company.

For our friends' anxieties about snakes, there might seem to have been some justification. We were, after all, living in what was no more than a clearing in the jungle; we had a right to expect – or others had a right to expect on our behalf – that now and again a creeping thing would find its way into our garden, if not into the house itself. Snakes are, however, exceptionally nervous creatures; they show little inclination to exchange confidences with man. They have the most marvellous sense of hearing: a footfall fifty yards up the track and they will slither away into the undergrowth. Step on one while it's asleep, or venture too near a nest, and you may be in trouble, but neither of these things happens very often. In the whole of our time in the country I saw one snake – a corpse, done to death by the boys on the College playing-field.

*   *   *

One was gratified to have one's contract, originally for two years, extended by a year. The idea, it may be recalled, was that a British Principal having got things going, would hand over to a Pakistani. Maurice Brown, for instance, after monumental work at Fauzdarhat Cadet College in

Chittagong, had already returned to New Zealand, and Lt. Col. Hussain, a most delightful West Pakistani, had succeeded him.

Pleased, then, to be given an extra twelve months to round off work so far accomplished, I was rather less pleased – in fact, like the Mother Superior who found the seat up, I was deeply shocked – to get back from U.K. leave to find my successor already *in situ*. He was a West Pakistani, Lt. Col. Ali Ansari, 6 ft. 2 in. high, and so slenderly built that to view him sideways-on called for concentration.

I wondered if this totally unexpected turn of events was a bit of mischief-making on the part of my old friend Col. Rahman. The situation was certainly a difficult one both for Col. Ansari and for me. A hand-over from one boss at the end of a tour to his successor is a reasonable, sometimes advisable, practice – of a few days' duration, perhaps a week or two at the outside. But a year . . .

First problem was what on earth to give the Colonel to do, and I never really found the answer to this. Not that it greatly worried him, for he was a man of languid disposition. An office of his own seemed essential – two principals in one office is one too many. I found him a small sanctum not too close to mine, and hoped that we would not get in each other's hair. It occurred to me that here was a wonderful opportunity for disappointed litigants – there was no shortage of them – to take their wounded pride off to the other principal-sahib on the off chance that the latter might take steps to redress the balance. This no doubt happened, but repercussions were minimal – much to Ali Ansari's credit.

My wife and I grew fond of Ali; we were soon on first name terms. He must often have been lonely – he, the Adjutant and three of the five havildars were the only West Pakistanis for miles around – and he would not infrequently pay us an early evening call, draping his willowy frame along a sofa, sipping a chotah peg and bemoaning the climate and the rigours of life in East Pakistan. He was reticent about his own wife and family, though we gathered they existed somewhere in distant Lahore. On the domestic front, he disapproved strongly of the open plan system we had adopted in the house. No doubt, as soon as we left, curtains and partitions were thrown up, little enclaves created for the disposal of his womenfolk.

Ali was absolutely obsessed by the desire to lay hands on a length of Harris Tweed – the genuine stuff, no cooked-up substitute would do – at all costs it had to be authenticated by the Harris Tweed label. Towards this end he pursued us relentlessly, seeing in this British connection an opportunity to satisfy his ambition. My eldest daughter, Angela, resident near Harrod's and good at Getting Things Done, was recruited into the team. Acquiring the stuff presented few problems: it was getting it out to Bengal that worried Ali sick. He would have no truck with official channels; in his eyes that way spelt ruin, for the precious material – a sports jacket-to-be of surpassing splendour – would, he assured us, certainly be purloined somewhere along the route.

We had to await, therefore, the return from leave of some Britisher who was prepared, out of the kindness of his heart, to lug the stuff 7,000 miles on a restricted air baggage allowance (by this time, sea-travel was no longer the norm.) Ali could not understand why people were not positively queueing up in their anxiety to undertake 'this little commission' as he delighted to call it. Inevitably it took time to find a willing emissary.

'Michael, (or 'Helen' if she were within earshot) when will my stuff be here? Why the delay?' Since it was his caution that ruled out parcel post, we got rather tired of his petulant query, repeated daily, and many times a day at that. Almost we began to think that we were somehow to blame . . .

However, I made a little political capital out of it. Very occasionally, Ali would be 'difficult', badgering me to get some decision reversed, some favour bestowed. I had only to suggest that the Harris Tweed Affair was getting snarled up to an extent that the whole business would have to be called off – I had only to hint at this for Ali to come smartly to heel. It could be said, I suppose, that I was learning fast.

At last contacts were established; a returning businessman agreed to bring the parcel, and all was well. Alas! we never saw the jacket, as the tailoring of the cloth proved to be an even more long drawn out affair than its acquisition.

Sometimes Ali would have himself driven into Dacca, where he would disappear for days on end, doing goodness knows what; I would simply get a polite message for a car to be sent to fetch him home. He affected to despise Col. Rahman, but they seemed to spend quite a lot of time in each other's company, and I was never sure what the two colonels might be up to.

Ali enjoyed a measure of ill health, and was frequently *hors de combat* with 'head pains' or stomach ache. He found endless fascination in my wife's little store of medicine, and would seek her advice on disorders often of a somewhat intimate nature. On more than one occasion he confessed to me that he had little relish for the task ahead of him. Poor Ali! It was impossible not to like him. We had our occasional disputes, but it was, I suppose, a feather in both our caps that we got through the year without coming to blows.

The astute fellow was wise enough to be on leave in Lahore when the disasters of 1971 erupted through the Province. He was luckier than the gentle Col. Hussain in Chittagong. There the Cadet College Principal was a prime target for the mob that rampaged through the campus looking for West Pakistanis: Col. Hussain, his wife and small children were cut to pieces.

*   *   *

A highlight of our last year was a visit from staff and boys of Jenaidah Cadet College. This had been started up – very successfully – by a Pakistani colonel, who had then handed over to Lt. Col. John Smitherman, late of the British Army, thus reversing the normal practice. The distance between our two colleges was only a hundred and fifty miles, but in the Ganges Delta distances can be deceptive. The waterways create problems: huge diversions, voyages on ferries, unpredictable delays at embarkation points, speeds clipped to 20 m.p.h. by poor road surfaces. Thus we were faced by an adventure rather than a bus drive, and the wise man allowed a good twelve to fourteen hours for such a journey. With so much effort involved, it seemed sensible to make a real go of it: a three-day visit was arranged with various matches and entertainments laid on to keep the fun fast and furious.

Centre-piece was a 'Grand Concert in honour of our friends from Jenaidah Cadet College.' I have the programme in front of me as I write this many years after the event. Our troupe, calling themselves the Momen-shahi Music Makers, put on twenty turns, all based on music and dance. I welcomed the whole thing as an opportunity for the Bengali to demonstrate his undoubted flair for artistic presentation, and, with some misgiving, took it upon myself to act as a sort of impresario/producer/director.

Our boys were much taken up with pop. This was the time – the middle sixties – when the Beatles were at their height, and the names of Ringo Starr and John Lennon were household names down the corridors of our Bengal fastness. There was an obvious paradox between the sort of society depicted by Western pop, and the sort of society in which our pupils lived, moved and had their being – a Muslim state with unequivocal attitudes towards sexual behaviour and the place of women in the community (it is a conflict which remains unresolved to this day). We were at pains to string together a balanced programme: I wanted, and got, plenty of Eastern music. One of the memorable performances was a duet by Y.F. Rahman and Rahim Khan, sitting cross-legged in priest-like robes, playing the Tabla; memory, perhaps mercifully, brings no recall of 'The Dance of the Six Sweet Sisters', save that they were certainly not girls. There was lively chorus work in 'John Brown's Body', and (grand finale) 'Marching Through Georgia'; an Urdu song by Rahmatullah and His Rascals, a pop group (Michael Gomes and His Gang), led, appropriately enough, by the only Christian pupil on our books.

We went for pretty elaborate staging, as the credits on the back of the programme suggest. Lighting soaked up a crew of eight, stage management under the Lecturer in Bengali, Mr. Abdullah-el-Amin, five. The Adjutant ran the Costumes Department, Mr. Gaffur, Physics Lecturer, the Sound Effects. Uncle was not left out of things – he was one of two Dance Arrangers. Our new V.S.O., lately arrived from U.K. – Martin Johnson – showed his worth as Chorus Leader.

It was, I recall, a colourful affair, a lot of fun to put on. The audience – guests of honour, John and Enid Smitherman – made the most piercingly appreciative noises at the end of it all.

*   *   *

To – Mr. and Mrs. Pitt
　　　Momenshahi Cadet College.

Dear Sir/Madam,
　　　I, on behalf of the Fare-Well Committee will be Highly Obliged if you would kindly give us a list of your friends and their address for inviting them in the Fare-Well Party to be given on the eve of your departure.
Thanking you sir/madam
Yours Obediently,
Mohammend Ali,
Plumber
On behalf of the Fare-Well Committee

The Bengali takes a farewell very seriously indeed. When the time came for us to cry enough, we found ourselves on the receiving end of a barrage of letters and invitations, of which the above was a typical example. From the manager of the village Drug House came:

'Though you leave us, your mercy and kindness will remain alive in our inner most heart forever'.

From the Mess Manager, our Mr. Barbhuyan, in a huge screed marked Personal and Confidential, we had, inter alia:
'It is learnt that you are leaving this College shortly for goods. This news has saddened all and everyone of this College's but to me, this has come as a bolt from the blue. This fatal news has rendered my heart to the extreme and I can not help shedding tears'.
One's reaction, I recall, to so much supercharged emotion, was mainly one of hopeless inadequacy. What had one really done to ease the lives of these humble people, many of whom existed in a state of desperate poverty? What possible justification was there for such regard? One recollected with shame the moments of quick temper, the hasty judgments, which from time to time had erupted in the stress of the moment. Really one would have liked to have one's time over again on the off chance of doing rather better . . .
Meanwhile there was nothing for it but to put on a bold face and let events take their course. Splendid parties were laid on – speeches, gifts, more speeches. From the boys we received a model in silver of a Bengali river boat, on its sail the inscription –'*To Mr. M.V. Pitt, Founder Principal, Momenshahi Cadet College, from the Cadets of 1965-67*'. The Staff gave my wife a filigree silver necklace with ear-rings to match. There was much more – photographs, cups, flowers, this Farewell Address:

> The Principal, Mr. M.W. Pitt, M.A. (Oxon)
> On the Eve of his Departure from
> Momenshahi Cadet College, Mymensingh
> East Pakistan.

Beloved Sir,
    With a heavy heart we have assembled here this evening to bid you farewell from amongst us at the end of your tenure of your service in this College. Our hearts bleat when we think of your departure at this moment.
    Sir, this College was fortunate to get a gigantic and towering personality like yourself, and it stands as a living monument of your leadership and organising ability.
    Sir, the staff of this College, irrespective of rank and file, always received your fatherly guidance and unstinted help and support. You were at all times a constant source of inspiration to them as a friend, philosopher and guide.

Sir, your affable manners and charming personality over-whelmed us in all circumstances. Your keen sense of judgement and prompt and correct decision always worked as a beacon light and shall remain as a model to us for years to come.

Sir, physically you will no longer be with us, but our souls will ever-blossom with your memory and our hearts shall be with you wherever may you be.

Sir, we are now choked with feelings of grief and sorrow at the thoughts of your departure.

Before we conclude, Sir, we once again extend our heart-felt gratitude to you for all that you did for us. We sincerely pray to the Almighty for your future happiness, peace and prosperity.

We remain, Sir,

Your beloved employees,

Momenshahi Cadet College.

On the last morning, a huge crowd assembled outside the house. One of the College vehicles, polished and adorned with ribbons, awaited us, Driver Nazir never more stiffly at attention, never more splendidly accoutred. The College band struck up and we were off, towed by the senior Cadet class with Uncle in charge on a slow, clamorous ride through the campus. We sat there beaming, heavily garlanded, aware that we might not quite be rising to the occasion as the situation demanded; that feeling of inadequacy was never sharper. Baby Nickler stood in the back, chaplets about her neck: what she was making of it all, I could not imagine. Outside the dining hall, our Mr. Barbhuyan had mustered the Furies, dressed overall in clean white and holding aloft the banner: 'Fear Well.' Himself was rigid in a salute, which, save for lack of a hat, would have won approval on Horse Guards. A last look at one's office, the Office Superintendent waving wildly from the verandah – the band belting out marches fit to burst – the crowd, now swollen, assuming cup-tie propor-tions – there, the main road just ahead. Driver Nazir switched on the engine. The boys fell aside, frantic shouts and waves, and we were round the last corner, the College and all its human content for ever gone from sight.

Three hours later, as the Boeing carried us clean and swift across the plains of India, I wrote this:

'It is unlikely that Deenat, Daniel, Cyprian, Ahmed the first mate, Major Rashid, Uncle, Abdul the cook, our Mr. Barbhuyan, the

Bursar, Mr. and Mrs. Ahmed Khan, Izzy, Capt. Wasiq Khan, little
Dr. Shaha, the Office Superintendent, Mr. Alam, Mr. Shamsul,
the sinister Mr. Malik, Col. Ali Ansari, the Furies, Mr. Decorum
Ltd., Driver Nazir, Mr. Rahman, the Splendid Havildars, Mr.
Hamid and all his family, the Cadets of '65-'67, Mr. Shaha and
little Abdul will ever read a word of this. Which is a pity in a
sense because they are the people who matter in the story, they
are the meat in the sandwich. We British are visitors to their
country, transients, here to-day gone to-morrow, leaving scarce a
wrack behind. If they in their innocence think that we have done
something for them, they are wrong – or perhaps one should say
wrong in one essential: it is really the other way round . . .'

This was written when the emotional temperature was high. Yet, looking
at the words years later, I could see no cause to alter any one of them. We
had been living in a densely populated land. Not surprising, therefore, that
one's memory, reaching back to those years, saw a canvas dominated by
people – their whims, their fancies, their unpredictability.

I remembered the words of General Ismay who, when serving on
Mountbatten's viceregal staff in the chaotic blood-bath at the time of
partition, made the point that the one safe rule was to expect the unexpected. In a gentler and infinitely less consequential setting, I had learnt
the wisdom of this rule. I recalled, too, the words of Sir Paul Sinker:
'You're taking on an extremely tough job'. Had it been worth it? To the
extent that one had been taught a whole crop of lessons about the
strengths and weaknesses of human nature – not least one's own – there
could only be one answer: emphatically, yes.